The ♦ Religious ♦ Dimensions ♦ of

C ♦ O ♦ N ♦ F ♦ U ♦ C ♦ I ♦ A ♦ N ♦ I ♦ S ♦ M

SUNY Series in Religion
Robert Cummings Neville, Editor

The ♦ Religious ♦ Dimensions ♦ of

C ♦ O ♦ N ♦ F ♦ U ♦ C ♦ I ♦ A ♦ N ♦ I ♦ S ♦ M

Rodney L. Taylor

♦ State University of New York Press ♦

Published by
State University of New York Press, Albany

© 1990 State University of New York

For information, address State University of New York Press,
State University Plaza, Albany, N.Y., 12246

Library of Congress Cataloging-in-Publication Data

Taylor, Rodney Leon, 1944-
    The religious dimensions of Confucianism / Rodney L. Taylor.
        p.   cm. — (SUNY series in religious studies)
    Includes bibliographical references.
    ISBN 0-7914-0311-4. — ISNB 0-7914-0312-2 (pbk.)
    1. Confucianism.   2. Confucianism—Relations—Buddhism.
3. Buddhism—Relations—Confucianism.   I. Title.   II. Series.
BL 1852.T39   1990
299'.215—dc20   89-21724
                                                                    CIP

10   9   8   7   6   5   4   3   2   1

For Judith

Contents

Foreword

Professor Taylor, in his Acknowledgments, tells his version of the story of the origin of this volume. He's right about the heat, the conference, and the enthusiasm for his essays I evinced as an alert series editor on the scout. He fails to note, however, that the conference itself was preoccupied with the question, whether Confucianism is a religion, and had formulated that question in terms of the issue of transcendence. An elaborate dialectic had developed contrasting Christianity as "transcendent transcendent" with Confucianism as "immanent transcendent," or maybe it was "transcendent immanent." This debate reflected the old and elsewhere discredited strategy of defining religion primarily in terms of monotheism and then asking whether non-theistic traditions are analogous enough to share the label. Our frustration with this debate, in the context of a truly significant and enlightening conference, caused us to ask one another, how *should* we frame the question of whether Confucianism is a religion? Of course we both knew, but he had the documents to show it: hence, this volume.

A religious tradition has at least three essential elements, each handed down and developed in the multitude of ways traditions transmit. One element is a mythic, philosophical, or theological cosmology defining the fundamental structures and limits of the world and forming the basic ways in which cultures and individuals imagine how things are and what they mean. As a cognitive element, this part of religion has been analyzed in detail by Peter Berger and other sociologists of knowledge, and there is no doubt that Confucianism has such a cosmology. The ancient Confucian writings expressed both heaven/earth and moral-origins dimensions to cosmology, and the Neo-Confucian writers elaborated these with elegant philosophic arguments, presenting the Confucian tradition as an explicit alternative to Buddhism and Taoism.

A second essential element of religion is ritual. Rituals are a finite set of repeatable and symbolizable actions that epitomize things a tradition takes to be crucial to defining the normative human place in the cosmos. Early layers of ritual epitomize the hunt, nurturing of agricultural fertility, acknowledgment of political authority (worship of gods as lords), acts of commitment to other individuals, and so forth. There is no doubt that the rituals involved in filial piety qualify Confucianism as a major religion, as Matteo Ricci and other Christian missionaries found when they tried to incorporate the rituals of filiality into Christianity as incidental additaments.

The third essential element is that a tradition have some conception and practical procedures for fundamental transformation aimed to relate persons harmoniously to the normative cosmological elements, a path of spiritual perfection. In theisms this usually means salvation, a right relation to God. In Buddhism it means transformative enlightenment about the truth of change and suchness. Does the Confucian path of the sage count as a religious path of spiritual perfection? This is the precise question of Rodney Taylor's book.

The negative answer is urged by those who see Confucian social practice as conformation to normative ways of life, perfecting certain important social relations. The path of the sage, according to this interpretation, is exhausted in the social agenda. The positive answer is given by thinkers such as Tu Wei-ming, Anthony Cua, and Cheng Chung-ying who argue some version or other of the classical Neo-Confucian thesis that true humanity is fully achieved only when the usual run of life is transformed so as to manifest Principle (*li*) in a full and perspicuous way. The essays by Professor Taylor here add up to a multidimensional analysis of the way of the sage and the institutions of that way, for instance the use of scripture and quiet sitting. This volume discusses these topics with explicit attention to the sense in which they are or are not religious. Some of the essays are explicitly comparative in raising the question, and the comparative issues are in the background of the other issues. In the sum, this is a richly argued and conclusive answer to the question of whether Confucianism is a religion, and in what senses. I take great pleasure in introducing it to the audience of this volume.

Rodney Taylor's earlier monographic study of Kao P'an-lung, *The Cultivation of Sagehood as a Religious Goal in Neo-Confucianism* (Scholars Press, 1978), set the major guidelines for the study of sagehood and established him as an authority on the issue of the relation between the religious and the "humanistic" in Chinese thought. Building on the case of Kao, Professor Taylor here addresses the question of the volume generally, but with approaches coming from many angles. As Charles Peirce pointed out, a good argument is not a chain with successive links but a rope with many overlapping strands. The diversity of approaches in the essays of this volume makes a stronger argument than would result from a monographic biography, or a study of scripture, or of meditation, or of sagely discourse, alone. This is a book to ponder carefully.

Robert Cummings Neville

Boston University

Acknowledgments

The idea for this volume first began on a hot and steamy bus ride from my hotel up to the campus of the Chinese University of Hong Kong during the International Conference on Confucianism and Christianity in the World Today in June 1988. I was sitting with Bob Neville discussing the literature available on the religious nature and interpretation of the Confucian tradition. I suggested that assembling a selection of my previously published essays together with some recent and as yet unpublished work, to present in book length form a full discussion of the religious dimensions of the tradition, might be appropriate. He encouraged me with great enthusiasm. The eventual result is the book for which I am now writing the acknowledgments. This book would not have come into being without Bob's encouragement and enthusiasm and I gratefully acknowledge my gratitude to him.

"Confucianism and the Political Order: Religion Poised in Risk" was originally presented at the national meeting of the American Academy of Religion, Atlanta, Georgia, 1986. I want to thank my colleague Ira Chernus for drawing me into the topic of risk-taking and inviting me to present this paper.

"Scripture and the Sage: On the Question of a Confucian Scripture" is the result of an invitation from my colleague Frederick M. Denny, initially to a paper presentation and then to join him in the editing of a book on the subject. I have benefited greatly from discussions with him on a number of aspects of the question of scripture. This essay, under a slightly different name, was published in *The Holy Book in Comparative Perspective,* eds. Frederick M. Denny and Rodney L. Taylor (Columbia, S.C.: University of South Carolina Press, 1985). Copyright 1985 by University of South Carolina, and reprinted with permission.

"The Sage as Saint: A Study in Religious Categories" was published, under a slightly different title, in *Sainthood: Its Manifestations in World Religions,"* eds. Richard Kieckhefer and George Bond (Berkeley: University of California Press, 1988). Copyright 1988 by the University of California, and reprinted with permission. This paper was initially presented on a panel dealing with the nature of sainthood in world religions at the national meeting of the American Academy of Religion, San Francisco, 1981. I am grateful to Richard Kieckhefer and George Bond for the work that went into the original panel and the eventual publication.

"The Centered Self: Confucian Religious Autobiography" was published, under a slightly different title, in *History of Religions* 17, nos 3 & 4 (February and May, 1978), pp. 266-83. Copyright 1978 by The University of Chicago, and reprinted with permission. This essay was first presented at the 30th International Congress of Human Sciences in Asia and North Africa, Mexico City, 1976 and later at the Regional Seminar in Neo-Confucian Studies, Columbia University, 1978, where I benefited from the seminar's discussion of the role of religious autobiography in Confucianism.

"Proposition and Praxis in Neo-Confucian Syncretism" was published, under a slightly different title, in *Philosophy East and West* 32, no. 2 (April 1982), pp. 187-99. Copyright 1982 by The University Press of Hawaii, and reprinted with permission. This was first presented at a national meeting of the American Oriental Society, San Francisco, 1980.

"The Sudden/Gradual Paradigm and Neo-Confucian Mind Cultivation" was published in *Philosophy East and West* 33, no. 1 (January 1983), pp. 17-34. Copyright 1983 by The University Press of Hawaii, and reprinted with permission. This was first presented at the Conference on the Sudden/Gradual Paradigm in Chinese Thought, Los Angeles, 1981, and I am grateful to Robert Gimello for the invitation to participate in this conference. I have particularly benefited from conversations with Tu Wei-ming on a number of issues in this essay.

"Meditation and Ming Neo-Orthodoxy" was published, under a slightly different title, in the *Journal of Chinese Philosophy* 6, no. 2 (June 1979), pp. 149-82. Copyright 1979 by D. Reidel Publishing Company, and reprinted with permission. This essay was originally presented at a national meeting of the Association for Asian Studies, Toronto, 1976, as part of a panel on "Modes of Self-Cultivation in Traditional China." I benefited from discussion with all members of the panel: William Theodore de Bary, Judith Berling, Anne Ch'ien, Chün-fang Yü, and Tu Wei-ming.

"The Problem of Suffering: Christian and Confucian Dimensions" was presented at the International Conference on Confucianism and Christianity in the World Today, Hong Kong, 1988. I am particularly grateful to Peter Lee and John Berthrong for their roles in the organization of this conference. The paper has benefited greatly from comments by Langdon Gilkey, Tu Wei-ming, William Theodore de Bary, John Berthrong, Judith Berling, and Robert Neville.

"Modernity and Religion: A Contemporary Confucian Response" was presented at the International Symposium on Confucianism and the Modern World," Taipei, 1987. This paper has benefited from discussions with William

◆

Theodore de Bary, Tu Wei-ming, and, of course, would not have been possible without the willingness of Okada Takehiko to speak to a number of the issues of modernity from his own perspective. The material from Okada is based upon my recent book *The Confucian Way of Contemplation: Okada Takehiko and the Tradition of Quiet-Sitting* (Columbia, S.C.: University of South Carolina Press, 1988).

The following publishers have generously given permission to use extended quotations from copyrighted works: From *Confucius: The Analects (Lun-yü)*, translated by D. C. Lau (Middlesex: Penguin Books Ltd., 1979). Reproduced by permission of Penguin Books Ltd. From *Mencius*, translated by D. C. Lau (Middlesex: Penguin Books Ltd. 1970). Reproduced by permission of Penguin Books Ltd. From *Reflections on Things at Hand*, by Wing-tsit Chan. Copyright © 1967 Columbia University Press. Used by permission. From *The Confucian Way of Contemplation: Okada Takehiko and the Tradition of Quiet-Sitting*, by Rodney L. Taylor (Columbia, S.C.: University of South Carolina Press, 1988. Used by permission.

I consider myself very fortunate that for a number of years I have had the teaching, advice, and counsel of both scholars of Confucianism and Confucian scholars. I want to acknowledge my gratitude to William Theodore de Bary, Okada Takehiko, Wing-tsit Chan, and Tu Wei-ming. I also want to express my thanks to Mary Evelyn Tucker, John Berthrong, Julia Ching, and Judith Berling— colleagues who take seriously the religious dimension of the Confucian tradi- tion—and Paul W. Kroll, friend and colleague. I want to thank, as well, Risa Palm, Dean of the Graduate School and Associate Vice Chancellor for Research, University of Colorado at Boulder, for her constant support of my scholarly work. My work as always has been made far more meaningful through the abiding support of my family, Judith, Meghan, Annika, and Dylan, and now the memory of a certain Num.

Introduction

Some years ago, at a national meeting of the American Academy of Religion, I was presenting a paper on the religious dimension of Confucianism. During the discussion of the paper someone asked me whether, in the Confucian literature I had surveyed, there was a single occurrence of a term for *religion*; that is, a word that could be directly translated as *religion*. The answer, of course, was that there was no such term, though this was hardly an answer unique to the Confucian tradition as the work of Wilfred Cantwill Smith has suggested.[1] This was apparently what the individual who asked the question wanted to hear, and it substantiated a still too frequently found characterization of the Confucian tradition as lacking a religious character. In answering the question, I responded by saying that my entire paper had been about the occurrence of religion, not the term *religion*. In fact, this was the very point I was trying to make. That the term itself for religion was not there or, for that matter, that other terms frequently associated with religion may have been absent, should not in and of itself have precluded the question of religious dimension from the tradition. When we examine the Confucian tradition, we are not necessarily going to find those structures of religion that we have grown most accustomed to encountering in the study of religious traditions. We need to be sensitive to different ways in which a religious tradition can express its religious dimension.

The question of whether Confucianism is a religion or not is not a new question. It has been asked for many years and a number of attempts have been made to define the religious character of the tradition.[2] The essays that compose this volume are merely one approach to this question. The volume is built upon the premise, however, that the Confucian tradition is profoundly religious. From this point of view, those interpretations that have sought to define Confucianism as a form of humanism devoid of religious character have failed to realize the central feature that persists throughout the tradition. I

1

argue that a single thread runs throughout the tradition, and this thread is religious.

The religious nature of the tradition not only must be identified, but utilized in the interpretation of the unfoldment of the tradition as a whole, if we are to fully understand the nature of Confucianism. If a religious core is found at the very center of the tradition, then all that flows from it is part of that religious meaning. One still finds interpretations of East Asian cultures that implicitly understand Buddhism to be the great religious tradition of China, Korea, and Japan. Confucianism from this point of view, while recognized as an ideology of major import to the history of these cultures, continues to be considered primarily as an ethical system or humanistic teaching. Let us make no mistake, Confucianism is an ethical system and humanistic teaching. It is also, however, a tradition that bears a deep and profound sense of the religious, and any interpretation that ignores this quality has missed its quintessential feature. Rather than arguing that East Asian cultures have been largely free of the dominance of religion precisely because Confucianism was the salient form of ideology, one might well argue that East Asian cultures are in part religious because of this dominance. It is time for Confucianism to assume its rightful place amongst the major religious traditions of East Asian cultures and, in turn, the religious traditions of the world.

If Confucianism is going to be recognized as a religious tradition, however, it is necessary to identify that element of the tradition that may be described as deeply and profoundly religious. This element revolves around the Confucian understanding of *T'ien*, Heaven, the traditional high god of the early Chou people. The religious core itself is found in the relationship of humankind to Heaven. Heaven for the Confucian tradition is not thought of, as some have argued, as an abstract philosophical absolute devoid of religious meaning. In the Classical Confucian tradition Heaven functions as a religious authority or absolute often theistic in its portrayal. In the later Neo-Confucian tradition Heaven, or the Principle of Heaven, *T'ien-li*, also functions as a religious authority or absolute frequently monistic in its structure.

It seems clear that Heaven, or the Principle of Heaven, functions as an absolute for the tradition. Because it is an absolute, however, does this necessarily, make it religious? For something to be religious, there may need to be something more than simply the identification of an absolute. In this sense, the abstract philosophical absolute may be quite satisfying as a philosophical structure, but it may for some remain largely if not entirely devoid of religious meaning. What, however, can be added to provide religious meaning that is not already included in the identification of an absolute? The one area that seems to offer some usefulness is the identification of an absolute with a provision for a relationship. For a religious tradition, the absolute must provide for a relationship with the individual, although that relationship can differ widely, whether discussing theistic, monistic, or the spectrum of traditions possible. In a very fundamental way, theism and monism describe first and foremost a relationship. Often they are thought of primarily in terms of the nature of the absolute they represent, and they do describe an absolute. Beyond the representation of the absolute, however, they describe a relationship to the absolute. In a practical sense, and this is a highly relevant question for religion, one might say that theism and monism as descriptions of the absolute are meaningless unless they can provide a relationship. This relationship becomes, then, an essential and defining characteristic of religion.

Relationship, however, may be inadequate as a term to describe fully the essential and defining characteristic of religion. For that, we need to employ the term *transformation*. Religion provides not only for a relationship with what is defined as the absolute, but provides as well a way for the individual to move toward that which is identified as the absolute. This movement toward the absolute is a process of transformation, and because the goal is the absolute, the process can be spoken of as ultimate transformation. The direction of this argument depends heavily upon Frederick Streng's definition of religion as a means toward ultimate transformation,[3] a definition I have used as a central element of my work on the religious dimensions of the Confucian tradition. This process of transformation is the salvational or soteriological element and the quintessential characteristic in the identification of a religious tradition.

To discuss an absolute as a religious absolute, that absolute must, in its relation with the individual and perhaps other living things, provide a means of salvation or soteriology; it must provide a means for ultimate transformation. The question for the Confucian tradition is the degree to which Heaven, or the Principle of Heaven, establishes a relationship with humankind that provides a means of ultimate transformation, such that humankind might realize a transformed relationship and thus enter into a transformed state of being. Such a process of ultimate transformation appears to exist in both Classical Confucianism as well as Neo-Confucianism in the figure of the sage, *sheng* or *sheng-jen*. Thus, in the relationship between Heaven as a religious absolute and the sage as a transformed person, we have the identification of a soteriological process and, as a result, the identification of the religious core of the tradition. In turn, the soteriological relationship between Heaven and the sage becomes a religious model for the tradition as a whole. As each person has the capacity to emulate the way of the sage, if not to become a sage, the possibility exists for soteriological transformation of the individual. A life lived within this salvational hope and committed to its achievement is a religious life.

As this religious core is recognized, other elements of the tradition take on religious significance as they relate to this central meaning. The essays assembled in this volume deal with a variety of elements of the tradition and invite a religious interpretation. They deal in large part either with issues well-known in the tradition but not normally interpreted in religious terms, or uncommon elements of the tradition closely associated with religious elements. In either case, the intention is to draw together various elements of the tradition within a religious interpretation and to suggest the religious depth and richness of the tradition for the cultures in which it has played a major role.

Chapter I begins with an introduction to the basic teachings of Confucius (551-479 B. C.) and Mencius (372-289 B. C.) within the political framework of late Chou Dynasty society. It discusses the long-standing questions of the nature of the advice offered by the Confucian teachers to the political rulers of the day. The framework of interpretation is, however, religious. It sees their advice as welling forth from a religious faith and suggests that when these teachings are understood as religious teachings, the risk that the teachings demand of the political rulers is not insecurity, but a leap of faith. As political advice, the teachings of Confucius and Mencius have often been regarded as rather naive. When seen as religious counsel, however, the risk the Confucian teacher demands becomes a profound reflection of religious commitment.

Next is an introduction to the Confucian Classics and several prominent Confucian writings in Chapter II. The question posed is a simple one. If this tradition is at its core religious, then is there a need to look at these writings as scripture? As with the history of scripture, there are questions of the origin of these works and the role that they have played in the history of the tradition, both as sources of orthodoxy and orthopraxy. By continuing to think of them only as Classics, and thus not as scripture, is there something inherently meaningful in a religious sense that is being precluded?

Chapter III deals at some length with the sage, the origin of the term, the way the figure is understood in the early tradition and the increased relevance of the ideal of the sage for later Neo-Confucian forms of learning and self-cultivation. Rather than treating the sage in isolation, however, the chapter explores the relation with what has often been thought of as a very different form of figure, the saint. In one sense, the distinction drawn between them is often around the very term religion itself. The saint is obviously religious. The sage is not so clearly religious. When these figures are placed in comparative perspective, are there substantial commonalities? And are the commonalities such that the sense in which the sage has been seen as not religious is in need of rectification in our interpretation of the term?

Chapter IV presents the autobiographical writings of the late Ming Dynasty Neo-Confucian Kao P'an-lung (1562-1626). Though certainly not of the magnitude of the founders of the Neo-Confucian tradition during the Sung Dynasty, Kao P'an-lung is an important figure in the history of the tradition because he is a follower of Chu Hsi (1130-1200) and yet comes after the major challenge to the Chu Hsi school by Wang Yang-ming (1472-1529). His thought and practice is thus an attempt to maintain the Chu Hsi teaching, but he is, at the same time, influenced by the teachings of Wang Yang-ming. He is also very much a product of the Ming period with its heightened sense of the learning and self-cultivation of the individual. As a result, his writings dwell at great length on questions of learning and self-cultivation and engage in processes of self-examination and self-reflection which makes them highly relevant to questions of religious practice and religious interpretation of the tradition.

Within the autobiographical writings of Kao P'an-lung, we find a self in search of itself. This is truly the task of autobiography. An additional element surfaces, however, that is not usually associated with the interpretation of Confucian writings. The journey of the self in search of itself is the path to becoming a sage. The sage and his relation to Heaven reveals the religious nature of the tradition. Thus, the path to becoming a sage is a religious journey and the account of this path becomes then the subject matter of not just autobiography, but religious autobiography. This offers the possibility of placing a number of Confucian writings in a very different perspective, one that begins with a respect for the degree to which the writing is a form of expression of the inner religious life.

Chapter V continues the theme of autobiography, examining some of the autobiographical writings of Hu Chih (1517-1585). It goes on, however, to analyze a particular feature of Hu Chih's life of learning and self-cultivation. Hu Chih studied both Confucianism and Buddhism, and he discussed his experiences with both traditions at some length in his autobiography. He is often cited as an example of one for whom the different traditions were merged in a syncretic unity. The nature of this syncretism is the main subject of this chapter. *Syncretism* is a term frequently used to discuss a number of Neo-Confucians. The study of Hu Chih's syncretism raises the question of the appropriateness of this term in the Neo-Confucian context as a description of the relationship between religious traditions and the faith of an individual.

The relationship between religious traditions and the practices and methods of learning associated with them has perhaps nowhere been more questioned in Neo-Confucianism than in the development of the Neo-Confucian form of meditation. This is often interpreted as the clearest sign of adaptation of Buddhist practices. Chapter VI analyzes this in terms of Neo-Confucian forms of learning and self-cultivation with particular attention to the Neo-Confucian form of meditation, *ching-tso*, quiet-sitting. Confucian methods of learning and self-cultivation have a wide range of differences. For some meditation is acceptable; for others it is strongly opposed. These differences in methods of learning and self-cultivation have, at times, been spoken of in terms of a classic Buddhist distinction in methods of learning, the difference between sudden and gradual learning. The essay analyzes the appropriateness of this model and the implications of Buddhist influence upon the development of Neo-Confucianism.

Quiet-sitting was an important form of meditation practice for many Neo-Confucians. The history of the practice spans nearly the length of the history of Neo-Confucianism itself. Chapter VII analyzes the practice of one individual by returning to Kao P'an-lung and his writings on quiet-sitting. Kao has some of the most extensive extant writings on the practice and has been a major influence upon others.[4] Through a study of these writings, one can glimpse the actual practice and the role it played in the larger framework of study and learning as well as the responsibilities of daily life.

Chapter VIII returns to the tradition as a whole and places it in a comparative framework with Christianity. The focus of this comparison is the problem of suffering and its interpretation. Suffering has been described by some as the very reason for the existence of religion and by others as the proof of the argument that religions' claims of a meaningful universe are unfounded. The chapter attempts to understand the ways in which the occurrence of suffering is understood in Christianity and then applies this to the Confucian tradition. In one sense, Confucianism is unique amongst world religions for the degree to which it does *not* address the question of suffering. In another sense, however, it speaks directly to the issue, although one must listen with sensitive ears for its cry. Recognizing its cry, however, the response to suffering is a central component of the religious dimension of the tradition. It is an expression of deep religious faith in the moral order of the universe and anguish at the occurrence of suffering.

The final chapter brings the Confucian tradition to the stage of modernity, seeking to clarify the relation between the pressures of modernity and the life and vitality of a tradition viewed for many as moribund in the modern world. The point of departure is Tu Wei-ming's view of the possibility of a future of the tradition, what he calls the third epoch of Confucianism, in which the concerns of Confucianism have transcended East Asian cultures and become global in perspective. My own study of Okada Takehiko,[5] a contemporary Japanese Confucian, is the primary context, and raises the question, in chorus with Tu Wei-ming, of a premature judgement of moribundity. As long as we study the tradition as history, its only existence is historical. As soon as we recognize its present life, we can begin to discuss its future life.

What brings all of these essays together is that with which I began, the sense of a common thread running throughout the tradition, a common thread defined in terms of a basic religious response to the world. My hope is that through this study and the work of other scholars, this element of the Confucian tradition will be more commonly recognized. As a result, the richness and depth of the Confucian religious experience will join company with the world's religious heritage.

CHAPTER **I**

Confucianism and the Political Order:
Religion Poised in Risk

Confucianism has traditionally sought to advise political rulers in the course of action the state might pursue to establish a polity genuinely reflective of the ethical nature of humanity. This early role of the tradition, and a major activity of Confucius himself, was in large part made up of the effort to offer such advice. Standardly, the teachings offered by the Confucians have been seen as a form of humanism, often against a background of emerging human-istic tendencies within Chinese society. [1] All too infrequently have Confucian teachings and their roots been presented in the framework of a religious super-structure that views humankind as a potential mirror of the ways of T'ien, Heaven, the source of religious authority within the Confucian tradition. It is, however, from a religious context that Confucians have traditionally called upon political rulers to emulate the Way of Heaven for the betterment of humankind. This involves components of faith and risk-taking not often understood for the central role they play, even in the matter of political decisionmaking.

For purposes of this chapter, I am defining faith as a way of thinking and acting that is motivated primarily by a religious commitment. A religious com-mitment is a total commitment of the entire person toward that which is regarded as absolute, a definition influenced by Joachim Wach's discussion of the characteristics of religious experience.[2] It is also soteriological in that it offers ultimate transformation, following the definition of *religion* by Frederick Streng suggested in the Introduction.[3] Faith is not primarily a matter of know-ing, although unfortunately it is most often taken as a form of knowledge that lacks proper empirical verification. Streng has discussed faith as a way of liv-ing, not a way of knowing, in which all things are related to one's religious life,

7

not compartmentalized into specific epistomological categories.[4] Thus, a life lived with religious commitment is a life of faith. It involves much more than simply the way in which things are known.

Risk-taking is not usually discussed as a category of religious dimension, and it is not the defining characteristic of the presence of religion. In many situations it may have nothing to do with religion. Situations exist, however, where it seems an important extension of faith. If we think primarily of faith as a way of thinking and acting within the context of religious commitment, then there will be those recommendations for action that appear to call for risk-taking. In such a situation faith may find itself in intimate association with risk-taking. One can think of numerous historical examples that would sub-stantiate this. Is it, however, actual risk-taking? The answer is both yes and no. Religious commitment can call for certain forms of action, the outcome of which is very uncertain. That is a risk. Loss, suffering, and even death may be involved. That is a risk. Advice given may appear to ask for action that chal-lenges the very basis of one's security. That is a risk. In any of these cases, the risk may still be taken precisely because of the religious commitment. And the consequences suggested can follow.

On the other hand, because in this case the primary motive to initiate the risk-taking is the religious commitment, the "risk" may only be a risk to one who does not share that religious commitment. After all, the risk for loss in each of the cases posed is loss of some thing in particular, even if that involves life, but it is not the loss of religious commitment. The religious goal may override any other form of commitment: at the very least, this appears to be the case for a religious person. Thus, the judgment that something is a risk is far more subjective than we normally chose to consider and is highly dependent upon the goals set by the individual.

The advice that the Confucians offered the various political rulers called for a risk, in a sense an ultimate risk, although they promised as well a security were the risk to be taken. While the political rulers wanted advice that would ensure them of the maintenance of political power and perhaps the enlarge-ment of their own political base, the Confucians repeatedly cautioned that it was not political power in itself that brought security. If anything, such political power brought the threat of greater insecurity because of its precarious nature. Being a political leader was an insecure business, and the stakes were high for one's own demise. The answer lay not in an increase in political power, but from the Confucian point of view, in a radically different direction. This differ-ent direction was a return to the ways of moral virtue. For the Confucian, this was the moral virtue of the sage kings of the past. In a religious context, this was also the moral virtue of the Way of Heaven itself.

The various political rulers found, however, small comfort in the model of the sage kings of the past or the fact that this was the Way of Heaven itself.

Their concerns were more immediate—the need to respond to a bellicose enemy, a rebellion within one's borders, the struggle for power within one's own court. And it was answers to such dilemmas that the political leaders sought from the Confucians and in a sense have always sought from the loyal Confucian ministers. The answer the Confucians gave, however, was in a sense unnerving and unsettling. It suggested that political solutions in themselves were inappropriate and inadequate. Instead, the solution lay in the return to the way of moral virtue. This was the risk. In the face of a seemingly insurmountable adversary, the Confucian suggests that one does not respond in kind, but instead radically alters the course of political action to a self-reflective mode of internal learning. The root of the problem is not with the external adversary, but with the internal level of one's own moral nature.[5]

The political leader responds, "I must meet my enemy, build my military strength to a greater level than my adversary, and provide security for my people." The Confucian response over the centuries has been that no amount of political and military strength will ensure security; the only thing that will ensure security is the proper attention paid to the cultivation of the moral nature of each individual. The risk suggests that the application of the moral nature of humanity to governance and rulership will disarm the armed. The risk of returning to the moral nature of humanity, from the Confucian point of view, is the only basis upon which an outward and external security may be built. This was the risk posed, a risk poised in religious commitment, and it has been at the very heart of Confucian teachings throughout much of its history.

Genesis of Religious Faith

It is a matter of methodological consideration to understand the basis upon which Chinese history and the Chinese political order might be interpreted in religious terms. If there has been any one dominant mode of interpretation, it has tended to argue for the largely secular character of Chinese society and worldview, and thus the general paucity of religious dynamics.[6] While this is far too large a topic to respond to in an appropriate fashion in the present chapter, I want to comment upon a single aspect of this issue, one highly relevant to our understanding of the Confucian tradition. This is the religious character of the early Chinese political order.

It is commonly understood that Confucius advised rulers of his day to return to the ways of the ancient sage kings. Less common is the understanding of the religious import of this advice. That the sage kings lived in a world impregnated with religious meaning has played a surprisingly small role in the interpretation of the early political state, but even less in the interpretation of the arising of the Confucian tradition. Methodologically, the failure to understand the religious roots of the tradition has remained a critical problem for Confucian studies, and one might argue, the general understanding of much of Chinese thought. The problem, a frequently encountered one in the history of religions, is the reductive interpretation given to the role of religion. Religion occurs, but it is often seen either as secondary to other factors or even in a fundamentally manipulative role, upholding the authority of those in power and circumscribing the will of those without power. If instead of this role, religion were seen as the authentic and absolute worldview for the inhabitants of China at the time, what would the interpretation of the early emerging political order in China resemble? Were religion viewed in this way, it would, of course, become the central characteristic of the worldview, for religion when present is never a secondary feature.

One interpretation of the early political order that has allowed for its religious dynamic is that by David Keightley.[7] Keightley argues that religion is at the very center of the Shang political order. This suggests that religion for Shang culture is not secondary, not derivative, not manipulative, but quintessential to the defining character of the Shang worldview. As such, the Shang political state is a religious state and we misinterpret that political state as long as we fail to understand the religious dynamics that underpin it, support it, and provide its very life. At the center of this religious dynamic lay ancestor worship and a perception of what Keightley calls the *generationalism* of its order and structure. By this term, Keightley means "the necessity to conceive of the world in hierarchies of power based upon the relative age of generations."[8] It is the Chinese commitment to hierarchy, authoritarianism and bureaucratic structure that, for Keightley, has its origins and continued allegiance in a religious dynamic. Thus, the political state is propelled by a religious commitment and its growth and development fed by a religious dynamic. Keightley says, in this respect: "The form that political authority, and the civil theology supporting it, eventually took as political culture became increasingly secularized in Chou times continued to manifest a commitment to the hierarchical, authoritarian, quasi-magical, bureaucratic features whose presence may be discovered in the characteristic generationalism and contractual logic of Shang ancestor worship."[9] The importance of this issue is not the character of the religious dynamic itself, but the possibility of seeing its role as the dominant element in the worldview.

For Keightley, this element remains as the driving force in political ideology and the functioning of the political state, even in those periods where religion appeared to play a less dominant role. "A religious faith in the validating efficacy of classification, hierarchy, number, and contract persisted, remaining behind in secular areas of life after the inundating flood of Shang religious belief had receded."[10] This suggests a need to understand the religious dynamics at work in a given period and the misunderstanding that can occur if we fail to take this element into account, even in later periods. "We misunderstand the new, more differentiated values, attitudes and institutions of Chou and Han if we view them in purely secular terms."[11]

This has profound implications for the study of Confucianism. From this perspective Confucianism can be seen against a backdrop charged with religious import. Its own religious dimension develops out of this background, not in opposition to it. We know that the later Chou state cannot maintain the same religious dynamic as that of the Shang before it. There is a weakening in the power of the Chou state with the arising of the strength and independence of the individual states. It is in this setting that we see the arising of the so-called hundred schools of thought and the genesis of the Confucian school.

Confucius advised that there be a return to the ways of the ancient sage kings. This advice takes on a different meaning in light of the religious interpretation of the political order. Might one not argue that Confucius is primarily motivated by his own perception of a religious dynamic still existing, though but a faint shadow of its form from an earlier age? And is not his mission not only the continuation of this religious dynamic, but the attempt to reinstate it as a central component in the world in which he lived? One could argue that with the arising of the independent states, there is a loss of the central religious dynamic of the Chou political order. With this loss of the central religious dynamic, the states gain power, but the power remains largely disenfranchised from its religious roots. Confucius, however, remains driven primarily by this religious dynamic, what he saw as the quintessential feature of an earlier culture and the element most important to emulate and implement if the world was to be rectified. It is this religious dynamic he sought to transmit. As Keightley concludes, "The strength and endurance of the Confucian tradition, ostensibly secular though its manifestations frequently were, cannot be fully explained, or its true nature understood, unless we take into account the religious commitment which assisted at that tradition's birth and which continued to sustain it."[12] A religious interpretation of the Confucian tradition is thus not an isolated phenomenon, for the Confucian tradition itself has its own religious genesis in an already-established religious dynamic at the very heart of the early political order. Confucius' motivation was to return to this religious dimension, but the political reality he faced was one of men of apparently small faith and a dominance of political ideologies with the disintegration of the central religious component of the Chou worldview.

Confucius and Government by Moral Example

Much of Confucius' life was spent in what often seems a futile attempt to advise the rulers of his day in what would bring an end to the strife and turmoil of a war-torn Chou dynasty and a return to the ways of peace and harmony. Repeatedly, his advice was a return to the ways of the ancient sage kings. If, from his point of view, the rulers of his day could but follow the ways of the ancients, then there would be the creation of peace and harmony. And what was it that these rulers possessed that the rulers of Confucius' own age did not possess? First and foremost, it is what was referred to as the ruler's *te*, translated as moral virtue. The quality of *te* as it referred to the ancient sage kings meant primarily a special relation established and maintained between the ruler and *T'ien*, Heaven.[13] It was in a sense an attitude; the ruler's whole being standing in proper relationship to *T'ien*. This is often spoken of in terms of the ruler's special mission as an intermediary for Heaven and thus his possession of *T'ien-ming*, the Mandate of Heaven, which was Heaven's continued favor for the ruler as long as the ruler was himself virtuous.[14] In turn, the ruler is frequently addressed as *T'ien-tzu*, Son of Heaven, to indicate the closeness between the ruler and Heaven, assuming that the ruler continued to hold Heaven's favor. The *te* of the ruler was identified specifically in the actions carried out by the ruler. If they were truly *te*, then they were themselves a reflection of the Way of Heaven.

From Confucius' point of view, the rulers of his own day were no longer exemplifying *te*. They were instead morally corrupt and thus no longer the intermediary between *T'ien* and humankind. Confucius' primary advice was to suggest that the rulers of his day return to this earlier model, that they reestablish their *te*, their proper relation to Heaven. The primary method whereby this could be accomplished for Confucius was for the individual to cultivate and develop his own inner moral nature. It was the responsibility of the ruler to be moral exemplar to his people, and Confucius saw his role as prodding the ruler on to awareness of this responsibility.

Time and time again, however, Confucius found a less than enthusiastic response on the part of the ruler. The rulers reminded Confucius that they found little usefulness and practicality in what they considered to be abstract moral discussions. Their problems were, instead, immediate and practical. Confucius responded by suggesting that his moral teaching was not irrelevant to these problems, and that, in fact, unlike the advice they sought, a moral solution was the only solution that was actually relevant and ultimately practical!

The moral teaching of Confucius is focused around often-found descriptions of the paradigmatic moral figure. This is the *chün-tzu*, the noble person, virtuous person, gentleman or exemplary person.[15] Originally a term suggesting birth into the aristocratic ranks, Confucius changed its meaning from nobility by birth to nobility by virtue—moral virtue. As such, it came to mean a level of moral achievement. Confucius stresses repeatedly that anyone can become a *chün-tzu*, anyone can achieve the development of his moral nature. It is not easy; it requires diligence and perseverance, but each individual has the capacity for its achievement. And it is to this goal that the ruler must strive. This, for Confucius, is the only way that peace and harmony will return to the world.

Let us look at several examples of the description of the *chün-tzu* given by Confucius.

The gentleman understands what is moral. The small man understands what is profitable.[16]

While the gentleman cherishes virtue [*te*]; the small man cherishes possessions.[17]

He puts his words into action before allowing his words to follow his action.[18]

The gentleman devotes his mind to attaining the Way and not to securing food.[19]

If the gentleman forsakes benevolence [*jen*], in what way can he make a name for himself? The gentleman never deserts benevolence, not even for as long as it takes to eat a meal.[20]

A number of other passages could be cited, but these are sufficient to see some of the key concepts and terms introduced in terms of the characterization of the *chün-tzu.*

First, there is a sharp contrast drawn between what is right, *i*, and what is profitable, *li*. These continue to be held in sharp contrast to each other and are mentioned frequently in the characterization of the true ruler from the false. The way Confucius uses the term *i*, right or righteous, suggests a moral capacity inherent within human nature. Its chief character is to distinguish right from wrong and it is often used in a way that would suggest the term *conscience*, a kind of inner judge of right and wrong.[21] The contrast of *i* and *li* stresses that the petty man is only concerned for material gain. With *li*, the end is defined exclusively in terms of such material gain, and there is no concern for the means employed to reach the end. There is certainly no consideration of either moral ends or means by the person so motivated, the *hsiao-jen* or inferior person. By contrast, the *chün-tzu* sees ends and means as intimately linked and each thoroughly rooted in moral consideration.

Second, we see the focus upon *te*, moral virtue, and its contrast with material possessions. The call is for the ruler to develop his capacity of *te*, to reflect his true relation to the Way of Heaven, rather than his own selfishness in personal aggrandizement of power and material possessions. Third, we see the contrast drawn between the Way, *Tao*, and making an end of one's livelihood. There is a higher call than mere subsistence where subsistence is not a mark of economic level, but of economic commitment. The Way is a religious commitment and other commitments pale by comparison.

Finally, there is the emphasis upon *jen*, goodness, probably the most frequently discussed virtue by Confucius. It has been translated as goodness, humanity, humaneness, or benevolence. Its meaning, rooted in its philological structure, suggests literally the relation of one person to another, that is, the proper relation, or moral relation, of one person to another. It is described in the *Analects* as the single thread that runs throughout Confucius' teachings.[22] It is also further defined by two other virtues—*chung*, reciprocity, and *shu*, empathy.[23] It was this paradigm of virtue that Confucius sought to teach the rulers of his own day.

Several passages in the *Analects* find Confucius advising the rulers of his day on the benefits of a model of rulership by moral virtue: "The master said, 'Guide them by edicts, keep them in line with punishments, and the common people will stay out of trouble, but will have no sense of shame. Guide them by virtue, keep them in line with rites, and they will, besides having a sense of shame, reform themselves.' "[24] Confucius is quite clear in distinguishing edicts and punishments from moral virtue and rites and suggests a rulership of inward moral capacity rather than outward political sanctions. Confucius is, in a sense, daring the ruler to appeal to his own inner moral virtue, suggesting that while political control and authority very well may be retained by edicts and punishments, it is a government of coercion and control rather than a naturally felt respect for moral virtue. The key is the use of the term *shame*. Edicts and punishments will keep the people in line, that is, the state will be ordered, but there is no sense of shame. With moral virtue and rites, there is a sense of shame. Confucius is using the term *shame* not to emphasize, as we might, shame as a response to a condition of socially constructed disgrace,[25] but as an indicator of the fiber of the inner moral nature of man. Shame is an outward form of an inwardly established capacity for rightness. Thus Confucius' comments suggest that a rulership of *te* and *li*, rites or propriety, allows the individual to develop his own capacity for moral conscience rather than coercing a conformance to a preestablished legal and punitive code. This point is made even more strongly in the following passage:

> Chi K'ang Tzu asked Confucius about government, saying "What would you think if, in order to move closer to those who possess the Way, I were to kill those who do not follow the Way?" Confucius answered, "In administering your government, what need is there for you to kill? Just desire the good yourself and the common people will be good. The virtue of the gentleman is like wind; the virtue of the small man is like grass. Let the wind blow over the grass and it is sure to bend."[26]

To Chi K'ang Tzu, the solution is simple—eliminate those who do not follow the Way, and then we will have the Way! The Way for Chi K'ang Tzu is an external standard to be applied as if it were a law or, in turn, a punishment. Chi K'ang Tzu's mistake, from Confucius' point of view, is that he fails to see that the implementation of the Way does not depend upon his success in demanding conformity, but upon his own inner and subjective realization of the Way. This is why he can distinguish between the goal of the Way and the means for its realization, why he can state that one simply eliminates those who do not conform. Confucius' response is to shift the problem from external standards to internal process. "Just desire the good yourself and the common people will be good." Instead of worrying about the elimination of those who do not share your perspective of the Way, just become good yourself. Become a *chün-tzu*, become a ruler of virtue, and the world itself will follow. The people may be forced to adhere to the laws of the state, but unless they see the goodness and the moral virtue of the ruler, the capacity of rulership remains superficial and only effective to the degree it demands conformance. But this is coercion, and it does not solicit the hearts and the minds of the people. However, if one is a ruler of goodness and virtue, then the people will give not only their allegiance, but their hearts and minds. With moral goodness, there is a trust from the people, an element of no small significance for Confucius.

> Tzu-Kung asked about government. The Master said, "Give them enough food, give them enough arms, and the common people will have trust in you."
> Tzu-Kung said, "If one had to give up one of these three, which should one give up first?"
> "Give up arms."
> Tzu-Kung said, "If one had to give up one of the remaining two, which should one give up first?"
> "Give up food. Death has always been with us since the beginning of time, but when there is no trust, the common people will have nothing to stand on."[27]

The last element to be given up is the trust of the people. This is what the ruler must establish if he is to be a true ruler, and not simply a tyrant. This trust ultimately depends upon the ruler's capacity of moral virtue. This, from the Confucian perspective, is all that is needed.

If this inner character of moral virtue can be developed and brought to fruition, then governance itself is almost effortless. According to Confucius, "If a man is correct in his own person, then there will be obedience without orders being given; but if he is not correct in his own person, there will not be obedience even though orders are given."[28] The obedience springs forth from trust in the morally correct person and is itself a sign of each person's moral development. The dark side of the coin suggests that without this correctness one may force obedience, but such obedience is not a product of a natural inclination of moral response.

In describing the sages of antiquity, Confucius suggests that little effort was required in the art of rulership. "If there was a ruler who achieved order without taking any action, it was, perhaps, Shun. There was nothing for him to do but to hold himself in a respectful posture and to face due south."[29] This passage has received much comment, and I do not want to minimize the complexity of terms and phrases, but one point that seems quite clear is the quality of effortlessness exemplified by Shun. Because he possessed *te* and thus stood in the correct relation to Heaven, there was little, if anything, he had to act upon. The phrase found in the passage, taking no action, *wu-wei*, suggests not so much "no action" as "non-action." The difference is the differentiation of the cessation of all action, which the phrase does not mean for either Taoist or Confucian, from a very special kind of action, an effortless action. The ruler's *te* is itself enough to effect action and most importantly to effect the manifestation of moral virtue in action. The ruler himself is essentially at the center in a kind of still point with his *te* fully manifest.[30] Action proceeds, gravitating around this paradigmatic manifestation of *te*. As the wind bends the weeds, so is there no one who is not influenced by this center of *te*.

Such *te* is the key to rulership, not the outward implementation of laws and punishments, and this can be seen in Confucius' attempt to define the word for government or to govern. "To govern [*cheng*]," Confucius says, "is to correct [*cheng*]. If you set an example by being correct, who would dare to remain incorrect?"[31] His statement is a philological explanation of the term. The major part of the character for govern, *cheng*, is the word *cheng*, to correct or rectify. This suggests that the very process of governing is itself a process of rectification, moral rectification.[32] From the Confucian point of view, the model of government as moral rectification continues to stand in contrast to a government of laws and punishments.

Confucius' own frustration in attempting to convince rulers of his day of the ultimate correctness of his point of view is echoed perhaps in one passage of the *Analects*. "I suppose I should give up hope. I have yet to meet the man who is as fond of virtue as he is of beauty in women."[33] Yet it is also a mark of Confucius' teaching that he does not give up hope. There is a very strong undercurrent of thought that suggests Confucius believes Heaven itself has given him this mission.[34] Eventually someone will stop and listen and instead of asking for political and military strategy, will recognize that the only solution lies in taking that risk of returning to the ways of virtue; of risking what appears to be everything upon the belief that moral goodness will overcome the evil adversary, of taking the risk that the ends do not justify the means, but that the means are themselves determinations of the very nature of the end to be reached. The risk is high; the cost possibly great.

Confucius sees the risk and weighs the risk. He is aware that such risk may involve the loss of one's own life, and yet he is prepared to take this step. "For gentlemen of purpose and men of benevolence while it is inconceivable that they should seek to stay alive at the expense of benevolence, it may happen that they have to accept death in order to have benevolence accomplished."[35] This I would suggest is risk, and it is clear that what Confucius is posing to the various rulers of his day is an invitation to enter into this risk-taking, to defy the precedent of the age and strike out in a radically new way of acting and thinking, to act upon the belief, or more properly the faith, that the universe is morally good and that human nature has the capacity for such goodness, a moral goodness that can transform the world. It is risk-taking in his own age, but it is merely a confirmation of the faith of the sage kings from Confucius' point of view, a faith of great magnitude in relation to the political realities of his own day.

Mencius and the Moral Nature

Mencius, considered since the thirteenth century as the orthodox interpreter of the teachings of Confucius, maintains the same basic themes we have seen in Confucius. He roots them rather more firmly, however, in a theory of human nature that attempts to articulate the moral components of human nature and then employs this theory for its capacity to argue a political transformation based upon moral learning and self-cultivation. The *Mencius* begins, however, by arguing as Confucius earlier had for the benefits of the ruler adopting moral virtue rather than persisting in personal and selfish pursuits and interests.

> Mencius went to see King Hui of Liang. "Sir," said the King, "You have come all this distance, thinking nothing of a thousand *li*. You must surely have some way of profiting my state?"
> "Your Majesty," answered Mencius, "what is the point of mentioning the word profit? All that matters is that there should be benevolence and rightness. If Your Majesty says, 'How can I profit my state?' and the counselors say, 'How can I profit my person?' then those above and those below will be trying to profit at the expense of one another and the state will be imperiled. When regicide is committed in a state of ten thousand chariots, it is certain to be by a vassal with a thousand chariots, and when it is committed in a state of a thousand chariots, it is certain to be by a vassal with a hundred chariots. A share of a thousand in ten thousand or a hundred in a thousand is by no means insignificant, yet if profit is put before rightness, there is no satisfaction short of total usurpation. No benevolent man ever abandons his parents, and no dutiful man ever puts his prince last. Perhaps you will now endorse what I have said, 'All that matters is that there should be benevolence and rightness. What is the point of mentioning the word profit?' "[36]

Mencius, as Confucius before him, distinguishes between, on the one hand, the virtues of *jen*, goodness, and *i*, rightness, and, on the other hand, profit, *li*, chastising the king for his emphasis upon profit. The argument from this passage becomes an important one throughout the history of Confucian thought. If the ruler is motivated by profit, then how can he expect any other motive for any other person in his kingdom? If the people from high rank to low witness the king questing after profit, then they, in turn, will follow the same course. Mencius counters this with an alternative. "All that matters is that there should be benevolence and rightness. What is the point of mentioning the word profit?"

In other words, all that is necessary is benevolence and rightness. Following the themes we have seen Confucius develop, Mencius is suggesting that it is benevolence and rightness alone that are responsible for rulership. If, however, the ruler insists upon seeking his own profit, then he can expect nothing other than competition and struggle in all the ranks of society, and order will be maintained only by the implementation of laws and punishments. How much simpler to revert to the ways of virtue, to say nothing of its cost efficiency!

Mencius describes how his return to virtue might attract the attention of the people and how, in turn, it would begin a process that would transform society itself.

> It was through losing the people that Chieh and Tchou lost the Empire, and through losing the people's hearts that they lost the people. There is a way to win the Empire; win the people and you will win the Empire. There is a way to win the people; win their hearts and you will win the people. There is a way to win their hearts; amass what they want for them; do not impose what they dislike on them. That is all. The people turn to the benevolent as water flows downwards or as animals head for the wilds. ... Now if a ruler in the Empire is drawn to benevolence, all the feudal lords will drive the people to him. He cannot but be a true king.[37]

The argument is a simple one, but central to Confucian thinking. To lose the hearts of the people is to lose the Empire itself. In what is essentially constructed as the opposite argument of the first passage, Mencius argues that instead of the divisions created by profit, the application of virtue will unite the people with their ruler. The critical element is to win the hearts of the people. This is the product of virtue and virtue alone.

To Mencius, the power of virtue is immeasurable. If virtue alone is employed, the ways of the world will be healed once again as they were in the time of the sage kings. To the ruler the challenge is to adopt such ways of virtue. But if they are adopted, the results are extraordinary. Several passages address this issue. In the first, King Hui of Liang, the same ruler who asked Mencius what he brought that might profit his state, questions the relation of the weak state to the strong, seeking Mencius' advice on how to remedy his own weaknesses.

> King Hui of Liang said, "As you know, the state of Chiu was second to none in power in the Empire. But when it came to my own time we suffered defeat in the east by Ch'i when my eldest son died and we lost territory to the extent of seven hundred *li* to Ch'in in the west, while to the south we were humiliated by Ch'u. I am deeply ashamed of this and wish, in what little time I have left in this life, to wash away all this shame. How can this be done?"
>
> "A territory of a hundred *li* square," answered Mencius, "is sufficient to enable its ruler to become a true king. If your Majesty practices benevolent government

towards the people, reduces punishment and taxation, gets the people to plough deeply and weed promptly, and if able-bodied men learn, in their spare time, to be good sons and good younger brothers, loyal to their prince and true to their word, so that they will, in the family, serve their fathers and elder brothers, and outside the family, serve their elders and superiors, then they can be made to inflict defeat on the strong armor and sharp weapons of Ch'in and Ch'u, armed with nothing but staves. . . . Hence it is said, 'The benevolent man has no match.' I beg of you not to have any doubts."[38]

A ruler of a small state complains bitterly of his fate to be sandwiched between militarily strong states. He tells Mencius of the defeats he has suffered and seeks Mencius' advice on what course of action he might pursue to remedy his situation. Echoing the first passage of the work, however, he is still asking Mencius how he might profit his state. Mencius' response is to suggest that considering military responses is unnecessary, that ultimately the only response is a moral response. He must cease looking at the strength of his enemies and turn his gaze inward upon himself and the condition of his own moral virtue. The answer lies in his becoming a true king, a benevolent ruler. If he does this, he will win the hearts of the people as well as their faith and trust. With their hearts committed, the people will fight valiantly for him against military forces far stronger than their own. However small or weak the state, if such policies are adopted, it will become the state of true strength. As Mencius says, there is no match for the strength that comes from moral virtue, and he begs that the ruler might accept this possibility.

Mencius offers the ruler the belief that if he were to adopt such ways, there will be little doubt as to his recognition by the people as the true king: "Now if you should practice benevolence in the government of your state, then all those in the Empire who seek office would wish to find a place at your court, all tillers of land to till the land in outlying parts of your realm, all merchants to enjoy the refuge of your market-place, all travelers to go by way of your roads, and all those who hate their rulers to lay their complaints before you. This being so, who can stop you from becoming a true king?"[39]

The model of moral rectification is ultimately based upon the view of human nature, a view that has played a central role in the history of Confucian thought. It is Mencius who is primarily responsible for the classical form of discussion of human nature, arguing that human nature is inherently good. This is a position that often seems assumed in the writings of Confucius, but it was not a topic actually discussed by Confucius directly. With Mencius, however, we find a much greater attention paid to trying to describe and define human nature. Mencius argues that human nature has certain beginnings of goodness within it. This is not to say that human nature is at birth fully good and nothing else needs to be done. Rather, there is an intentionality toward goodness, an incipient goodness that suggests human nature has the beginnings of goodness. In one of Mencius' classic debates with the philosopher Kao Tzu, Kao Tzu has argued that human nature is like water, it will flow in whatever direction a channel is opened.[40] That is, human nature is morally neutral, and it depends upon environmental circumstances to develop its capacity for goodness or for evil. Mencius replies that while water may flow east or west, it always flows downward. This is its natural proclivity, just as it is the natural proclivity of human nature to be good. This proclivity toward goodness is discussed by Mencius as the so-called Four Beginnings—qualities that if developed will lead toward the virtues of *jen, i, li* and *chih*, goodness, rightness, rites, and wisdom.[41] The most famous example that Mencius uses to support his argument is that of a child about to fall into a well.[42] His argument is that any person upon seeing a child about to fall into a well would seek and rescue the child. They do it for no other purpose than the response of their own human nature which cannot bear to see the suffering of another. This reduces itself to a basic Confucian moral axiom that states that it is a part of our human nature that we cannot bear to see the suffering of another. Interestingly enough, this ethic is tied directly to the sage kings. "Mencius said, 'No man is devoid of a heart sensitive to the suffering of others. Such a sensitive heart was possessed by the Former Kings and this manifested itself in compassionate government.' "[43]

This is not to say that there are not evil acts, and, for that matter, evil persons and potentially evil states, but to suggest that such evilness is the product of external circumstances, rather than the inherent nature of the individual. The ramifications of this are important, for it suggests that the core of human nature remains good even when clouded by a capitulation to circumstance. Mencius would suggest that on the basis of this theory of human nature, the inherent goodness can be appealed to, not in every case, but in a number of cases. Perhaps there are some who simply are too encrusted with the evilness of their ways, but for most, if given the proper circumstance and opportunity, there remains the possibility of appealing directly to the inherent goodness and engaging the individual in the development and emergence of such goodness.

What Mencius is doing is posing a risk! He is asking the ruler to change his course of action from a rule of law and punishment to a recognition of the universality of moral virtue. He is asking the ruler to recognize that it is a part of the very nature of an individual that he cannot bear to see the suffering of another, and he is asking that this moral principle be incorporated into the process of governing itself. We again see the dynamics of the relation between risk and security. From the ruler's point of view, security is to be found in adequate laws and punishments to order the state and adequate military defenses to defend the state. From the ruler's point of view, the risk Mencius poses—to adopt a moral principle—only presents a picture of a total lack of security. To give up the legal and military underpinnings of society in order to follow some general moral principle seems only to offer the possibility of throwing away all security as well as common sense!

The response of Mencius is essentially to argue that the adoption of moral rectification is a risk, but it is a risk worth taking for several reasons. First, the present context of security is a false security. To think that through the political subjugation of one's subjects and military subjugation of one's neighbors, one has achieved a genuine security is simply wishful thinking. The fact of the matter is that while one might exercise control over subjects and neighbors, one has neither the trust nor faith of subject or neighbor. Thus, one cannot trust him, and at any opportune moment such subjugation will well forth in rebellion. The current path, while it might appear secure, has seeds of ultimate insecurity imbedded within it. Second, if this is the case, then the risk itself is of less magnitude when one realizes that the present policy is itself a risk, although it has been thought of as the only policy to pursue to gain a security. The risk worth taking is to turn away from a policy that involves a genuine insecurity and the risk of perpetuating such insecurity. What then is the risk, or in other words, wherein lies the actual risk? Does this risk lie with starting out on a new path of policy, one that admits to the moral nature of man, or does the risk lie with treading the same path of building a false security and having to rebuild such security to convince oneself that one is actually secure?

Finally, there is a sense that while there is risk in adopting something new and it appears idealistic at best to suggest this turning back upon the moral nature of the individual, such risk is only an apparent risk, for it arises from a profound faith in the truth of the moral nature of humanity. Here is where the risk in a sense appears as risk to the ruler, but not to Mencius, for it is the ruler who does not believe that human nature is good. Nor does the ruler remember his legacy in the religious nature of the earlier political order. The early political order, as we have seen, was in intimate association with religious authority. The political order reflected the religious order and the religious order reflected the political order: neither could be divorced from the other. For the Confucian, this is an article of faith. Lacking that faith the risk factor appears high if not insurmountable to the various political leaders with whom Confucius interacted. From the Confucian point of view, however, the moral nature of humanity is true, and if the ruler takes the risk and adopts himself to policies that recognize this moral nature, then he too will see that if given the opportunity humanity will respond in moral ways.

In summary, the weight of religious faith plays a critical role. The Confucian tradition assumes not only the moral goodness of human nature, but the larger context of religious authority, the Way of Heaven, which from the Confucian perspective is the ultimate moral order of the universe itself of which humankind is but a microcosm. As the Way of Heaven is morally good, so in turn is the way of human nature. This is an article of faith held by the Confucian tradition and one that serves as the basis for acting in the world. This is the foundation from which Confucius, Mencius, and much of the later tradition can invite the ruler to risk the implementation of moral government. It is, after all, no risk at all, for what appears to be a risk of political insecurity in fact represents the ultimate security of the way of humankind matching the Way of Heaven itself. From the Confucian point of view, political considerations are ultimately a matter of individual religious and moral learning as they were for the sage kings. The degree to which the political order is divorced from these concerns is the degree to which the facade of security is created and maintained by political power alone, a security that matches neither the true nature of humanity nor the Way of Heaven. It is for this reason that the Confucian tradition over the centuries has sought to take the risk, acting out a deep religious faith in the goodness of human nature as a reflection of the Way of Heaven.

CHAPTER II

Scripture and the Sage:
On the Question of a Confucian Scripture

One component of the Confucian religious life that has remained virtually unexplored is the role of the holy book or scripture.[1] In fact, in many ways its mere mention seems almost inimical to the tradition itself: a Confucian scripture or holy book? One is tempted to ask whether this is not simply the wrong term! And yet having demonstrated the religious dimension of the tradition and delineated salient features of the religious life of the Confucian, it is appropriate to take a new and fresh look at the role of scripture in the Confucian tradition. It is, after all, frequently observed that the Confucian tradition is one that emphasizes the role of learning, specifically book learning. In light of the religious dimension of the Confucian tradition, there is a need to look anew at the nature of the authority these works possess, as well as the role they play for the tradition and the individual.

The Sage—Source of the Literary Tradition

The exemplar of the understanding of Heaven from the Confucian point of view is the sage, *sheng*, a designation assigned to early rulers of Chinese antiquity and increasingly applied by later Confucians to major figures of their own tradition. The books that can be described as the scripture or holy books of Confucianism are intimately linked to this tradition of the sage. They are a record of the deeds and in some cases the words of the sages. For the later tradition there was an attempt to see Confucius himself, a sage from the point of view of later generations of his followers, as instrumental in the process of the formation and transmission of these works. First, however, I want to focus upon the figure of the sage, and why it was of such importance that there be a record of his activities.

The word *sage, sheng,* is defined in the earliest and standard etymological dictionary, the *Shuo-wen,* as *t'ung,* a word meaning either "penetrate" or "pass through."[2] The general meaning of the term suggests that the sage is one who thoroughly understands things. To penetrate thoroughly or understand things means primarily that the sage understands Heaven or the Way of Heaven. It is on the basis of this knowledge of the Way of Heaven that he is an able and wise ruler.

The meaning of the word itself indicates something more of the complex nature of the sage and in turn the extraordinary status both historically as well as religiously associated with the designation. In the commentaries to the *Shuo-wen* provided in the *Shuo-wen chieh-tzu ku-lin* we find a fuller explanation of the term.[3] The character is composed of two parts; the phonetic *ch'eng,* glossed by Karlgren as "manifest" and thus "disclose" or "reveal,"[4] and the radical or signific, *erh,* the word for ear. With the signific *erh* playing a prominent role, we have the sense of the sage as the one who hears. As Boltz has suggested,[5] there is an intriguing contrast to be made between China and the classical antiquity of Europe in terms of the visual and auditory metaphors of wisdom; while the Greeks saw, the Chinese heard! Thus the sage hears the Way of Heaven. There is also a very close philological relation between the word for sage, *sheng,* and the word *t'ing,* to hear, to acknowledge, to listen. In fact the word sage was often written as *t'ing,* emphasizing the capacity of the sage to hear.

It is somewhat more speculative to suggest a semantical significance in the phonetic component; however, it is perhaps telling that the phonetic alone carries the meaning of "manifest." If there is a significance to the meaning of this phonetic, then the sage is he who hears the Way of Heaven and in addition manifests or reveals it to humankind. As the *Hsi-ch'uan t'ung-lun* commentary to the *Shuo-wen* says, "There is nothing he does not penetrate . . . The ear component does not mean simply to use the ear; it means instead that the mind penetrates the feelings of all things as the ear penetrates all sound . . . It is said that the sage penetrates the feelings of Heaven and earth and understands the nature of humanity and the world."[6] As such, those works that record the deeds of the sages bear a major import for the development of the individual and society alike, for they represent the deeds of those who understood the Way of Heaven.

The term most generally used to describe the literary works that record the deeds of the sages is that of *ching,* translated most frequently as "classic." It suggests even in translation a work that stands the test of time, a work that has an appeal as well as an importance to each new generation. This is also, however, the word that frequently renders scripture in both Taoist and Chinese Buddhist tradition.[7] The question is whether the term carries for the Confucian tradition a significance correctly understood as scripture or holy book. The term itself is quite clear in its etymology. Its origin, as evidenced by its signific which means thread, is within the context of weaving. It means warp, as opposed to weft.[8] Karlgren glossed the term as rule, law, or norm, suggesting the underlying sense of warp as that which creates continuity as well as regularity in a piece of cloth.[9] The extended meanings are orthodoxy and heterodoxy for warp and weft respectively.

The term *ching* has been applied to various groupings of writings at different points in the history of the Confucian school. The designation can also be applied as a group designation even when a work does not actually bear the term in its title. There are groupings of Five Classics, Six Classics, Nine Classics, Twelve Classics and Thirteen Classics. The most essential collection, the Five Classics, includes: the *I-Ching, Classic* or *Book of Changes*, a divinatory work with philosophical commentaries which explain the patterns of change inherent in the universe; the *Shih-Ching, Classic* or *Book of Poetry* or *Odes*, a collection of some 300 poems thought to exemplify the quintessential expression of poetic beauty and moral virtue; the *Shu-Ching, Classic* or *Book of History*, a record of the deeds of the early sage-kings; the *Li-Chi, Book of Rites*, detailed accounts and philosophical meanings of the rituals of the ancient sage-kings; and the *Ch'un-Ch'iu, Spring and Autumn Annals*, a record of the events in the state of Lu, the native state of Confucius.

The collection of Six Classics adds to these five a work no longer extant, referred to as the *Yüeh-Ching, Classic of Music*, which purportedly discussed the philosophical meaning of music. By the T'ang dynasty this collection had expanded to twelve, including the basic Five Classics. Two additional ritual texts, the *Chou-Li* and the *I-Li* were added to the *Li-Chi*. The *Ch'un-Ch'iu* which had already included the *Tso-chuan* commentary had two additional commentaries added to it, the *Kung-yang chuan* and the *Ku-liang chuan*. The *Hsiao-ching, Classic of Filial Piety*, the *Erh-ya*, an early lexicon, and the *Lun-yü, Analects* of Confucius, were also added to bring the number to twelve. Finally within several centuries the *Meng-tzu* or the *Mencius*, the works of Mencius, was added, bringing the total to thirteen. Each of these texts has its own significance as a Classic and each in turn is connected with the tradition of sages. Let us begin, however, by returning to the founders of the tradition, Confucius and Mencius, to understand their attitudes toward the literature that purportedly came from the age of the sages.

Confucius and Mencius on the Classics

Both Confucius and Mencius focused in their teachings upon a return to the virtuous ways of the sage-kings, particularly the founders of the Chou dynasty. The literature that was thought to be the record of the times of such paradigmatic figures of the early Chou period was what they felt themselves responsible for transmitting. It is this literature that became for later Confucians the Classics. For Confucius and Mencius the significance of this literature seems to rest less with a sense of textual authority, than a living contact with the virtuous sage-kings of China's past.

To Confucius the study of this literature, what he referred to as *wen*, litera-ture in its broadest category, was critical, for it was seen as the means whereby individual and society alike might become fully humane and virtuous. The ideal of the *chün-tzu*, the noble person, virtuous person or exemplary person, who has developed his own inner sense of humaneness, *jen*, and displayed it through the outward perfection of propriety was, as we have seen, central to the teachings of Confucius. The literature, *wen*, is invoked by Confucius as the means whereby such development could take place. Confucius says, for exam-ple, "Be stimulated by the *Odes*, take your stand on the rites and be perfected by music."[10] The reference may well be to the *Book of Poetry* or *Odes*, the *Book of Rites* and the *Classic of Music*, although little indication of the form in which these would have been seen by Confucius is found. However, the direction of Confucius' remark is clear; a person will develop and perfect their moral nature through a thorough learning and assimilation of such sources. In describing the *chün-tzu*, Confucius says, "The noble person widely versed in culture but brought back to essentials by the rites can, I suppose, be relied upon not to turn against what he stood for."[11] An additional passage from the *Analects* is an indication of Confucius' expression of faith in the *Book of Poetry*'s ability to contribute to the learning as well as moral and spiritual development of the individual. "Why is it none of you, my young friends, study the *Odes*? An apt quotation from the *Odes* may serve to stimulate the imagination, to show one's breeding, to smooth over difficulties in a group and to give expression to com-plaints. Inside the family there is the serving of one's father; outside, there is the serving of one's lord; there is also the acquiring of a wide knowledge of the names of birds and beasts, plants and trees."[12] The study of literature which had been transmitted from the period of the sage kings was viewed as the method through which humankind would return to virtuous and moral ways, ways in accord with the Way of Heaven.

Confucius' interpretation of the *Book of Poetry*, the only such interpreta-tion he offers of a Classic, suggests that the salient and overriding meaning of the *Book of Poetry* is its purity and uncorruptedness. "The *Odes* are three hun-dred in number. They can be summed up in one phrase, 'Swerving not from the right path.' "[13] This short passage goes a long way toward explaining Con-fucius' attitude toward *wen* or literature and, in turn, sets the ground for the approach by later Confucians to the Classics themselves. Confucius believed in the moral and spiritual purity of this collection of poems. This is based upon the presupposition that the age out of which this poetry emerged was itself an age of purity, for it was the period of the founding sage kings of the

Chou dynasty. This is an article of faith, but one central to Confucian teaching. Thus, from the Confucian point of view these poems embody the very spirit of their age. In turn, if one thoroughly studies such works, they will have nothing short of a transforming effect on the individual. This approach to the *Book of Poetry*, which will be mirrored by later Confucians with this Classic as well as other Classics, is the very seed from which the Confucian scriptural tradition developed.

Mencius referred to the Classics far more frequently than Confucius, quoting or referring to the *Book of History* and the *Book of Poetry* extensively and, to a lesser degree, the *Ch'un-Ch'iu* and *Li-Chi*. In addition to quoting or referring to these works, he also discussed the significance as well as the interpretation of the *Book of History* and the *Book of Poetry*. It is through these discussions that we have perhaps the clearest view of how these works were understood. In the case of the *Book of Poetry*, Mencius suggested in one case that an interpretation by a contemporary who had suggested a poem's limitations and accused it of expressing bigotry was inaccurate. From Mencius' point of view the poem displayed true goodness, *jen*.[14] Without analyzing specific content of the poem itself, Mencius' correction of the interpretation suggests a good deal about his own approach to the *Book of Poetry*. In a similar fashion to Confucius, Mencius viewed the work as the embodiment of virtue. The key to interpretation was to be seen in the uncovering of moral content. In another passage, Mencius agreed with Confucius that the author of one of the poems was versed in the Way itself, again suggesting the degree to which the founders of the Confucian tradition presupposed the immediate connection between such works and the age of the sages.

This might lead one to think that there is a literal and unquestioning acceptance of these literary sources as the works of the sages themselves. To a large degree, the admiration and veneration seem unceasing, yet Mencius also expressed a qualification on the interpretation of the *Book of History*, and suggested that a literal interpretation could under some circumstances lead to misunderstanding. He noted a passage in the *Book of History*, which stated that the blood of the people flowed unmercifully when fighting on behalf of a benevolent prince[15] and argued its inaccuracy. The text is not, therefore, infallible for Mencius. Yet he retains, on the other hand, a belief that the Way of Heaven is inviolable. The blood of the people would not be spilled unmercifully for a benevolent prince. Thus, it is not a question of unqualified acceptance of the authenticity of the sources, but it indicates the degree of belief in the Confucian teachings that Heaven operates in moral ways and any violation of this principle could only indicate an inaccurate source.

The literary sources that became known as the Classics were for Confucius and Mencius an immediate link to the age and the teachings of the sages. The transmission of the Classics was critical to the moral and spiritual learning

Confucius and Mencius envisioned as vital to the reshaping of individual and society. Yet for all the importance these works play, there is a strange paucity of reference to the overall significance the works possess. We have cited most of the references that give some general sense to the interpretation and significance of the Classics. This is all the more marked when contrasted with Hsün-tzu, for whom the conscious articulation of the significance of the Classics was significantly more important.

Hsün-Tzu and the Articulation of the Classics

Unlike Confucius and Mencius, Hsün-tzu (fl. 298-238 B.C.) seems to be far more conscious or at least conversant with the significance of the Classics as texts and as a group. We find, for example, the following statement in his writings. "The *Shu* records political events. The *Shih* establishes the standard of harmony. The *Li* sets forth the rules governing great distinction, and is the regulator of social classes . . . The reverence and elegance of the *Li*, the harmony of the *Yüeh*, the comprehensiveness of the *Shih* and *Shu*, the subtleties of all creation."[16] There is a sense of wholeness about the Classics from Hsün-tzu's point of view; they each make their contribution, but together they provide for the total development of individual and society. A statement from Tung Chung-shu (c. 179-104 B.C.), one of the major Confucians of the Han dynasty, suggests a similar admiration for the Classics taken as a group. "The *Shih* describes aims, and therefore is pre-eminent for its unspoiled naturalness. The *Li* regulates distinction, and therefore is pre-eminent in the decorative qualities. The *Yüeh* intones virtue, and therefore is pre-eminent in its influencing power. The *Shu* records achievements, and therefore is pre-eminent concerning events. The *I* takes Heaven and Earth as its basis, and therefore is pre-eminent in calculating probabilities. The *Ch'un-Ch'iu* rectifies right and wrong, and therefore stands pre-eminent in ruling men."[17] Other examples indicate the same shift in focus to the significance of the total grouping of texts, particularly among generations of Confucians during the Ch'in and Han periods. Considering the prominence of Hsün-tzu during this period, it may be no exaggeration to pinpoint this effort to him specifically.

Why did Hsün-tzu feel the need to speak in terms of the Classics as a group when this was of little or no concern to either Confucius or Mencius? The answer lies, in part, in the different political and ideological climate faced by Hsün-tzu. In Hsün-tzu's day the Confucian school was in more direct competition for dominance in the marketplace of ideas. Various schools of thought had arisen, the so-called hundred schools, and most were competing to influence the political rulers of their day. The claim to the Classics as the source of one's ideas necessitated major attention to the texts themselves as the source of authority. This does not minimize Confucius' and Mencius' admiration for the

Classics, but it does suggest that the focus for both remained primarily the teachings of the sages rather than textual authority. The situation for Hsün-tzu was different. He felt the necessity of defending and preserving the learning of the sages and, from his point of view, the very foundations of civilization itself, perhaps primarily from the Taoists whom he saw as antithetical and inimical to the preservation of culture. As part of his response there arose the gradual recognition of the need to articulate a body of teachings and support these teachings with the authority of a textual tradition.

The Establishment of Confucianism—Canon and Cult

During the Han dynasty, Confucianism was officially established as state orthodoxy. There are several aspects to this official establishment: the emergence of a state orthodoxy, a Confucian canon, and an official cult of Confucius. During the reign of Emperor Han Wu-ti (140-87 B.C.), we see much of the activity responsible for the emergence of the Confucian tradition to a position of major significance. Acting at the suggestion of the noted Han dynasty Confucian Tung Chung-shu, the Emperor Wu-ti sought to carry out measures that would virtually guarantee a major role for the Confucian school. He established the position of "Scholar of the Five Classics," *wu-ching po-shih*, and on the basis of the recommendation of Tung Chung-shu, sought to exclude from office those who did not share a Confucian perspective. The "Scholars of the Five Classics" served in the capacity of advisors to the emperor as well as teachers.[18] Their role as teachers was enhanced by the establishment and opening under Emperor Wu-ti of an imperial university, *t'ai-hsüeh*, in 124 B.C. The university was to provide a training center for learning in the Classics and those who achieved expertise were given official positions. The result was the eventual civil service system so well known throughout Chinese history: training in the Classics at the imperial university, the passing of a series of examinations, and official appointment to governmental position. With the increased role of the Confucian scholar and the official recognition of their status, the Confucian school became a dominant and major element of the Han period and the texts it focused upon achieved the status of revered and authoritative writings.[19]

At the same time that these efforts were being undertaken, much of the focus of the Confucian school itself was directed toward the editing of texts and the attempt to establish definitive editions. Subsequent to the infamous "burning of the books" carried out by the first emperor of the Ch'in dynasty, Ch'in Shih Huang-ti (reign 221-210 B.C.), and the appearance of two versions of many of the texts, the New Text and the Old Text versions, there was a need to settle questions of variant texts. The emperor eventually commissioned a committee of scholars to deal with the variant versions and produce a definitive edition. The eventual result of this effort was the production of orthodox versions as well as interpretations of the Five Classics. As an indication of the official establishment of a canon, the Five Classics together with the *Analects* were engraved in stone.

The fact that the *Analects* was included among those works engraved in stone is not surprising when one realizes the increased role and status given to Confucius. With the emergence of Confucianism to a position of prominence was an equal elevation in the status of its founder. Some of the ways in which he was elevated were only short-lived, particularly the tendency of Tung Chung-shu and his school to suggest hagiographic features in Confucius' biography. Within a matter of years such interpretations were declared heterodox and subsequently Confucius remained a founder remarkably human in personality and character. One of the features that did, however, play a lasting role was the establishment of an official cult and subsequent temple to Confucius. Confucius had already been the patron of scholars prior to the official establishment of Confucianism during the Han dynasty, but with official recognition the cult of Confucius became a regularized part of official state orthodoxy and in particular state orthopraxy. Scholars offered sacrifice to Confucius and the ritual came to be included among those sacrifices officially performed by the emperor himself.[20] Although the attempt to deify Confucius was declared heretical, he remained at the center of a cult that was eventually institutionalized as the Confucian temple. As a cultic object, Confucius appears to have remained human. Sacrifice was simply viewed as the perfection of ritual, not a sacrifice to Confucius. The cultic ritual provided a means for perfecting one's own ritual or propriety and thus one's moral and spiritual nature. It also provided a focusing upon the teachings of the founder. Nothing more was to be involved.

As an outgrowth of the New Text interpretation, which had far reaching ramifications, Confucius himself was assigned a far larger role in the composition and editing of the Classics. Ssu-ma Ch'ien's (c. 145-86 B.C.) biography of Confucius in his monumental *Shih-Chi* shares in this influence by suggesting that Confucius was instrumental in the composition of all of the major Classics.[21] Tung Chung-shu, a direct follower of the New Text interpretation, stated that Confucius was the author of the *Ch'un-Ch'iu*. The *Shih-Ching* was described as being edited by Confucius. Confucius was given a major role in the composition of the commentaries, or wings, of the *I-Ching*. The *Chin-ssu lu, Reflections on Things at Hand*, a major source of Neo-Confucian teachings, states this same view succinctly, saying that the Classics were the product of the writing of the Sage, that is, Confucius.[22]

We have then the confluence of several factors at this stage of the official establishment of Confucianism. On the one hand, the tradition has engaged in conscious self-reflection in which it views itself as a repository for the preservation and interpretation of the teachings of the sages. On the other hand, it sees its own founder as a critical link, what the later tradition will call *tao-t'ung*, the transmission of the Way, in the establishment of the proper sources of authority to transmit such teachings, the Classics themselves.

The Confucian Canon: Classics or Scripture?

The official establishment of Confucianism during the Han dynasty was a major development in the clarification of the role of canon in the Confucian tradition. This official establishment goes hand in hand with the concern for clarification and adjudication of variant versions of the texts, the intention of which is the production of an authoritative version of each of the Five Classics. The question may well be asked whether the issue here is simply to have correct versions of the texts, such that the student of the Classics will have a consistent body of knowledge for the examination system or whether deeper concerns exist.

It might still be argued that the establishment of a canon and the attending questions of variant and authoritative texts indicates nothing more than a concern, although a very genuine one, with the establishment of the correct teachings and practices as Confucianism assumes its role as state orthodoxy and orthopraxy. On the other hand, the Classics must be something more than this if they are to be described as scripture or holy books. The designation canon in itself may be misleading by implying too readily the religious orientation of the works. The works studied by Confucians are, no doubt, classics in the full sense in which we use that word, a cross-generational statement that remains basic to the entire cultural milieu. It is a very different question, however, to impose upon these works the category of scripture.

To a large degree, the primary difference between a classic and a scripture lies in the locus of religious authority ascribed to the latter. It is a simple fact, not a tautology, that a scripture is a holy book and the designation "scripture" carries religious authority. Beyond the statement that a scripture is a holy book, and even that might be subject to closer scrutiny, especially when dealing with "holy books" in nonliterate traditions,[23] different scriptures may have little in common. Certainly their origins are very different, depending upon the particular religious tradition, or even within the same tradition, upon differing theological perspectives.[24] Not all scripture, in this sense, is revealed. To some religious traditions scripture is without revealed origins and in turn revelation itself can mean many different things depending upon particular theological interpretations.

To describe scripture as a holy book is not begging a definition, but suggesting that scripture must be related to our basic understanding of religion itself. We have discussed religion primarily in terms of its capacity for soteriology or ultimate transformation. The key to the interpretation of a work as scripture must be its ability to possess and hold authority within a tradition that can be defined in terms of a religious dimension or a soteriological capacity. The Classics are not revealed scripture, at least in the sense in which the term is usually employed, but this does not exclude the possibility of their religious dimension. The religious dimension must be established in terms of the tradition as a whole and thus, in this case, the tradition the Classics are a part of and serve.

This religious dimension has been defined in terms of the goal of the Confucian tradition, the Way of Heaven, the sage, the figure who represents the fulfillment of this goal, and the transformative relation between them. The Way of Heaven and the sage as the embodiment of Heaven are directly relevant to the question of whether these works are classics or scripture. The sage is a religious figure in the tradition and is directly involved in the Classics either in terms of exemplifying his own deeds or contributing to the composition itself. As such, while not "revelation," the sage is he who hears the Way of Heaven and manifests it to the world. Thus, the Classics become the repository of such manifestations. They bear an authority as well as a source that is religious in nature. On the basis of the primary religious dimension, even though this dimension for the Confucian may be seen primarily in terms of nonrevelatory ethical and humanistic tradition, discussing the Classics as holy books is, therefore, appropriate. Their official recognition in the establishment of Confucianism as state orthodoxy and orthopraxy may then be interpreted as the establishment of a Confucian canon with its implication of religious authority as well as religious dimension.

The New Scriptural Tradition of Neo-Confucianism

Neo-Confucianism was in many ways a reaffirmation of the basic teachings of Confucius and Mencius, although with increased philosophical speculation. One of the many features of the Neo-Confucian movement, and one particularly relevant to the present discussion, was a gradually increasing doubt as to the authority of the Classics.[25] During the T'ang dynasty, an orthodox interpretation of the Five Classics had been established in a work entitled *Wu-ching cheng-i, The Correct Meanings of the Five Classics.*[26] It was this interpretation that the Neo-Confucians rejected, suggesting instead that the interpretation of the Classics was a far more individualistic matter. Thus, new commentaries appeared, commentaries that differed substantially enough to warrant the designation "new learning," *hsin-hsüeh.* For Ch'eng I (1033-1107), one of the major Neo-Confucians of the Sung period, a commentary on the *I-Ching* was simply an occasion for the expounding of his own point of view. Thus, the commentary became a philosophical essay in its own right.

Wing-tsit Chan has suggested that in addition to a challenge to the orthodox interpretation of the Classics, there was also a growth of skepticism toward the authenticity and authority of the Classics themselves.[27] Ou-yang Hsiu (1007-1072), for example, doubted the authenticity of the commentaries, or wings, of the *I-Ching* as well as the introduction to the *Shih-Ching* and the three commentaries connected with the *Ch'un-Ch'iu*. Chu Hsi also shared in this same general attitude though, as Chan is careful to point out, he still worked closely with the Classics and wrote commentaries to at least four of them.[28] However, his attitude toward them had changed. It is this change that is critical for the Neo-Confucian movement. Chu Hsi was skeptical as to questions of authenticity of the texts and he was also flexible and individualistic in his interpretation. This can be seen, for example, in the following statements from the *Chin-ssu lu*[29] "In reading books, we should not rigidly stick to one meaning because the words are the same or similar. Otherwise every word will be a hindrance. We should see what the general tone of the passage is and what the preceding and following ideas are."[30] Or the following: "The Six Classics are vast and extensive. At first it is difficult to understand them completely. As students find their way, each establishes his own gate, and then returns home to conduct his inquiries himself."[31] Limits exist as well, however, in the process of interpretation of the Classics. "In interpreting the Classics, there is no harm in differing from their original meaning, except for important points, on which we must not differ."[32] Such passages represent a challenge to the authority of the Classics, a challenge which, as Chan argues, reaches its height in the viewpoint that the Classics might not be necessary at all.[33] Quoting Chu Hsi, "We make use of the Classics only to understand principle. If principles are understood we do not have to depend upon them."[34] Or even further: "If we understand principle, we do not have to have the Classics."[35] The meaning of the Classics shifted from the concreteness of the historical deeds of sages of antiquity, to a philosophical capacity to reveal principle, *li*, the underlying metaphysical structure revealed in all things. Even further, according to Chu Hsi, with the understanding of the Principle of Heaven, the source itself becomes unnecessary. The effect was to diminish the authority of the Classics. The result, however, was not perseverance in the light of skepticism, but the establishment of a new source of authority, specifically a new scriptural authority.

The new scriptural authority was found in a new collection of writings, the *Four Books*. The works that comprise the *Four Books* were not new, but the combination as well as the authority given the collection were all very new. The *Four Books* were composed of the *Analects*, the *Mencius*, and two chapters from *Li-Chi* which had for some length of time been considered as having philosophical merit as separate works, the *Ta-hsüeh* or *Great Learning* and the *Chung-yung* or *Doctrine of the Mean*. From Chu Hsi's point of view, as Chan has analyzed, at least three major differences are found between the *Four Books* and the Classics.[36] First, the Classics remained secondary in comparison to the actual teachings of Confucius and Mencius. It was the teachings of Confucius and Mencius that were central to Neo-Confucianism and in this regard the Classics were secondary. Second, Chu Hsi considered the *Four Books* as the source of knowledge of principle, *li*. They provided solid and pragmatic teachings for the ethical and religious growth of the individual as well as the implementation of the individual's moral nature into the daily affairs of the world. These concerns, from Chu Hsi's point of view, were simply not met in the Classics. Finally, it was Chu Hsi's opinion that the grouping of the *Four Books* provided a unique combination of works that served as an entire program of learning and self-cultivation. The whole was greater that the sum of its parts, and taken together, the works served the needs of the individual and society in their entirety.

The *Four Books* were also arranged to reflect a cumulative learning experience. The *Great Learning* was placed first because it provided a general framework for learning. The *Analects* was placed second to reinforce the primacy of Confucius' teachings as the foundation upon which learning was built. The *Mencius* was placed third to indicate its basis as the interpretative tool and elaborative text of the basic Confucian teachings. Fourth was the *Doctrine of the Mean*, a text that was appreciated for its subtlety and abstraction as well as the depth it displayed. In terms of the process of learning Chu Hsi stated, "I want people first of all to read the *Great Learning* to set a pattern, next to read the *Analects* to establish foundation, next to read the *Book of Mencius* for stimulation, and next to read the *Doctrine of the Mean* to find out the subtle points of the ancients."[37]

What is particularly important for our purposes is the new authority Chu Hsi places in the *Four Books*. Comparing the *Four Books* and the Classics he states, "The student should first read the *Analects* and the *Book of Mencius*. If he has studied them thoroughly, he will get the fundamental points. He will save a great deal of effort if he reads other Classics on the basis of these. The two books are like the measure and the balance."[38] The *Four Books* were thus the proper interpretative tool with which to approach the Classics. In such a case, however, the authority rested with the *Four Books* rather than the Classics and one might even suggest that much of the interest stopped with the Four Books as well. "The student should use the *Analects* and the *Book of Mencius* as the foundation. When these have been well studied, the Six Classics can be understood without study."[39] Chu Hsi's commentary upon this passage stated, "The *Analects* and the *Book of Mencius* require less effort but will yield more result, whereas the Six Classics require more effort but will yield less result."[40]

The actual approach to the texts themselves was for Chu Hsi and other Neo-Confucians an individualistic enterprise within certain limits. For Chu Hsi, the understanding of a text was not an exercise in philology, which was why he tended to ignore the T'ang commentaries, but a lesson in moral and spiritual self-cultivation. The unearthing of meaning in a text was measured, from the

Neo-Confucian perspective, in terms of the ability to penetrate to the deepest
layers of one's own nature; to establish a correlation between self-understanding
and the understanding of the text. In the metaphysical language used by Chu
Hsi, all things were said to contain principle, *li*, the underlying moral nature
immanent in the phenomenal world. Humankind's task of learning was to discover this principle through a process linked in Chu Hsi's mind to the investigation of things, *ko-wu*, and the proper attitude of reverent seriousness, *ching*.
The meaning of a text became almost a subjective experience, for it was a
matter of adjudicating inner dimensions of the self with the text itself. From
Chu Hsi's perspective, the *Four Books* represented the quintessential expression
of *li* or principle and as such could serve as a guide for the interpretation of the
Classics, but more importantly as a template to the unraveling of the depth of a
person's moral and spiritual core, his true nature and mind.

Chu Hsi, drawing upon the *Great Learning*, focused upon the underlying
li within things and one's own nature, which was to be understood gradually
through the process of *ko-wu*, the investigation of things. This school became
known as the School of Principle, *Li-hsüeh*. A challenge was offered to this
school by Lu Hsiang-shan (1139-1193) during the Sung dynasty and in particular Wang Yang-ming during the Ming dynasty,[41] suggesting that the investigation of things for principle only served to miss the fundamental metaphysical
importance of the mind as the true repository of principle. While the Chu Hsi
school focused upon learning, particularly book learning, necessary to accumulate an understanding of *li*, the School of Mind, *Hsin-hsüeh*, suggested that
learning and self-cultivation were primarily a process of realization of what
was already the ground of the mind. This led men such as Lu Hsiang-shan to
say of the Classics that they were merely footnotes to the mind.[42] Still, the
learning and the reverence shown the Classics and in particular the *Four Books*
in most cases seemed to change little. There were differences in interpretation,
but neither school rejected the authority of the *Great Learning*, nor the other
texts that make up the *Four Books*.

In his study of the nature of Neo-Confucian orthodoxy during the Sung
and Yüan dynasties, William Theodore de Bary has pointed to the major importance attached to the *Four Books*, particularly in those years of struggle to
establish Neo-Confucianism in the several generations following the death of
Chu Hsi.[43] Followers of Chu Hsi such as Chen Te-hsiu (1178-1234) during the
Sung and Hsü Heng (1209-1281) during the Yüan displayed extraordinary commitment to the *Four Books*. This was at a time when, as de Bary suggests,
Neo-Confucianism had not emerged into a position of prominence and in many
ways resembled a religion of the oppressed.[44] Hsü Heng represents perhaps the
clearest example of an almost fundamentalist approach[45] toward the *Four Books*
as well as several other writings he felt captured the essential Confucian teaching. Hsü had a virtual conversion experience and adopted in its totality the

Neo-Confucian point of view. He recommended to his disciples that they study *only* the *Four Books* and a work called the *Hsiao-hsüeh*, the *Elementary Learning*: all other works were deemed unimportant and unnecessary. He wrote to his second son, "I revere and have faith in [these books] as if they were divine."[46] The response is not atypical and suggests the degree to which these works were accepted as scripture within the living day-to-day context of the life of a Confucian.

Confucian Scripture in Daily LIfe

The daily life of moral and spiritual self-cultivation and learning of the Neo-Confucian is perhaps no more exquisitely expressed than in the following passage from the *Chin-ssu lu*, "The way of the Sage is to be heard through the ear, to be preserved in the heart, to be deeply embraced there to become one's moral character, and to become one's activities and undertakings when it is put into practice."[47] The focus of the religious life is the realization of one's own internal moral and spiritual nature. The vehicle for such learning is in part the relation of teacher and disciple, a model central to the tradition, following the paradigmatic relation of Confucius and his disciples. It is also in part the individual efforts of learning and self-cultivation, efforts that for many indicated the sheer pertinaciousness of the religious life. Both of these pursuits return to the fundamental authority of the *Four Books*, the Classics, and other selected writings dependent upon the particular interests of the individual. Thus, to hear the way of the sage was to understand the teachings preserved in the scriptures of the tradition.

This scripture was to be thoroughly internalized by the individual through repetition and memorization as well as self-understanding. Repetition and memorization in themselves were always viewed as empty and sterile. The *Chin-ssu lu* cautions against considering learning as a mere process of memorization. "In studying books, search for moral principles. In compiling books, appreciate what ultimate purposes they have. Do not just copy them."[48] A further and similar point: "Master Ming-tao considered memorization, recitation and acquiring extensive information as 'trifling with things and losing one's purpose.' "[49] The commentary on the passage states, "Merely to memorize what one has recited and to have extensive information, but not to understand or to reach the point of thorough understanding and penetration, is to chase after what is small and to forget what is great ... "[50] The focus of one's efforts was self-understanding. Some efforts, at least for certain individuals, were directed towards the successful passing of the civil service examinations, exams that were based upon the knowledge of the Classics and the *Four Books*. Orthodoxy, however, is a rich and diverse phenomenon.[51] While there was an official state orthodoxy there was also an orthodoxy that served the individual. For a Chen Te-hsiu or Hsü Heng embracing the Confucian perspective was a religious act. Such a motivation is also illustrated by works such as the *Chin-ssu lu,* as well as the often contemplative lives of individual Neo-Confucians who chose not to serve in government, but to pursue their own form of learning and self-cultivation.[52]

There is a certain tension within the character of the scholar-official. On the one hand, a certain amount of basic memorization and recitation of the Classics and the *Four Books* was essential to pass the examination system, and this remained as an important, if not critical step, within the individual's maturation process.[53] On the other hand, however, to have as the goal only a successful placing in the examination and thus the assurance of a prestigious appointment was not characteristic of the noble person, the *chün-tzu,* who had remained the paradigm of the Confucian tradition. Thus, while rote learning is necessary, so, too, is the preservation of a larger motive, one that sees learning as the way to the realization of one's own moral nature and thus the way to accord with the Way of Heaven. We find the following kind of statement exhorting the student on to study. "The Six Classics must be gone through one after another, in repeated cycles. The student will find that their moral principles are unlimited."[54] Or a very personal statement about the nature of reading and the way in which it should deeply penetrate one's nature: "In reading a book, one should recite it silently. Often excellent thoughts will come to him at midnight or while he is sitting in meditation. If one has thoroughly understood the great foundation of a book, however, it will be easy to remember."[55]

Based upon statements such as this it is easy to see why the practice of copying passages or phrases from the Classics, the *Four Books* or various Confucian authors, became a central activity in study and self-cultivation. This was the art of calligraphy and one that the Confucian scholar practiced frequently in the quiet of his study. Calligraphy was not simply to perfect certain styles of writing as an end unto themselves, nor was the focus a method for the memorization of passages and phrases. It was seen as a direct means to deep and profound understanding of the wisdom of the Classics or other sources and the reflection of such wisdom in the gradually developing moral nature of the individual. To write the words was to identify with the words and to manifest in one's own nature the meaning of the words. Thus, calligraphy too was seen as a part of the path of self-cultivation toward the goal of sagehood. Others, in a autobiographical genre, expressed the manner of resolution of a life, a life with purpose and fulfillment from a gradually increasing understanding of the writings of the sages.[56] To call the source of inspiration of these various kinds of activity anything less than scripture and holy book is simply to miss the full significance of the Confucian religious life and its focus upon the realization of the Way of Heaven.

◆ ——————————————————— CHAPTER **III**

The Sage as Saint:
A Study in Religious Categories

In an article on saints and martyrs in the 1922 edition of *Hasting's Encyclopedia of Religion and Ethics* it was suggested that the sage rather than the saint was paradigmatic of Chinese religious traditions.[1] The inference is that sage and saint are separate categories in terms of a typology of religious functionaries; the saint is a religious figure, the sage perhaps more of a wise man who may even preclude the question of religious dimension. We know already that the sage, is a figure of extraordinary importance to the Confucian tradition. There is virtually no Confucian who has not addressed the teachings of the sages, the lives of the sages, and the role the sages play in the restoration of humankind and the world to the ways of virtue, the Way of Heaven. This attention to the sage is rooted in a profound faith in the perfectabilty of humankind. As Tu Wei-ming has expressed, "The Confucian conviction that virtue can be learned and that the highest exemplification of virtue, sagehood, is attainable has been a source of inspiration for both the educated elite and the general populace in China."[2]

This chapter analyzes the Confucian sage as a religious figure.[3] The approach is fundamentally historical and will analyze the term *sage* within its earliest context of Classical Confucian material. In turn, it studies the changing relevancy of the ideal as well as image of the sage within the development of Neo-Confucianism. Whether the Confucian sage is compatible with the category of saint will depend in large part upon the salient characteristics that emerge in a typology of the figure. The question of the sage as saint rests as well, however, with an analysis of the nature of the saint. If the term can be freed from its specific role in the history of Christianity, it may be useful in

39

describing a certain type of figure whose role can be defined within a number of different traditions.[4] As a type of religious person, the saint suggests characteristics of both "otherness" or inimitability, associated with the veneration of the saint, and exemplariness or imitability, resulting in the emulation of the saint by his followers.[5]

This characterization of the saint is not unlike religious traditions themselves, combining elements of imitability and inimitability. The Confucian case is a fascinating one in this respect, however, for Confucianism seems to have consciously minimized the expression of "otherness" or inimitability through miraculous and supernatural means. The Confucian tradition more frequently finds its religious dimension within the process of an individual's learning and self-cultivation, and the perfection of his moral nature. The sage is the exemplar of such perfection, but the record of his deeds often suggests a degree of "ordinariness" rather than "otherness." As a result, hagiography takes on a very different content in the Confucian context. From the Confucian point of view, it is being most human that is the measure of people's religious dimension. Does this particular form of religious dimension permit us to call the Confucian sage a saint?

The Sage and Confucius

Confucius as sage was the exemplary teacher of the Way of Heaven. As Tu Wei-ming has said: "He was a sage to his followers but not to himself, and for that reason he became the exemplar of sagehood itself."[6] To himself he was merely an individual struggling with the perfection of his own moral nature. He saw the world in moral decline and sought to remedy its ways. To accomplish this he turned to the sages of antiquity and the teachings they had left. It was not his own experience but theirs he sought to transmit to his own generation. He was, as he said, not a creator, but merely a transmitter.[7] He was not a sage, he merely loved learning,[8] and found through learning the teachings he firmly believed held the key for the return of humankind to the ways of virtue.

The sage for Confucius was, thus, of the greatest significance, and the attempt to articulate the way of the sages to his own generation remained Confucius' primary goal. The term *sage* occurs in the *Analects* only eight times, four as *sheng*, sage, and four as *sheng-jen*, sagely person. I want to briefly summarize these occurrences. *Analects* 6:28 is a reference to the ideal ruler. Confucius says that any person capable of transforming the state to peace and order would be, without doubt, a sage. The focus is upon the Confucian virtue *jen*, goodness, or humanity, and the sage's ability to enact it, thereby transforming the entire empire. *Analects* 7:33 is a reference to the distance that separates Confucius from the sages. Confucius claims for himself only an unwearying effort to pursue learning. Nothing is suggested of Confucius himself being a sage or, for that matter, anyone in contemporary times. *Analects* 9:6 contains two references. A disciple is asked whether his teacher Confucius is a sage. The answer suggests that, from the disciple's point of view, Confucius is at least very close to being a sage. *Analects* 7:25 finds Confucius lamenting that he can find no sage in his own generation. He states that he would be fortunate even to find a *chün-tzu*, much less a sage. In *Analects* 16:8, the noble person is said to stand in awe of three things: the Mandate of Heaven, great men, and the words of the sages. In *Analects* 19:12, the sage is said to possess beginnings and endings; that is, he possesses the ability to penetrate or understand all things, and is suggestive of the *Shuo-wen*'s definition of sage as *t'ung*, penetrating.[9]

Who, then, are the sages in the context of the *Analects*? It appears that only the sage kings of antiquity achieve the status of sage. Yao and Shun are described in the *Analects*, for example, as the highest standard of humankind.[10] Yao is described as equal to Heaven, Yü is sublime and yet humble.[11] What of the Duke of Chou, the constant paradigm of virtue from the Confucian perspective? Even given the extraordinary status assigned to the Duke of Chou by Confucius, he is never spoken of as a sage. The same might be said for King Wu. Although a paradigm of virtue, King Wu needed ten ministers to govern, whereas the sage Shun needed only five.[12] The category of sage seems thus to be limited to the figures Yao, Shun, and Yü for Confucius. The paradigms of virtuous rule, Kings Wen and Wu, as well as the Duke of Chou, by not being given the designation sage, serve to indicate the extraordinary level of achievement intended by the term *sage*. What is particularly apparent in the context of the *Analects* is the separation of the sage from the capacities of ordinary persons. There is no attempt to suggest that one can reach the state of sagehood. There is no reason to believe that another sage might not appear, but there have been none since the sage kings of antiquity, and for Confucius at least, the sage was identified with this period of antiquity. They remain as figures removed from ordinary time and place. Centered in antiquity, they were thought to have acted on the basis of their direct apprehension of the Way of Heaven. This did not, however, minimize their impact upon Confucius nor upon what he felt their influence could be in his own time. They remained as exemplary figures, a high ideal for humankind to emulate, however distant the actual achievement of the state of sagehood. The sage was, as Hawley as suggested for the saint, an example both of *something*, as an embodiment of the Way of Heaven, and an example to *someone*, as a model for emulation.[13]

Mencius, Humanity, and the Sage

Mencius, as Confucius, saw the sage as an example of someone who had fulfilled the potentiality of human nature; that is, the sage was someone who

was fully, deeply, and profoundly human. To have achieved this level of humanity meant that one was not only a moral person, but an exemplar of humanity's
capability of being moral as the highest goal of humanity itself. This, in turn,
was a reflection of the Way of Heaven. Mencius shared Confucius' optimism in
the perfectability of humankind and saw the sages of antiquity as paradigmatic
figures whose remoteness did not lessen their significance for his own generation. The sages remained as examples of the fulfillment and perfection of human
nature and as examples to all those for whom the ideal of moral perfection was
as yet unrealized.

As exemplar of human perfection and a reflection of the Way of Heaven,
the sage played a key role in Mencius' unfoldment of Confucian teachings. The
term for *sage*, for example, played a far more prominent role in the writings of
Mencius than in the *Analects*. Forty-seven occurrences of the word *sage* are
found in the Mencius text. These can be summarized under several general
themes. First, the sage for Mencius is also for the most part represented by the
sage kings of antiquity. Mencius comments in several passages that Yao and
Shun were of the age of sages and after them the way of sages fell into decline.
Even Confucius himself cannot without difficulty measure up to the sages of
the past.[14] Second, Mencius expresses a hope that sages will once again appear,
presumably to guide humankind to act in accordance with the Way of Heaven.[15]
Third, a number of passages give characteristics of the sage, suggesting the
possibility of a definition and characterization of the sage's role and nature. For
example, Mencius says of the sage that he exhibits perfect human relations,[16]
he employs instruments with perfection—that is, he has practical skills[17]—he
has a "transforming" influence upon others,[18] and there is a sense of wonder
when in the sage's presence.[19] Fourth, although there is an idealization of the
sage kings of antiquity, there is also a movement of the figure of the sage out of
antiquity. Unlike Confucius' view, the Duke of Chou is for Mencius a sage.[20]
With this recognition of the Duke of Chou as a sage, the concept has broken its
time barrier. Although the age of Yao and Shun is still the preferred context, the
sage can now be found in different periods. This seems to have its effect in
the interpretation of Confucius himself who, from Mencius' point of view, is
a sage.[21]

Finally, for Mencius a very different relation is established between the
sage and the capacity of the ordinary person than seems suggested by Confucius. As the ideal of the sage breaks free of its sacred time referent in antiquity,
the relation of the nature of the sage and the nature of ordinary or normal
human capacities becomes more relevant. No longer is it possible to distinguish
the ordinary person and the sage solely on the basis of a temporal context.
How, then, does one adjudicate the nature of the sage and the nature of the
ordinary person? Mencius first argues that the sages of the past and those of
the present have the same nature, *hsing*,[22] an important premise to indicate

that there is no difference in the use of the term *sage*. Thus, whether referring to Yao and Shun or to the Duke of Chou and Confucius, to call them sages is to say the same thing about each. In another passage, Mencius argues that sages are the same in kind with others, but stand out through their capacity to manifest their character.[23] For example, the sage realizes and thus manifests his nature of righteousness *before* the ordinary person.[24] The critical argument states that sages and ordinary persons are by nature, *hsing*, the same.[25] Its appropriate and significant conclusion follows—that *any* person might become a Yao or Shun.[26]

With this statement, the ideal of the sage changed from a figure locked in antiquity to a potentially realizable goal for any person. This change in the interpretation of the sage was predicated upon the understanding of human nature and suggested that all humanity possessed the same basic nature of goodness that was instilled in each by Heaven. Mencius, in suggesting that anyone could become a Yao or Shun, left open the possibility that through rigorous learning and self-cultivation one could, in fact, become a sage. The state of sagehood is the product of one's own efforts. And if one doubted this possibility, there was the example of Confucius himself. The sage remained, for Mencius, an example of one who had fulfilled his humanity, and he was in some sense at least an accessible role model. Whereas for Confucius, such role models remained just that, that is, they could be emulated but not fully realized, Mencius molded the Confucian tradition to the appreciation of the human capability for the realization of its own perfection in sagehood. This ability of humanity to perfect itself in terms of the realization of the goal of sagehood became the central and driving force for learning and self-cultivation in the later Neo-Confucian tradition.

The Neo-Confucian Quest for Sagehood

For the Neo-Confucian, sagehood was no longer an ideal of the past. Rather, it had become an ideal that stood as the end point of the cultivation and learning process.[27] Fundamentally, it was thought to be realizable within one's own lifetime. The *Chin-ssu lu* represented a kind of guidebook to the learning necessary for the realization of the goal of sagehood.[28] It was a work oriented not to the Confucian state orthodoxy and examination system, but rather to the individual's own search for sagehood. The second chapter begins, for example, with the sentence, "The sage aspires to become Heaven, the worthy aspires to become a sage and the gentlemen aspires to become a worthy."[29] In this expression and others similar to it, sagehood stood as the goal of the learning process, and, for many Neo-Confucians, the focus of their lives became this quest for sagehood. Chang Tsai (1021-1077), for example, "Often told" his students "the way to understand the rule of propriety, to fulfill one's nature and to transform one's physical nature, and told them not to stop learning until they were equal to the sage."[30] According to the *Chin-ssu lu*, Ch'eng I and Ch'eng Hao (1032-1085) even in their early teen years possessed the desire to pursue the goal of sagehood.[31] There was general agreement as to the relevancy of the goal. The question concerned the nature of the goal and how one would describe sagehood, or for that matter, recognize it.

Although sagehood is a very broad category encompassing many schools of interpretation and individual expressions, certain common and recognizable features can be identified. Most commonly, the state of sagehood refers to the full realization and development of the potential of human nature or mind. I am using the terms nature, *hsing*, and mind, *hsin*, to refer here to the most broadly based distinction in Neo-Confucian learning, that between the School of Principle, *Li-hsüeh*, associated with Chu Hsi and Ch'eng I, and the School of Mind, *Hsin-hsüeh*, associated with Wang Yang-ming. Human nature or mind, depending upon the particular perspective, is thought to share in the basic moral nature of the universe. In many ways this is simply a development of the Mencian point of view, for Mencius had said that by coming to understand one's own nature, one could understand the Way of Heaven.[32] Humankind's moral nature is seen as a microcosm of the Way of Heaven, the macrocosm. Within the framework of Neo-Confucianism this relationship is spoken of in terms of Principle, or the Principle of Heaven, *T'ien-li*, which is shared by humankind and the universe in common. In elaborating on the Principle of Heaven, the Neo-Confucian raised the Way of Heaven to a conscious metaphysical structure and in so doing laid the groundwork for a philosophical understanding of the relation of humanity and the universe.

The state of sagehood is also frequently spoken of in terms of a sense of "oneness" with all things. Specifically, this involves the recognition of humankind's moral nature and, in turn, the realization that the basic nature of goodness found in human nature or mind is shared with all things. It is in this sense that we can talk about the commonality of the microcosm, the individual in this case, and the macrocosm, all other things, for they share in the same underlying moral nature of the universe. Thus, Ch'eng Hao speaks in terms of the essential unity between himself and the universe. "The humane man forms one body with all things comprehensively."[33]

Oneness has, however, many shades of meaning. This is a term that can also be easily misused to overemphasize a form of mysticism, in itself a term of extraordinary complexity, but characterized more often than not by the psychological character of an experience.[34] What we are referring to in these passages is for the most part a point of understanding that saw the interconnectedness of all things through a common and shared moral nature. It need not have any particular mystical implications in terms of a certain type of experience, often described as apophatic in character, that directly and instantaneously perceives such unity. On the other hand, some Confucians recorded experiences that have the character of genuine mystical experience, and thus this dimension cannot be totally ignored.[35] For the most part, however, the term connotes a sense of interconnectedness and in many ways emphasizes the moral responsibilities this relationship bears and the ways in which one should act, rather than the psychological dimensions of the experience itself.

Chou Tun-i (1017-1073) uses the term *oneness* primarily as a description of a mental attitude necessary to permit one to act, that is, to act in a moral way. He emphasizes the relation between oneness and moral action in response to a question on how one becomes a sage:

> The essential way is to attain oneness [of mind]. By oneness is meant having no desire. Having no desire one is "empty" [absolutely pure and peaceful] while tranquil, and straightforward while in action. Being "empty" while tranquil, one becomes intelligent and hence penetrating. Being straightforward while active, one becomes impartial and hence all-embracing. Being intelligent, penetrating, impartial, and all-embracing, one is almost a sage.[36]

Chang Tsai suggests, in another dimension of oneness, that the sage is capable of entering into all things. "By enlarging one's mind, one can enter into all things in the world. As long as anything is not yet entered into, there is still something outside of the mind. . . . The sage . . . fully develops his nature and does not allow what is seen or heard to fetter his mind."[37] Another passage in the *Chin-ssu lu* focuses upon the basic feature of unity: "Combine the internal and the external into one and regard things and the self as equal. This is the way to see the fundamental point of the Way."[38] The basis of this unity, whether spoken of in terms of the transcendence of the dichotomy of internal and external or the ability of the sage to penetrate into all things, remains the common moral nature shared by all things. It is this same shared moral nature that Wang Yang-ming called the innate good knowledge. It is that which at the metaphysical level united the microcosm and the macrocosm and what the sage, who has fully penetrated his own nature or mind, directly comprehended.

Even with the increasing relevancy of the ideal of sagehood, seldom was there a claim to its achievement. There are a few exceptions to this, but not many, and most of these represent a certain philosophical interpretation of the state of sagehood.[39] For the vast majority, sagehood precluded self-affirmation just as its goal eluded any simple realization.[40] It was something imitable and yet its realization remained in the realm of the inimitable. However, it was not beyond the capacity of Neo-Confucians to assign at least a near status to former and major figures of the tradition.

How does one determine sagehood in someone? There is the full realization and development of the moral nature and a sense of oneness with the universe, as we have seen, but what do these mean in terms of recognizable features within the individual? How would the sage appear, and how would he act? As William Theodore de Bary has pointed out in his seminal study of spiritual practice in Neo-Confucianism, by far the greatest number of characteristics associated with the sage are essentially personality traits.[41] In other words, no lengthy descriptions of the realized state of sagehood are found. It is not the state of sagehood that seems to be of concern, but rather the life of the sage, and it is this life that is the telling comment upon realization of the goal. With this in mind, it is surely no coincidence that the final chapter of the *Chin-ssu lu*, "On the Dispositions of Sages and Worthies," contains biographies of those thought to have realized or at least partially realized the ideal of sagehood. Included among the biographies were not only sages of antiquity, although this was the briefest material, but Confucius, Mencius, and various prominent Confucians as well as Neo-Confucians across the centuries. This is not an addendum to the text, seeking to provide biographical information on a number of major Confucians. In fact, the information provided is very brief and not even in a sense of major biographical interest. Most of what is included might best be described as brief insights into the personalities of the figures mentioned. The role of this material, however, remains central to the mission of providing a guidebook of learning and self-cultivation for the realization of the goal of sagehood. It creates the subject matter of Confucian hagiography, and the chief function of such hagiography is to provide an example for emulation.

The sense of caring and commiseration on the part of the sage was a salient feature of the biographies of sages and worthies contained in the *Chin-ssu lu*. Of Ch'eng I it was said, for example,

> The master not only possessed an unusual nature by endowment, but his own nourishment of it was in accordance with the Way. . . . His conscientiousness and sincerity penetrated metal and stone, and his filial piety and brotherly respect influenced spiritual beings. As one looked at his countenance, one found that in dealing with people he was as warm as the spring sun. . . . He saw penetratingly and made no discrimination between himself and others. As one tried to fathom his depth, one realized that it was as great as a boundless ocean.[42]

Of Ch'eng Hao it was said, "His self-cultivation was so complete that he was thoroughly imbued with the spirit of peacefulness, which was revealed in his voice and countenance. However, as one looked at him, he was so lofty and deep that none could treat him with disrespect. When, he came upon things to do, he did them with ease and leisure, and no sense of urgency. But at the same time he was sincere and earnest, and did not treat them carelessly."[43] And finally, Ch'eng Hao wrote of Chou Tun-i that he "did not cut the grass growing outside his window. When asked about it, he said, '[The feeling of the grass] and mine are the same.' "[44] Chu Hsi said of this passage: "You can realize the matter yourself. You must see wherein one's feelings and that of the grass are the same."[45]

In these and other passages the sage is portrayed as penetrating in his knowledge. He understood his own nature as well as the nature of the macrocosm and the depth of his understanding seemed as obvious in his countenance as in his actions. He was described as peaceful, warm, caring, utterly sincere and honest, serious and reverent, and displaying an extraordinary compassion for the life of others. In many respects, such images differed little from the earliest image of the term *sage*, although it was now accompanied by a metaphysical sophistication and a relevancy to the individual seeking his own self-understanding. With this development, the sage became in a sense a relevant and intimate image for the Neo-Confucian, and the *santus* of his presence was a model to all who sought to emulate the ideal.

The Sage as Saint

Is this figure of the sage, emerging amidst images of kindness and humility, peacefulness and reverence, equally describable as a saint? Many characterizations and descriptions of the saint are not irrelevant to this image of the sage. Although the technical definition of saint in its Christian historical context[46] has little or no meaning whatsoever in the Confucian tradition, the derivation of the word *saint* in terms of the Latin *sanctus*, Greek *hagios*, and Hebrew *qadosh* merely suggests that which is set apart and thus that which is thereby sacred.[47] In this broadest context, the saint may be described simply as the holy person of a given tradition. Even the Arabic for saint, *wali*, meaning a friend of God,[48] if viewed in terms of the relationship established between finite and infinite, is suggestive of the role played by the Confucian sage. The sage in this sense was the holy person of the Confucian tradition. According to the basic philological structure of the word *sage*, the sage penetrates the Way of Heaven and discloses it to humankind.[49] The saint, as the holy person of a given tradition, and the Confucian sage would thus appear to share a common role and common characteristic. However, the derivation of the term *saint* in terms of sacred and thus holy person only points to the broadest category of holy person in general. As the epitome of the religious dimension of the Confucian tradition, the sage is the full embodiment of sacredness and thus the holy person of the Confucian tradition. One must ask, however, whether the commonality at this level is significant? The question that remains, of course, is whether by establishing the category "holy person," we have sufficiently weakened the category "saint" to no longer articulate its distinctiveness. If the term *saint* is to be employed and not simply *holy person*, something more must be intended in the use of the term *saint*. It is one thing to refer to the

Confucian sage as a holy person, but it seems quite another to call the Confucian sage a saint.

G. van der Leeuw has addressed the category of sainthood in his now
classic study in the phenomenology of religion.[50] His sense of the potency of
power associated with the saint, particularly his corpse, is of little relevance to
the Confucian sage, however, he also emphasizes the activity of the saint on
behalf of humankind. The saint is he who takes on the trials and tribulations of
humankind, working for the betterment of the world and the elimination of
suffering. This is a characteristic of the saint that would not apply to all religious functionaries who might otherwise be spoken of as holy persons. When
we observe the role of the Confucian sage, we find the sage's commitment to
benefiting humankind one of the primary characteristics emphasized. The sage
is the epitome of such concern for the feeling of humankind. We have seen this
in terms of the images associated with the sage kings of antiquity for Confucius
and Mencius. In turn, such concern finds its quintessential reiteration in the
Neo-Confucian tradition in the *Western Inscription* of Chang Tsai in which the
sage is depicted as a brother to all living things. Fan Chung-yen (989-1052), a
Sung dynasty Neo-Confucian, summarized the characteristic by saying that the
ideal of the Confucian was to be the first to take on the troubles of the world
and the last in enjoying its pleasures.

What is particularly helpful about van der Leeuw's characterization is the
degree to which a central feature of the Confucian sage can be focused upon as
a distinguishing mark of sainthood. In this sense, it is possible not only to see
the sage as the epitome of the tradition's religious depth, and thus a holy
person, but in addition to suggest that the sage shares a critical feature with the
category *saint* as that category itself would be differentiated from the larger
context of *holy person*.

The work of Joachim Wach in the history of religions also permits us to
explore further the common ground of sage and saint. For Wach, the distinguishing characteristic of the saint is his or her personal character.[51] The influence of the saint, according to Wach, is a quiet and gentle one. This is to
distinguish the saint from the prophet whose role by definition is one of activity. The influence of the saint is by the exemplary character of his life, his
imitable facet, and thus his role as a model to the community. For Wach, the
saint's prestige and influence are not measured by achievements, by profes-
sional associations, or even by excelling in intellectual or practical talents.[52]
Wach continually returns to the quiet and exemplary life as the quintessential
expression of the saint. The driving force in this life is the basic religious
experience that has formed the foundation upon which the saint's life is built.

In his classic exploration of the psychological dimensions of religious experience, William James has suggested similar characteristics of the saint.[53] The
saint is one who, according to James, feels himself part of a "wider life," has a

sense of "friendly continuity of the Ideal Power with his own life," and has an immense elation and sense of freedom as well as the "shifting of the emotional center towards loving."[54] For James, the practical consequences in terms of the saint's life include asceticism, strength of the soul, purity, and charity. Obviously such categories are very broad. To avoid the broadest context of holy person, such characteristics can be placed within the framework of Wach's sense of the personal character of the saint. James has also said of saints: "They are impregnators of the world, vivifiers and animators of potentialities of goodness which but for them would lie forever dormant."[55] They provide, in other words, an exemplary life, and few if any who have contact with them come away unaffected.

The Confucian model of the sage seems most relevant within this context of the exemplary life. The Confucian sage also provides that exemplary life and a work such as the *Chin-ssu lu* speaks directly to the importance of this role. The Confucian sage lives his life within the framework of the Way of Heaven or the Principle of Heaven. The sage is he who is aware of the relation of his own nature with that of Heaven, and it is the concreteness of the life lived that serves as the exemplification of the sage's understanding and religious depth. Such a figure serves as a model or exemplar and his life itself is the measure of his understanding. The sage is both imitable and inimitable; imitable as a model and inimitable in terms of the depth of his understanding. The biographies of the sages and worthies found in the *Chin-ssu lu* serve to illustrate the importance placed upon the imitability of the sage, yet there is always the recognition of an inimitable dimension. Such biographies point to the features Wach and James discuss. The sage is quiet, at ease, serene, compassionate, and committed to serving fellow beings. The degree to which such features are prominent in the saint is the degree to which the sage and the saint share common ground.

There is a corollary to the exemplary life which may at first appear to differentiate sage and saint. The saint is known primarily for his humbleness, gentleness, and self-effacement, according to Wach.[56] He does not seem to be known for intellectual leadership or the exercise of power. The term *sage*, however, as we have already seen, seems to be easily extendable to such capabilities. For Confucius, the sages were primarily, if not exclusively, the sage kings of antiquity. That they were sage kings rather that simply sages is of importance. In this capacity as ruler the sheer exercise of the position involved more than humbleness, gentleness, and self-effacement. The definition of sage in the *Shuo-wen* is appropriate. The sage king is he who can rule because he possesses an understanding of the Way of Heaven. Does this role as a sage king exclude the saintly characteristics of humbleness, gentleness, and kindness? Not necessarily.

While the sage had a high degree of authority and power, the primary motivation and intentionality of the sage was to bring the way of humankind into accord with the Way of Heaven. Such authority and power were not ends in themselves but only by-products of the penetration and understanding the sage has acquired. In this sense the sage even for Confucius may have been a humble and gentle person, not perhaps in the outward demeanor of his role, but within his attitude in such a role. Yü after all is both sublime and humble.[57] The obvious difference between sage and saint is the difference in external role and thus capacity for manifesting humbleness, gentleness, and self-effacement. As an internal attitude the difference is potentially far less obvious.

The Neo-Confucians' view of the sage suggests a far stronger sense of commonality between sage and saint. For the Classical Confucian, the sage remained primarily a sage king, although even here the figure of the teacher in its paradigmatic form of Confucius himself emerged as a contrasting image of the sage. For the Neo-Confucian, conversely, the goal of sagehood was seen as something realizable within one's lifetime. This did not mean that one would become a sage king. The figure of the sage by this point included both those in authority and those holding no authority at all, but exercising their role as teachers or simply learners on the path to sagehood themselves.[58] The focus was the full development and perfection of one's humanity. Such perfection of one's humanity involved penetrating the roots of one's nature or mind, and this was accomplished through both internal or external modes of learning and self-cultivation. The personalities who were portrayed as having accomplished something of this goal were marked, as we have seen in the *Chin-ssu lu*, by a spirit of humbleness, gentleness, and self-effacement. Thus, what appeared to differentiate sage and saint is simply one further indication of the potential commonality to be found.

To focus only upon the gentleness and humbleness of the saint, however, may present only one dimension of a complex figure. Saints, too, have been associated frequently with processes of change and transformation.[59] A saint may act as a key component of a revitalization movement and as such is a symbol of change as well as involvement and activity. This does not make the saint a prophet, as Wach might suggest, but simply broadens the role played by the saint. Saint and prophet remain separate, not in terms of quietude and activity, but in terms of the style of pronouncement of knowledge. Thus, to describe fully the phenomenon of sainthood, it seems necessary to point to characteristics that include an active capacity as well as the contemplative and quiet modes, bearing in mind that nothing is necessarily inimical about the relationship between humbleness and activity.

The capacities of quietude and activity can serve as useful referents to the Confucian tradition as well. The Confucian sage can be portrayed in both active and passive contexts. Central always to the sage's composition was his ability to correct the ills of the world. This was reflected in the sage kings of antiquity who through their rule would be able to bring harmony into the world, and in the sage teachers, exemplified by Confucius himself, who through instruction and learning would be able to restore the ways of virtue to humanity. It was also reflected in the Neo-Confucian tradition in the unceasing notion that it was the responsibility of the Confucian to promulgate the Way of Heaven, whether serving in government or in teaching. There is perhaps a certain amount of tension between modes expressive of quietude and those focused upon activity. The dominant image of the sage for Confucius was primarily activity, although even here the issue was complex. The sage was first and foremost a sage king, but as a sage king there is a dimension of his strength that rested in quietude. This contrast is well-represented in the *Analects*: on the one hand, Confucius refers to the sage's capacity for bringing comfort to the entire population through active measures,[60] and, on the other hand, the sage rules by stillness and quietude.[61] Thus, the image of the Confucian sage has a broader dimension than the focus upon quietude alone would suggest. In the larger context, the ideal of sagehood has for the Neo-Confucian images of activity as well as quietude. In this respect, sage and saint continue to compliment each other.

What we have thus far seen would suggest a certain commonality of characteristics between sage and saint clustered primarily around the sense of exemplariness or imitability of the character of each. The saint seems, however, to maintain a delicate balance of exemplariness or imitability and "otherness" or inimitability. If the saint is he whose distinctive status is related to this balance of imitability and inimitability, can any common ground be maintained with the Confucian sage? After all, the Confucian tradition, as we have seen, has consciously minimized the expression of "otherness" through miraculous or supernatural means. This, however, does not preclude the category otherness from appropriate application to what at first appears to be *other* than otherness—that is, ordinariness. In other words, is not the notion of *otherness* itself perhaps applied with an already established theological framework suggesting a transcendent rather than immanent referent? The Confucian sage is an exemplar of the perfection of human nature. The records of the sage's deeds suggest an ordinariness in their focus, yet the ordinariness itself has the character of the religious when seen within the soteriological context of the tradition. To develop humankind's moral nature, from the Confucian perspective, is not only to realize its full potential, but to establish the essential relation between humankind and the Way of Heaven from the Neo-Confucian perspective. As such, precisely those activities centered upon the development of human nature have for the Confucian the character of otherness, if by *otherness* is meant not exclusively transcendence, but simply establishment of the relationship between the finite and the infinite, whether in transcendent or immanent modes.

Otherness as a recognition of the immanence of the absolute represents a dimension of the religious structure of the Confucian tradition. The sage possessed this capacity for otherness, but he also seemed to have reflected a dimension of otherness that fell into the more traditional usage of the term, that which was beyond description or ineffable. He was characterized by an imitability, yet his nature seemed to be inimitable as well. This sense of otherness seems to have been accepted as part of the complexity of the figure of the sage. An example of this ineffable quality may be seen in a description of Confucius found in the *Analects*.[62] Confucius' disciple Tzu Kung gives a description of Confucius by using the analogy of a wall and its height. He said that the walls surrounding the Master were so high that one could not look over them. It was only by entering through the gate that one could view the splendor of the interior, but, he said, those admitted through the gate are few. What Tzu Kung seemed to be attempting to describe was the inimitable and ineffable quality of the sage. There is extraordinary height and depth within his teacher. It is, in fact, beyond description. There is still much, however, that might be described of Confucius and his teachings and one can pursue a path of learning and self-cultivation to emulate Confucius, but that does not make one a Confucius.

Even with the recognition of the inimitable quality of Confucius, sagehood remained for the later tradition a goal that could be achieved. No doubt, the path of learning and self-cultivation was long and arduous, but a hope and faith remained in the realization of its achievement, even if something about the goal itself seemed beyond reach. The status of sage was in a sense distinctive, perhaps even unique, for while the path was imitable, the goal itself retained a certain dimension of inimitability.

With these decriptions of the sage and the recognition of the complex modalities of his being, the sage and the saint remain within a common mode of expression: the foci for both is found in the balance of imitability and inimitability. The application of the term *saint* to the Confucian context reaffirms the still often overlooked religious dimension of the Confucian tradition; and although any wholesale adoption of the term *saint* for *sage* is premature at best, the sheer possibility of commonality at least partially adumbrates the religious potential found within the Confucian sage.

◆ ————————————————— CHAPTER **IV**

The Centered Self:
Confucian Religious Autobiography

The self seeking to understand itself reconstructs through memory the development of its life, thereby engaging in the fundamental task of autobiography. If autobiography is to differ from a mere diary of facts, a chronological reckoning of the history of a life, then the endless maze of events and relations, must be sorted out and reorganized. Roy Pascal reminds us that "autobiography is a shaping of the past. It imposes a pattern on a life, constructs out of it a coherent story."[1] Not every event is recalled. An episode important in the eyes of a biographer may escape the purview of the autobiographer. Is the reason a failure of memory? Probably not. Rather, it is a result of the selective gaze of the autobiographer. Events for the biographer only partially explicated through historical context may become crucial turning points in autobiography. The difference is the perspective brought to bear on the life story. The autobiographer interprets the meaning of his own life; the order or consistency is the perspective within which he views himself.

When the autobiographical orientation is the self in religious perspective, the ordering of the life story is in terms of an individual's relation to his religious goals. For Saint Augustine, Saint Teresa, or John Woolman the selection and ordering of the autobiographical account is in terms of spiritual development.[2] In the self's journey into self and the self's relation to the world, experiences recorded contribute to defining a person and his spiritual foundation. The focus of religious autobiography is the centered self, an individual defining himself as a religious person.

53

Neo-Confucian Expressions of Self

The preoccupation with self is not exclusively the prerogative of Western culture, nor for that matter is the occurrence of autobiographical writing.[3] Sixteenth- and seventeenth-century China provides sufficient evidence of similar concerns. This chapter introduces Ming dynasty Neo-Confucian autobiography with an analysis and complete translation of Kao P'an-lung's autobiography, *K'un-hsüeh chi, Recollections of the Toils of Learning.*[4]

Within the development of Neo-Confucianism during the Ming dynasty, new-found emphasis is placed upon the importance of the individual and the examination of the self. While it may be said that Ming thought represents a decline in the metaphysical tendencies of Neo-Confucianism, it has also been pointed out that a new and creative perspective is established, one which is defined in terms of an emphasis upon an interior and self-conscious experience of the truth of the tradition.[5] Each person's potential is seen as the realization of his own nature in sagehood. A part of this process was a growing concern during the Ming for a concrete verification process within the setting of daily life.[6] What has not yet been explored fully is the relation between such tendencies of Ming thought and the popularity of several literary genres that illustrate a "self-conscious" perspective.

A number of Neo-Confucians compiled diaries and journals of various sorts. The travel journal, *yu-chi*, appears to be immensely popular during the Ming; and if we can judge from the example of Lu Yu (1125-1210) during the Sung,[7] by the Ming it seems to be far more concerned with the interior landscape than with external peregrinations. Diaries or daily records, *jih-chi*, records of day-to-day thoughts and actions, also seem to have been extremely popular. Autobiographical writings, while perhaps less common than diaries and journals, are still a serious literary form whose style and content are important for an interpretation of Ming Neo-Confucianism.[8]

Each of these forms of writing, although perhaps especially the autobiography, illustrates the Ming emphasis upon the self. At the same time, it should be abundantly clear that such genres are not themselves unique to the Ming period. As Wolfgang Bauer's study makes clear, the occurrence of autobiography in the Chinese tradition begins at an early point.[9] The difference between the Ming writings and earlier examples is the degree to which the former illustrate an individual's preoccupation with problems of self-cultivation and with the interior experience of understanding his own nature. The goal of sagehood is the daily subject matter of his life. Such writings explore the self fully, not as a tabloid of accomplishments but as a record of the pertinacity of searching and examining. The Ming autobiographical experience may be close to Stendhal's understanding of autobiography: "To note down my memories in order to guess what sort of man I have been."[10] The self is centered not with the intention of display but with the intention of discovering its true nature.

Mind, Principle, and Autobiography

If we examine in general terms two of the prominent Ming Neo-Confucian autobiographies several salient features of the autobiographical form emerge. These two writings share the same title, *K'un-hsüeh chi,*[11] an allusion to the *Analects'* discussion of differing capacities for learning.[12] Their respective authors represent contrasting philosophical points of view. Kao P'an-lung, a leading member of the late Ming Tung-lin reform movement and major exponent of Ch'eng-Chu orthodoxy, reflected upon his life, its direction and goals, in autobiographical form. As a representative of Tung-lin neo-orthodoxy, Kao was an outspoken critic of the Wang Yang-ming school. Hu Chih,[13] a disciple of Lo Hung-hsien (1504-1564)[14] and follower of the Wang Yang-ming school, represented many of the philosophical concerns Kao criticized. Hu also, however, felt the need to punctuate and articulate the experience of self in autobiographical form.

Kao P'an-lung and Hu Chih, while representing different points of view—ostensibly the polarity of the School of Principle and the School of Mind—share the larger concern for self-reflection, self-examination, and self-cultivation. The ground they share is demonstrated by the common features of their autobiographies. The focus of both autobiographies is the attainment or realization of sagehood. They both discuss in detail the process of learning and self-cultivation undertaken to reach sagehood. They both relate moments of doubt and crisis in their search for the true nature. They both describe breakthroughs to understanding, a form of self-transformation in which the individual's true nature is seen in a unitary relation with Heaven, earth, and the ten-thousand things. They both minimize family relations and political events and in this differ from the autobiography of the eminent Buddhist Te Ch'ing (1546-1623).[15] At the same time, they maximize the relation to teachers and friends who share the interest and practice of self-cultivation. Finally, they both state their involvement in alternative religious traditions, primarily Buddhism, and explicitly affirm or reaffirm their belief in and acceptance of the Confucian Way.

Kao P'an-lung—Centering the Self

For Kao P'an-lung the autobiographical perspective recounts incidents that contribute to the realization of sagehood pursuant to the unfolding of his own nature. His own record of his life illustrates the selection and interpretation of such experiences. Kao chooses to begin his autobiography at age twenty-five, later than both Hu Chih and Te Ch'ing.[16] For Kao, the commencement of the autobiography is the point at which his life may be said to acquire a significance, a significance measured in terms of the perspective from which he reviews his life in 1614. Here Kao's view differs from his own biographers. In the *Kao Chung-hsien kung nien-p'u, Chronological Biography of Kao Chung-*

hsien, by Kao's disciple Hua Yün-ch'eng (1588-1648)[17] and the *Hsing-chuang, Annals of Conduct*, by Yeh Mao-ts'ai (d. 1631),[18] Kao's life is recorded from the earliest incidents of his youth.

When Kao was twenty-five, he heard Li Yüan-ch'ung (1551-1608)[19] and Ku Hsien-ch'eng (1550-1612)[20] discuss learning. The significance of this experience is that a standpoint is established. It remains, though not without doubt and crisis, the perspective throughout the years Kao recounts. The standpoint is the direction and order around which Kao can see his life develop, the resolve to pursue the goal of sagehood.

The importance of this initial incident rests for Kao upon the resolve, *chih*. Kao's earlier years were not without learning and self-cultivation. Both biographies attest to his previous experiences.[21] Why were such experiences not included in the autobiography? They lacked the direction that Kao saw as central once the commitment to sagehood was established. Tu Wei-ming, in a perceptive article on the Confucian view of maturation, stresses the necessity of what he calls the "existential decision" to establish one's aim both at the commencement and during the learning process.[22] Autobiography as the self's view of maturation is a record of such decisions. With a standpoint established, the task of the realization of the nature can proceed with direction.

It is precisely at the establishment of this standpoint that we see the assimilation of the religious dimension of the tradition into the individual's life. As I have already suggested, the goal of sagehood might best be characterized as possessing religious dimension through its capacity to provide a means for ultimate transformation or a soteriology.[23] The commitment to sagehood is a commitment to the moral responsibility of becoming a person of goodness, an individual who, in reverential attitude, experiences a fundamental unity between himself and Heaven, earth, and the ten-thousand things. The degree to which this goal possesses a religious dimension is the degree to which the establishment of commitment becomes a process of religious affirmation.[24] As a statement of life ordered through such a commitment, we are dealing with the subject matter of religious autobiography.

The Pattern of Self-Reflection

Following the affirmation of his commitment, Kao recounts a number of incidents in his life. Difficulties and crises are encountered and are resolved, at least momentarily, until a new problem emerges. This is the pattern of Kao's autobiographical record up to the point of his enlightenment experience. In autobiographical retrospect, psychological tension builds throughout the incidents recounted to the occurrence of the enlightenment experience. What follows the enlightenment presupposes the enlightenment as verification for the truth claim of the commitment to sagehood.

The first difficulty recorded is the cultivation of *ching*, reverent seriousness. This attitude of reverent seriousness eludes Kao regardless of the efforts
he makes. With no resolution at hand a crisis of confidence develops. The
nature of the problem is Kao's understanding of *hsin*, mind; he had limited its
potential to the dimension of the physical heart and was thus unable to realize
a point of reverential attentiveness of both body and mind. Only when he had
found a description of mind as filling the entire body was the crisis resolved
and his motivation and commitment restored.

What follows is a period of contentedness, confidence, and, perhaps in
retrospect, overconfidence. Kao suggests a certain confidence in his ability to
do the good in whatever situation might arise.[25] He also recounted a momentary breakthrough in which he felt the utter sincerity or authenticity, *ch'eng*, of
the spontaneousness or immediate response, *tang-hsia*, of his nature.[26] Even
after he had learned of his banishment to Chieh-yang (Kwangtung) he claimed
an unperturbed mind.[27] From the perspective of the later enlightenment experience, these early experiences seem for Kao to be indications not so much of
insight gained as of shortcomings yet to be overcome.

Whatever confidence had been established dissipated rapidly in the re-
newal of crisis during the journey to Chieh-yang. Unresolved issues come to
the foreground and reactivate the feeling of a lack of self-understanding. Kao
speaks of the perennial conflict of principle and desire, the dichotomy of unself-
ish religious commitment and selfish motivation. In retrospect his uncertainty
is only exacerbated by the discussions he held with Lu Ku-ch'iao[28] and Wu
Tzu-wang.[29] Lu Ku-ch'iao, of whom little is known historically, asks Kao for a
description of the "original substance," *pen-t'i*, that is, the ultimate foundation
of his nature. Lu's question is pivotal for Kao for it precipitates Kao's recognition of his own lack of self-understanding. This is the time of Kao's spiritual
nadir, and yet out of this crisis a resolve emerges. In the setting of the Liu-ho
Tower, alone and alienated from friend and environment,[30] the resolve is made
to reaffirm the commitment: "If I don't penetrate it on this trip, then my life will
have been in vain."[31] What follows is a strict regimen of self-cultivation and un-
usually long hours of quiet sitting.[32] The result after days of indefatigable effort
is an experience Kao can call enlightenment, *wu*.[33]

> I passed by T'ing-chou [Fukien] and traveled on by land until I reached an inn. The
> inn had a small tower: to the front were mountains, to the rear a nearby rushing
> stream. I climbed the tower and was very much at ease. In my hand I held a book
> of the two Ch'eng brothers. Quite by chance I saw a saying by [Ch'eng] Ming-tao,
> "In the midst of the ten-thousand affairs and the hundred-thousand weapons 'joy
> still exists though water is my drink and a bent arm [my pillow].'[34] The myriad
> changes all exist within the person; in reality there is not a single thing."[35] Suddenly
> I realized this and said, "It really is like this, in reality there is not a single thing!"
> With this single thought all entanglements were broken off. Suddenly it was as if a

load of a hundred pounds had fallen to the ground in an instant. It was as if a flash of lightening had penetrated the body and pierced the intelligence. Subsequently I was merged with the Great Transformation[36] until there was no differentiation between Heaven and humanity, exterior and interior. At this point I saw that the six points[37] were all my mind, "frame of the body" was their field and "square inch of space" was their original seat. In terms of their spiritual or luminous character, no location could actually be spoken of.

The enlightenment experience is the watershed of the autobiography. As Kao recounts his life, a substantial difference appears in the events leading up to the enlightenment experience and those following. A foundation of self-understanding is established in the experience of enlightenment; such a foundation affects the outlook on succeeding events. The threat of spiritual crisis becomes instead the anguish of the toils of learning.

The Superiority of Confucianism

The postenlightenment stage begins in the autobiography with an account of the superiority of Confucianism over Buddhism and Taoism. The focus of Kao's attention is the relation between Confucianism and Buddhism.[38] The superiority of Confucianism is based for Kao upon its comprehensiveness as a way of life; it includes the subtleties of Buddhism and yet affirms the value of life and demonstrates its own ability to support it.[39] The question is the impact of this conclusion within the autobiographical context. What does this incident contribute to the perspective of the autobiography? As it is recounted there is no suggestion of a crisis of confidence in the Confucian Way that inexorably drove Kao to pursue alternatives. Instead, it is simply an affirmation of the correctness of his own commitment to Confucianism, the Way of Heaven, a commitment that had been solidified initially by the enlightenment experience but is reaffirmed by an examination of the alternatives. The alternatives are dismissed. The affirmation of Confucianism at this point is a reaffirmation of his own commitment.

Enlightenment's Legacy

The autobiographical perspective of a foundation established in the enlightenment experience is illustrated by Kao's discussion of the need for continued effort to meet the commitment of the learning process. In retrospect, the years between 1598 and 1606 exemplify the dominance of circumstance over effort. Kao, sensitive to his dual role as autobiographical subject and object, reveals the thoughts of a man weary with the toils of learning. His perspective at the time of writing becomes his own subject matter in the context of previous events. Looking back, he sees intervening and disrupting incidents that prevent his full effort from being concentrated upon the commitment to sagehood. Curiously enough, virtually the only mention made by Kao of his family is in this context of distractions.

Mitigating circumstances are found in the building of his hermitage, the Water Dwelling, *Shui-chü*, in 1598 and in the benefits he derives from the opening of the reconstructed Tung-lin Academy in 1604. There is no crisis of doubt, simply a profound recognition of the need to continue learning and of the difficulties of finding the proper circumstances for such learning: "With my own inferior endowment, what use could any expansive insight be in the absence of such exertion?"[40] Yet, regardless of the difficulties, the enlightenment experience persists as a foundation: "Fortunately ever since I have come into my own, I can take up a plan [to improve myself] and find the 'original state' there."[41] There exists a foundation to fall back upon and at the same time something to build upon.

Affirmations of Faith

The final events recorded in the autobiography appear as affirmations of major principles of the Confucian tradition. In 1606, Kao states that he has come to truly believe, *shih-hsin*, the principle of Mencius that human nature is good.[42] In 1607, he has come to truly believe in the principles of Master Ch'eng, "The hawk flies and fish swim," and Mencius, "You must work at it."[43] In 1611, he truly believes in the principle of the *Great Learning*, "Knowing the root"; and finally, in 1612, he truly believes the principle of the *Doctrine of the Mean*.[44]

Each of these contexts of belief presents its own complexities. The *Great Learning*, for example, remains an insoluble problem over a number of years for Kao.[45] His statement of true belief may be interpreted in one sense as a resolution to the problems the text presented for him. On the other hand, his true belief also expresses the commitment and maturation of the learning process.

The different principles referred to as "objects" of true belief suggest a progression in the maturation of Kao's learning. The learning builds from the foundation of the enlightenment and the affirmation of the superiority of the Confucian Way. First to be incorporated is the presupposition of the Confucian tradition, Mencius's theory of the goodness of human nature. With this established, the question of cultivating goodness is faced and assimilated. It is the balance, a balance that can shift depending upon the point of view, between spontaneousness and effort. Next is the assimilation of the *Great Learning*, a general schema of cultivation, and finally, the *Doctrine of the Mean*, a vivid image of the centering process and a suggestion of the subtle point of the Confucian religious dimension. Such principles of true belief serve as credos of faith in the ever-renewing function of religious affirmation.

The autobiography closes on a note of humility. The search for self has produced little. The perspective is established in the toils of learning. When Kao wrote his autobiography he was still in active retirement.[46] Had he chosen a later date to reflect upon his life one wonders if the fierce political events of the early 1620s could have escaped his autobiographical eye and, if they had been included, how the relation of the internal and external worlds would have been depicted. Why he chose to write his autobiography in 1614 is not known. The centered self remains only partially adumbrated.

Kao P'an-lung's *K'un-hsüeh chi* (*Recollections of the Toils of Learning*)

At age twenty-five, when I heard Magistrate Li Yüan-ch'ung and Ku Ching-yang discuss learning, I resolved to pursue the quest of sagehood. I considered that there must be a way of becoming a sage, though I was yet unacquainted with the methods. I had read the *Ta-hsüeh huo-wen*[47] and observed that Master Chu said there is nothing to equal reverent seriousness for entering the Way.[48] Therefore, I exerted all my effort toward respecting and concentrating on it, keeping the mind to a square inch of space in my chest.[49] I was aware, however, only of the oppression of my vital forces and restraint upon myself. It was decidedly unsatisfactory to me and so, subsequently, I dropped it, drifting again as before. I could find no remedy.

After quite a length of time I suddenly remembered that Master Ch'eng had said: "The mind must be retained within the bodily frame."[50] I did not know [however], what the bodily frame referred to. Was it really in a square inch of space or not? I searched for an explanation without success, then quite by chance I found it explained in the *Hsiao-hsüeh*[51] in the following manner, "The bodily frame is simply like speaking of the body."[52] I was very happy for the mind was not just a square inch of space, but the entire body was the mind. For a time my life was relaxed and contented. Then Lo Chih-an[53] of Chiang-yu [Kiangsi] came and spoke of Li Chien-lo's self-cultivation[54] as the foundation of learning. It was in line with what I took to be my own guide. I was increasingly happy, having no doubts. During this period, I spent all my effort working on "knowing the root."[55] This caused both body and mind to progress together and word and deed to be without error. After passing the examination of the *Chi-ch'ou* year of *Wan-li* [1589] I was even more aware that these ideas were progressing. When [I found myself] in mourning[56] [I] studied the [*Book*] *of Rites* and the [*Book*] *of Changes*.

It was in the *Jen-ch'en* year of *Wan-li* [1592], that I presented myself for appointment as a successful candidate.[57] Since in my daily life the sense of shame was very great, when I received my appointment[58] I took an oath to myself saying, "I have not yet perceived anything of the Way. I shall simply act upon my solitary knowledge. Right and wrong, good and bad: that which follows without [my having] acted, that comes from Heaven." In examining [my life], I found it very near to this. With a little insight into the mind, I vainly thought that whenever I saw what was righteous I would do it.

In the winter I traveled to the Chao-t'ien Temple[59] to practice the rules of ceremony. While quiet-sitting in a monastery seeking for the original substance, I suddenly thought of the sentence,[60] "He does away with what is false and preserves his integrity."[61] I felt that in the immediate response [of the nature] there was nothing false, but that all was sincere and I had no further need for seeking sincerity. In that moment I felt rapturous, as if all fetters were cast off.

In the *Kuei-ssu* year of *Wan-li* [1593], I was banished because I had spoken out on certain affairs.[62] It did not, however, disturb my thoughts. After my return [home] I tasted the ways of the world and my mind became once more agitated. In the *Chia-wu* year of *Wan-li* [1594] during the autumn I headed for Chieh-yang [Kwangtung]. I realized that within myself principle and desire waged battle upon battle without peaceful resolution. In Wu-lin [Chekiang] I talked for several days with Lu Ku-ch'iao and Wu Tzu-wang. One day Ku-ch'iao suddenly asked, "What is the original substance like?" What I said was vague though I answered by saying: "Without sound or smell." However this came only from my mouth and ears, not from a true understanding.

The night before I crossed over the river[63] the moonlight was pure and clear. I sat beside the Liu-ho Tower.[64] The river and the mountains were clear and inviting. Good friends urged me to drink more. In this most agreeable of times I suddenly felt unhappy, as if something were constraining me. I exerted myself to rouse my joy, but my spirit did not accompany me. Late in the night when the others had gone I went on board the boat and in a sudden realization said to myself: "How is it that today the scenery was as it was and yet my feelings were like this?" Making a thorough investigation, I realized that being totally ignorant of the Way, my mind and body had nothing on which to draw. Thus, I strongly affirmed: "If I don't penetrate it on this trip, then my life will have been in vain."

The next day in the boat I earnestly arranged the mat and seriously established rules and regulations. For one half of the day I practiced quiet-sitting while for the other half I engaged in study. During quiet-sitting, whenever I felt ill at ease, I would just follow the instructions of Ch'eng [I] and Chu [Hsi], taking up in turn: With sincerity and reverent seriousness consider quietude as fundamental; observe happiness, anger, sorrow, and joy before they arise; sit in silence and purify the mind; realize for oneself the Principle of Heaven.[65] Whether I was standing, sitting, eating, or resting, these thoughts were continuously present. At night I did not undress, and only when I was weary to the bone did I fall asleep. Upon waking I returned to sitting, repeating and alternating these various methods of practice. When the substance of the mind was clear and peaceful there was a sense of filling all Heaven and earth,[66] but it did not last.

The duration of the journey was two months and fortunately there were no normal involvements. The mountains and waters were clear and beautiful; my servant and I supported each other. It was very quiet. One evening I ordered a bit of wine. We stopped the boat before a green mountain and drifted to and fro beside a jade green mountain stream. I sat on a large rock for a time. The sound of the stream, the harmonies of the birds, flourishing trees and tall bamboo, all these things pleased my mind and yet it remained unattached.[67]

I passed by T'ing-chou [Fukien] and traveled on by land until I reached an inn. The inn had a small tower; to the front were mountains, to the rear a nearby rushing stream. I climbed the tower and was very much at ease. In my hand, I held a book of the two Ch'eng brothers. Quite by chance I saw a saying by [Ch'eng] Ming-tao, "In the midst of the ten-thousand affairs and the hundred-thousand weapons 'joy still exists though water is my drink and a bent arm [my pillow].'[68] The myriad changes all exist within the person; in reality there is not a single thing."[69] Suddenly I realized this and said, "It really is like this, in reality there is not a single thing!" With this single thought, all entanglements were broken. Suddenly, it was as if a load of a hundred pounds had fallen to the ground in an instant. It was as if a flash of lightening had penetrated the body and pierced the intelligence. Subsequently, I was merged with the Great Transformation[70] until there was no differentiation between Heaven and humanity, exterior and interior. At this point I saw that the six points[71] were all my mind, "frame of the body" was their field and "square inch of space" was their original seat. In terms of their spiritual and luminous character, no location could actually be spoken of. I ordinarily despised scholars who discussed enlightenment with grand display, but now I could see that it was something quite natural and realized that from now on it was suitable to apply my own efforts to this end.

In the spring of the *I-wei* year of *Wan-li* [1595], as I was returning from Chieh-yang [Kwangtung], I took up [the writings] of both Buddhists and Taoists to read them. The differences between the Buddhists and the [Confucian] Sages are very subtle. As for the points in which [the Buddhists] speak so well, Confucian teachings already have them all: they do not go beyond [the concept] expressed in the two words *wu-chi* [Ultimate of Nonbeing].[72] As for their defects, these have already been discussed by earlier Confucians and can be summed up in the words *wu-li* [having no principle]. Having studied the two [heterodox] schools, I appreciated all the more how worthy of respect were the teachings of the [Confucian] Sages. If the Way of the Sages did not exist, human life could not be sustained. Even the followers of these two schools depend on this Way for food, drink, and clothing without being conscious of the fact.

In the *Wu-hsü* year of *Wan-li* [1598], I built the Water Dwelling with the intention of practicing quiet-sitting and engaging in study there.[73] After the

Ping-shen year of *Wan-li* [1596] I had lost my parents, moved about, and saw my children getting married.[74] Those years allowed me no peace. In the midst of these activities, I tried to continue my practice of discipline but was only too well aware of the difficulties of transforming one's physical nature.

In the *Chia-ch'en* year of *Wan-li* [1604], the Teacher Ku Ching-yang first established the Tung-lin Academy. I was able to benefit from discussions with my friends. As I came to realize, I could do nothing without making the effort to concentrate on quietude. The maladies of each person are different. The Sages and the Worthies must have great spiritual capacity to enable them to master quietude in their ordinary daily lives. For the scholar whose spirit is deficient and whose physical nature is unstable several tens of years of effort are needed before quietude can be deeply established. The chief defect lies in one's youth, when one is without the benefit of a [proper] education in basic things.[75] Gradually one becomes used to worldly habits that are difficult to root out. One should bury one's head in study, allow the principle of righteousness to flow everywhere, transforming his own worldly flesh and bone. By purifying the spirit and sitting in stillness, one can cause worldly delusions to disperse. It is then possible to strengthen the right mind and the right spirit. With my own inferior endowment, what use could any expansive insight be in the absence of such exertion? Fortunately, ever since I have come into my own, I can take up a plan [to improve myself] and find the "original state" there.

In the *Pin-wu* year of *Wan-li* [1606], I came to truly believe in the principle of Mencius that human nature is good. This nature is neither old nor new, neither sagely nor common, for Heaven, earth, and humanity are one. Only with the highest grade of [nature], pure and clear and with no obscuration, can one begin to believe. The next grade is entirely dependent upon the effort of learning.[76] If a single speck of dust intervenes, it might as well be ten thousand *li*. This is why Mencius spoke of a medicine that causes a reaction.[77]

In the *Ting-wei* year of *Wan-li* [1607], I came to truly believe in [the principle of] Master Ch'eng, "The hawk flies and fish swim"[78] and also the [idea of Mencius], "You must work at it."[79] That which is called nature is entirely spontaneous, not from the effort of man. "A hawk flies and fish swim," who caused this to be? "Do not forget it, but also do not assist it."[80] This is an admonition to students. But in the case of the true primary substance that unceasingly flows and spreads in the past and the present, with no movement or rest, where can it be forgotten or assisted? Therefore, "one must work at it." Consider, for example, plants and trees. The roots, sprouts, flowers, and fruit change and transform of their own, yet they are cared for, watered, and fostered. If in the hard work of learning, one leaves everything to the natural, nothing will get done, no change or transformation will be accomplished and there will not even be anything natural.[81]

In the *Hsin-hai* year of *Wan-li* [1611], I came to truly believe in the *Great Learning* and its principle of "knowing the root." This is fully recorded in another work.[82] In the *Jen-tzu* year of *Wan-li* [1612], I came to truly believe the principle of the *Doctrine of the Mean*. Most surely words cannot describe this Way. Master Ch'eng called it the Principle of Heaven,[83] [Wang] Yang-ming called it innate knowledge. Neither, however, equals the two words *centrality* and *normality*. *Centrality* is what is appropriate and fitting; *normality* is what is ordinary and dependable. If even a slight transgression takes place nothing will be suitable or fitting. If there is only a slight amount of artifice or contrivance, it will not be ordinary or dependable. It is this way with the substance and it is this way with moral effort.

The Sage cannot fathom the limits of Heaven and earth. How much less people like us? How can there be a limit [to our efforts]? We should honor human relations, speak with care, act diligently and be cautious unceasingly until the day of our death. In the toils of study, the years mount up and the months accumulate with only more difficulties. And still there is nothing sufficient to bring a smile to the face of a wise man. For those who are deficient like me, they may find something useful in my account.

Recorded in the *Chia-yin* year of *Wan-li* [1614].

Chapter V

Proposition and Praxis in
Neo-Confucian Syncretism

Recent work has suggested that much of sixteenth- and seventeenth-century Chinese thought is marked by a syncretic character, perhaps best described as a fluidity between major religious traditions in the mid and late Ming periods. Indeed, such a type of activity appears to be taking place. Neo-Confucians are practicing various forms of Buddhist as well as Taoist spiritual cultivation,[1] and both Buddhists and Taoists express genuine interest in the problems of Neo-Confucian self-cultivation.[2] As such, practice seems to dominate over labels of differing traditions and their respective truth claims. The practice of self-cultivation is central, and the potential conflicting nature of truth claims from the various sources of such practices seems secondary. The character of this so-called fluidity between traditions is, however, far more complex than the term *syncretism* might suggest.

There is little doubt that Buddhism and Neo-Confucianism are deeply influenced by each other and that at the level of practice, methods from various sources are tried, borrowed, and interrelated.[3] Whether, however, the word *syncretism* is appropriate to describe the range of relationships possible between traditions is a rather different question. A good deal of the problem extends from the ambiguity inherent within the usage of the term *syncretism*. At root is the all too frequent identification of syncretism with a broad range of quite different types of relationships between traditions stretching from a strictly historical interrelationship to the creation of a genuine synthesis. A historical interrelationship involves the borrowing and blending of tenets and practices. A synthesis, by definition, suggests that the respective traditions held in syncretic relation have been transcended, or at the very least put aside, with the emergence of a new system of truth-claims. Thus, the usage of the designation syncretism has tended to focus upon practice and the relationships between various forms of practice of differing traditions. This focus has been to the virtual exclusion of questions of truth claims representing the traditions involved. The result has been to ascribe syncretism to a larger range of activities than may be the case. After all, if historical interrelationship is virtually synonymous with syncretism and syncretism becomes an ubiquitous phenomenon in the history of religions, this may say a good deal less about the history of religions than the fact that syncretism as a designation has lost its specificity and thus a major part of its usefulness. Perhaps an even more serious ramification is involved. When syncretism is used in its broadest capacity suggesting nothing more than historical borrowing and blending, its connotation of fluidity between traditions actually may be quite inaccurate. Such fluidity suggests religious faith lacking exclusivity and less distinct boundaries between religious traditions than might actually be warranted.

The Autobiographical Reflections of Hu Chih

In this chapter, I consider only one case, Hu Chih,[4] a prominent follower of Wang Yang-ming,[5] noted for his study as well as practice of both Confucianism and Buddhism. Hu Chih focuses his life upon the goal of sagehood,[6] and studies Confucianism, Buddhism, and Taoism for what each might contribute to his religious life. Hu, as with many thinkers of the Ming period, recorded his life of self-cultivation in a first-person genre, the autobiography,[7] and it is this source that forms the basis of the present comments.[8] What I am particularly interested in examining are the sections of the autobiography that discuss the relation between Confucianism and Buddhism. It is this relationship articulated by Hu that demonstrates the potentially syncretic nature of Hu's thought.

The early years of the autobiography record Hu's frequent setbacks in learning. He says of this period that there was no clear focus in his learning, that he was too carefree, and that his personal faults were too numerous. This condition appears to be rectified at least in part when, in 1542 at age twenty-six, he meets Ou-yang Te (1496-1554)[9] and accepts Ou-yang as his teacher. Hu says in the autobiography that he felt this presented the possibility of actually beginning his learning. The optimism, however, is short-lived for Hu soon finds himself in crisis, a crisis reflective of his own sense of the failure of his learning. His comment reflects the nadir of his feelings.

> When I looked at my own learning it lacked all effort and because of this I regretted the time that I had let slip by. My greatest weakness lay in loving lyrical composition and in addition there were my many hatreds and desires. These three stabbed me within my breast; it was like a battle in which I was not long able to endure.

This is the crime of not having established one's resolve [*chih*], there is nothing else to be said for it! At this time I was already thirty-one years old.[10]

At least a part of the explanation for this loss of commitment is to be found in his preparation for the *chin-shih* examination during 1543 and his subsequent failure at the examination of 1544.[11] In addition, however, is the realization of the distance between the goal of learning, sagehood, and the reality of the toils of learning of everyday life. The recollection in the autobiography is but a testimony to the time Hu has let slip by. He confesses that his resolve to pursue the goal of learning is not yet established, even though he is already thirty-one years old. The comparison is to Confucius, whose resolve to learning had been established at age fifteen and by thirty was firmly established.[12]

Hu responds to this crisis by pursuing alternatives in learning. He first studies under Lo Hung-hsien[13] learning Lo's principles of *chu-ching*, mastering of quietude, and *wu-yü*, freedom from desires, as well as practicing quiet-sitting.[14] However the major new departure for Hu occurs, when he travels to Shao-chou, [Kwangtung] in 1548 to teach in the Ming-ching Academy.[15] It is here that he undertakes the study of Taoism and Buddhism. Unfortunately, the record of his study of Taoism is virtually eclipsed by the magnitude of attention given to Buddhism and even strictly biographical accounts render no assistance at this juncture.[16] Hu says that he studied Taoism with the hope of curing an unidentified illness from which he had suffered for several years. A certain Teng Tun-feng, identified only as the major scholar in residence at the academy,[17] suggested that he would be cured of his illness if he should take up Buddhist meditation rather than Taoist.

Hu began his study of Buddhism ostensibly, at least, with the goal of curing his long-standing illness. His description of his study of Buddhism suggests he is studying Ch'an Buddhism, the most prominent form of Buddhism of his day, and that he is introduced to doctrine as well as practice. "I saw him [that is, Teng Tun-feng] daily. He would discuss the law of Karma with his assembled students and insisted that everyone sit in meditation together. Some would sit on their beds, some sat on mats on the ground. Frequently we would sit until midnight, sleep a little, and with the crow of the rooster resume our sitting. He emphasized resting the mind empty of distracting thoughts. The goal was to see into our natures [*chien-hsing*]."[18] In his autobiography Hu remarks that he encountered certain difficulties during the initial period of his study of Buddhism. These difficulties were ascribed to the lengthy period of travel prior to his arrival at the academy. "I had had a lengthy period of rapid travel and as a result for the first several months saw strange apparitions while sleeping."[19]

Teng Tun-feng assures him that such apparitions were without any reality and that with continued practice they would subside of their own, for they were nothing but the product of a mind still obscured with the affairs of the world. "You ordinarily desire wealth and fame and there is nothing but anxiety. It can change into such forms. . . . Have no doubt that when you have achieved your goal they will subside of themselves."[20] Hu states that the apparitions did subside, and furthermore, that his mind became calm, *chi-jan*.[21] He then goes on to describe the culmination of his study and practice—an experience of enlightenment, *wu*. "After six months [my mind] became calm. One day my mind was suddenly enlightened [*wu*]. There were no distracting thoughts within it and I could perceive that Heaven, earth and the ten-thousand things were all the substance [*t'i*] of my own mind. I sighed deeply and said, 'Now I know that Heaven, earth and the ten-thousand things are not external.' "[22] The effects of the experience are far reaching and Hu records the influence upon subsequent behavior. "From this time on whenever activities would arise there was no corresponding stirring up of my thoughts. . . . My whole body flourished with health and the disease of fire of the preceding ten years or more gradually disappeared. I was able to sleep during the night and my mind unknowingly became content."[23]

The intellectual context of the experience is Buddhism. It is this context that becomes increasingly important to Hu as he attempts to fit the experience into the structure of his religious life. Hu informs Teng Tun-feng of his experience. Teng's reply is simple and to the point; "Your nature is revealing itself."[24] To Teng, the experience Hu has called "enlightenment" is an experience of his own Buddha-nature; Buddhism, to use Frits Staal's terminology, is the "superstructure" of the experience.[25] Teng does not actually confirm Hu's "enlightenment." He only says that it is a beginning within the framework of Buddhist practice. It is Hu himself who claims the experience as an enlightenment and describes it as seeing all things in the substance of his own mind, *wo-hsin-t'i*.[26] From Hu's description the context or superstructure is actually quite ambiguous. It could be interpreted entirely within the terms and structure of Neo-Confucianism. In such a case, Hu is describing the original substance, *pen-t'i*, of the mind revealed through innate knowledge, *liang-chih*. It could also be understood, however, in strictly Buddhist terms, that is, the Buddha-nature of the mind revealed through introspective practice. In addition, the context of the experience could represent a synthesis, a common structure transcending the exclusive terms of either Neo-Confucianism or Buddhism.

At this juncture of the autobiography, Hu pursues the Buddhist connection further. He recounts effects of the experience upon himself and the response of Teng. "After a length of time even though I was sleeping, it was as though I was perceiving. Whenever I slept I could hear people's every word and step. Everything was clear and distinct. Tun-feng replied; 'This is the gradual process of penetrating day and night; if you push yourself on you will be able to leave the cycle of birth and death.' "[27] Teng Tun-feng's reply is strictly Buddhist. Hu asked Teng for further instruction in the meaning of liberation from birth and death and found it to be compatible with his own experience.[28] Hu then describes travel to various Buddhist sites with Teng as well as his intention to leave the world, *wang-shih*, that is, to become a Buddhist. "I had strange dreams and following that went so far as having the intention [*i*] of leaving the world."[29] Thus, he appears to be at the point of becoming a Buddhist.

The enlightenment experience seems firm within a Buddhist context, at least as Hu himself interprets it, and Hu appears intent upon pursuing the path of Buddhism not in conjunction with his Confucian past, but as an alternative to it. For Huang Tsung-hsi and Jung Chao-tsu, there is little that separates Hu from Buddhism.[30] Such conclusions are based upon an appraisal of Hu's mature philosophy. Had Huang Tsung-hsi and Jung Chao-tsu been characterizing this period of Hu's life, the question of the separation from Buddhism would have been even more problematical.

At the moment that Hu appears closest to accepting Buddhism he meets Ch'ien Te-hung (1497-1574),[31] a prominent disciple of Wang Yang-ming. Ch'ien was visiting Shao-chou and was invited to stay at the Ming-ching Academy. As Hu recollects this meeting with Ch'ien, it was an encounter that was to provide a crucial turning point for Hu. Even Ch'ien's appearance seems to act as a catalyst for serious self-reflection. Ch'ien was in mourning attire when Hu met him. "Within my own mind I was thinking, although I study all of this about leaving the world, I still yet can't say it is correct!"[32] Mourning attire might suggest the inherent suffering of the cycle of birth and death to a Buddhist; but to a Confucian it is a symbol filled with the depth of filial piety, and it is the decision to return home, a decision that for Hu is tantamount to leaving Buddhist practice. He finds, he says, that once this decision has been made he was no longer in possession of the enlightenment he claimed to have experienced,[33] suggesting the intimate relation between the experience and its context for Hu. His thoughts, he says, had become blurred, and he no longer had a perception of the substance, *t'i*, of his mind. He told Ch'ien Te-hung of these experiences following his decision to leave Buddhism. Ch'ien's response was to suggest that Buddhism was something that was not suited to Hu's intentions.[34]

What follows in the autobiography is the record of a second enlightenment experience. The second experience is described in similar language to the first. There is an experience of unity and the experience itself is of a sudden and dramatic psychological character, giving a sense of immediate and thorough knowledge of the interconnectedness or oneness of all things. The experiences, although virtually the same in their manner of description and suggestive of a common psychological core,[35] differ markedly in their interpretation. "Suddenly I was again enlightened and as a result Heaven, earth and the ten-thousand things were not external. I thoroughly examined the various philosopher's thoughts; Mencius' 'All things are complete . . .,'[36] Ch'eng Hao's 'The universe and I are one body,'[37] and Master Lu's 'The universe is my mind.'[38] There were none that were not the same principle."³⁹ Unlike the first experience, which found its superstructure or interpretative structure in Buddhism, the referents for the second experience are typically Confucian: Mencius, Ch'eng Hao, and Lu Hsiang-shan. In comparing the two experiences Hu says, "When I realized what I had seen previously, [this] was freshly penetrating."⁴⁰ If the first experience was an indication of Hu's approach toward or even acceptance of Buddhism, the second experience appears to restore Hu to the Confucian way. The eventual result is a clear rejection of Buddhism and a strong affirmation of Confucianism.

It is only at this point in the autobiography that Hu expresses his misgivings about Buddhism. "In examining myself I said, 'My fortunes have diminished and my sleep has been cut off; it is from following such a thing [as Buddhism]. Now I am even more bound up by the web of the world. Truly I have been turned upside down from following such corrupt worms.' "⁴¹ The tension between leaving the world and serving the world persists even as Hu returns home to attend to family affairs and to care for his aging mother. "My inner feelings were constantly ill at ease. I already possessed within myself the distinction between Confucianism and Buddhism, but I had yet to make the final decision."⁴²

At this point, the autobiography shifts its attention to two apparently minor incidents which in autobiographical perspective, however, bear the full weight of the decision Hu makes between Confucianism and Buddhism. Enroute to the capital to take the *chin-shih* examination again, the ship on which Hu is crossing P'eng-li Lake (Kiangsi), encounters a storm. "The boat heaved and rolled continuously. The passengers on board wailed throughout the night until the coming of dawn. I alone ordered wine and drank as if nothing were happening. I raised my voice in song and then slept soundly. As the sky brightened the wind diminished some and as I awakened my companions chided me for being such an unfeeling person, but that is the way I am."⁴³ When Hu returned home after once again failing the highest examination, he inquired of his teacher about the correctness of his actions while on board the boat. The teacher replied, "This is a very difficult matter, but I would say that it is not yet the essence of humanity [*jen*]."⁴⁴ Hu probed his teacher further, asking what the essence of humanity would have been in this particular situation. The teacher's reply was decisive to Hu: "To be near danger with an unmoved mind, but in addition to provide assistance and help, that is the essence of humanity."⁴⁵ The analogy is simple enough; Buddhism and Confucianism are being contrasted. To possess an unmoved mind suggests from Hu's autobiographical recollection the detachment of Buddhist meditation. But an unmoved mind is itself not enough. It must be motivated to action, in this particular case, the fulfillment of an individual's moral commitment to his fellow humanity. The moral commitment for Hu represents the return to the Confucian way.

A second incident involving a boat is recorded in the autobiography.⁴⁶ In this case, the threat is one of pirates. Hu portrays himself as once again retaining an unmoved mind. There is, however, a self-conscious difference between the two incidents. In the second incident, Hu retains his unmoved mind, yet he also devises a plan to render assistance to the other passengers if needed. In the perspective brought to bear by the autobiography, these two incidents suggest to Hu the decision he himself had already made. The second incident only confirms his own decision, a decision that rejects Buddhism and accepts Confucianism.

The remaining segments of the autobiography illustrate Hu's affirmation of the Confucian way. Having accepted Confucianism and rejected Buddhism, Hu examines the Confucian tradition in detail in an attempt to clarify what he regards as the true Confucian teaching. He examines the Chu Hsi school as well as the Wang Yang-ming school and expresses his misgivings about a number of tenets held by each.[47] Gradually out of this process, he clarifies his own point of view about the essence of the teaching of the Confucian school. What he formulates as the essential teaching of Confucianism he states as that which he comes to hold with true belief or faith, *hsin.*[48] With his point of view established and his faith expressed, the autobiography has completed its task. The task remaining for us is the clarification of Hu Chih's understanding of the relation between Buddhism and Confucianism. Much of this remains rooted in Hu Chih's two experiences of enlightenment and their interpretation, one Buddhist, and one Confucian. While the relationship between experience and interpretation is in itself an important feature of understanding Hu Chih's thought, I want to focus upon the relation between the two traditions that is implicit in Hu Chih's understanding. As such, the primary problem is the issue of syncretism, or, in turn, how the relation between Buddhism and Confucianism is best understood.

Syncretism—Its Use and Misuse

A standard definition of *syncretism* suggests an "attempted union or reconciliation of diverse or opposite tenets or practices, especially in philosophy or religion."[49] One of the few scholars who has dealt with the methodological problems in the use of syncretism, Robert Baird, has maintained that the essential difficulty in the employment of the term is the contradictory nature of its claim.[50] The term is defined as a union or attempted union of diverse tenets or practices. Baird maintains that to suggest that syncretism takes place when conflicting ideas or practices are brought together and united into a harmonious whole, "is to say nothing coherent."[51] He argues that: "if the original two ideas or practices are in conflict then they cannot, without modification, produce a harmonious unity. . . . To say that two originally conflicting concepts were harmonized is a contradiction."[52] This does not rule out the use of syncretism entirely, although its use is severely restricted. For Baird, the term *syncretism* is reserved for the case where such conflicting ideas and practices are brought together and persist without any principle of coherency.[53] Essentially, syncretism exists only where there is no consistency. The obvious difficulty with this particular formulation of the nature of syncretism is that those traditions or examples frequently cited as syncretic do not define themselves as devoid of consistency. In addition, the suggestion that syncretism implies self-contradiction or even lack of consistency runs the risk of pejorative as well as normative judgment.

Rather than focusing upon the self-contradictory nature of the claim of syncretism, a more fundamental question involves the truth claims of the respective traditions held in syncretic relation. Is truth-value ascribed to the traditions whose tenets or practices comprise the syncretism? At root, the question persists of where the truth claim rests. Because we are dealing with propositional truth,[54] our question ought to reflect that concern. Is there then assention to propositions of divergent traditions, or is the very nature of the question itself contradictory, as a ramification of Baird's methodological observation? Yet to maintain a true syncretism, if that is indeed a possibility, is it not essential that the status as well as the location of truth claims be settled? To maintain a syncretic point of view and not be guilty of the kind of self-contradiction or inconsistency Baird discusses, it is essential to ascribe truth-value to the propositions of the respective traditions in question. There are several possible alternatives to such a conclusion, however, their claim to true syncretism seems at best highly problematical.

On the one hand, it is possible that truth-value might be ascribed not to the separate traditions of the syncretism, but rather to the combination itself. Thus, the unity of the diverse tenets or practices would be given truth-value rather than the separate parts. Such a position simply begs the question of the self-contradictory nature of the tenets or practices in opposition, because truth-value is ascribed only to the point at which such diversity has already been united. The proper word for this is not syncretism but synthesis.[55] We are dealing with a synthesis emerging out of the diversity; the truth claims concern the synthesis, not the derivative traditions. What is being created is a new position and with it a new truth claim rather than a balance of diversity being held in syncretic relationship.

On the other hand, if syncretism is understood to apply to a level less than that of the essential truth claims and propositions of the traditions involved, its applicability is at the level of the borrowing and blending of ideas and practices. At this level, syncretism is equivalent to historical interrelationship.[56] It may very well be the case that a good deal of what is commonly called *syncretism* is, in fact, a historical interrelationship between traditions. However, if syncretism means nothing more than the borrowing and blending of ideas and practices that have taken place in the historical interrelationship of religious traditions, then it is so ubiquitous a phenomenon as to be virtually meaningless. Certainly, different types of historical relationships can be described between religious traditions, but there seems little justification in describing all of them as examples of syncretism if syncretism is only synonymous with such historical relationships. There would then be nothing about the use of the term in such a context to warrant a special designation. Its justification can only be found if there is more implied in the use of the term than a simple process of borrowing and blending. Whether this be a conscious or unconscious process bears little relevancy on the question when there is nothing more intended than a type of strictly historical relationship.

Syncretism must be reserved for a distinctive phenomenon if the term is to retain any usefulness at all. Its usage ought properly to be restricted to those examples of individuals and/or movements where equal attention is given to the propositions as well as the practices of the respective traditions held in syncretic relation. Ultimately, if the term *syncretism* is to be used at all, it must suggest the entertaining and attempted reconciliation of potentially divergent truth claims. Without attention to both proposition and praxis there is nothing more distinctive than a historical interrelationship between traditions. The problem most frequently encountered in the use of the term is a confusion in significance precisely between proposition and praxis. Praxis by itself does not suggest syncretism in any more significant a manner than does historical borrowing. Only the confrontation and attempted reconciliation with divergent truth claims suggests the potential uniqueness of the phenomenon of syncretism. As such proposition is primary and praxis secondary.

Whither Confucian-Buddhist Syncretism?

Hu Chih appears to fit the syncretic model of Ming thought for he studies and practices Buddhism as well as Confucianism and is deeply concerned with integrating practices from various sources into his religious life. Discussing syncretism with reference to proposition and praxis, Hu Chih may at first appear to fit the syncretic model, for he is concerned with both practice and the respective truth claims of Confucianism and Buddhism. Focus upon the truth-claims of each tradition excludes a simple borrowing and subsequent blending of practices into one of the traditions. Thus if Hu is a syncretist, he is a syncretist in a more meaningful way than mere historical borrowing and blending from diverse traditions. The claim for syncretism rests with his involvement with Buddhism and Confucianism at the level of their truth-claims. For Hu Chih to be a syncretist, however, there must be not only the involvement of proposition and praxis, but also the attempt to unify or reconcile the divergent or opposing tenets and practices. Here, Hu Chih is clearly not a syncretist. He does not attempt to unify or reconcile one tradition and its respective truth-claims with another. In fact, it is crucial to Hu to maintain the distinction between the traditions he studies and practices. Even though Huang Tsung-hsi in his critique of Hu maintains that Hu is very close to Buddhism,[57] he recognizes that Hu himself maintains a distance between himself and the Buddhists. Even at the level of Hu's two enlightenment experiences, one within the context of Buddhism and a second from a Confucian perspective, there is no attempt either to unify the experiences in a syncretic form or to find a unitary basis as a synthesis in anything other than common psychological features.[58] Within the context of Hu Chih's autobiography truth-value appears to be entertained for both Buddhism and Confucianism suggesting the potential syncretic form; however, such truth-value, if actually ascribed to these traditions, is ascribed at different points in his life. Assent to divergent propositions is then diachronic rather than synchronic, thereby eliminating the possibility of true syncretism. Lacking the attempt to unify or reconcile the traditions in question, the term *syncretism* seems quite inappropriate. Buddhism and Confucianism remain separate for Hu Chih at the critical level, the expression of his own religious faith.

Ramifications for a Syncretic Model

The question of syncretism for Hu Chih has potentially far-reaching implications for the so-called syncretic character of Ming thought. There is little doubt that in many ways Hu Chih's philosophy resembles what is called *syncretism*, yet it is also very clear that in fundamental ways he is not a syncretist. The ramification of this is the degree to which Hu Chih's case is paradigmatic.

There are those Ming thinkers who openly advocate the unity of the Three Teachings—Confucianism, Taoism, and Buddhism. The doctrine of the unity of the Three Teachings, *san-chiao ho-i*, would appear to fit the syncretic model precisely where Hu Chih fails to fit. However, the implication from the example of Hu Chih suggests that syncretism is most often mistaken for a simple borrowing and blending process, irrespective of their contextual truth claims. This may very well have ramifications for the so-called syncretism of the unity of the Three Teachings. Is the syncretic claim that is being made in the case of the unity of the Three Teachings any more than a claim for historical borrowing and blending? Of course, it will be argued that distinguishing between traditions and defining one's religious faith as assenting to the truth claims of one tradition in opposition to other traditions is categorically different from advocating the basic unity of various traditions, as for example, in the case of Lin Chao-en (1517-1598).[59] After all, the basic definition of syncretism rests with an attempted unity or reconciliation, although it may be the case that the word *attempted* is what ought to be emphasized in the definition. Certainly, it could well be the case that there are differences between Hu Chih and someone such as Lin Chao-en, however, the degree of difference may depend in large part upon the mode of expression intended by advocating the unity of Three Teachings.

What I am suggesting, even though it is contrary to the current model which ascribes syncretic character to much of Ming thought, is that distinguishing traditions and their truth claims may, in fact, be little different in intention or substance from suggesting the unity of the traditions when the model employed intends one tradition as the interpretative tool or truth claim base of the other tradition or traditions involved. If the truth claims rest with just one tradition of the supposed unity, such a unity is a unity only at the level of having *distinguished* rather than unified truth claims. Such a process essentially involves an adaptation at the level of historical interrelationship through the borrowing and blending of tenets or practices whose own truth claims have been subverted or rendered secondary in the face of the truth value of the primary or interpretative tradition. This process is quite clear in the case of Lin Chao-en. Taoist and Buddhist tenets and practices are incorporated into a Neo-Confucian mode of expression. The only question that remains in the case of Lin Chao-en is whether truth value is placed in the Neo-Confucian mode of expression or whether Lin's proposition and praxis represent a synthesis, begging the question of syncretism altogether.[60] Another appropriate model of syncretism often suggested is the *honji-suijaku* theory of the relationship between Buddhism and Shinto, a theory of distinctly Buddhist origin to "explain" the relationship between Shinto *kami* and Buddhist metaphysics. To suggest, as does the theory, that each *kami* has its Buddhist counterpart supports the truth claims of Buddhism, not Shinto.[61] Is it appropriate to call this or the other cases mentioned here syncretism? If the religious life is composed of more than practice and if propositional truth must be accounted for, then the usefulness, let alone appropriateness, of applying the designation syncretism will only be found in describing those systems that give equal importance to proposition and praxis. As such it may well be that the characterizing of Ming thought as well as other similar models as syncretic will be in need of adjudication. In addition, the religious character of the Confucian tradition may be accounted for without having to explain its existence as the product of another religious tradition. This is a complex problem, however, and one that is the focus of the next chapter.

♦ ——————————————— CHAPTER **VI**

The Sudden/Gradual Paradigm and Neo-Confucian Mind Cultivation

Okada Takehiko in his volume *Zazen to Seiza, Buddhist and Confucian Meditation,* a study of the relationship between Buddhist and Neo-Confucian forms of meditation, states the basic stereotype suggesting the application of the Buddhist sudden/gradual paradigm to Neo-Confucianism. "If the Chu Hsi learning and the learning of Wang Yang-ming are compared and if the Chu Hsi learning is spoken of in terms of Ch'an Buddhism, it should be called a learned experience and gradual cultivation. For Wang Yang-ming it should be called seeing into the nature and sudden enlightenment."[1] Okada's comment is suggestive of a common model for the interpretation of the inner workings of Neo-Confucianism. Although Okada himself has serious reservations about the import of Buddhism as an explanatory context for the development of Neo-Confucianism,[2] his suggestion places the primary issue of the sudden/gradual paradigm in proper perspective. To what degree do forms of Neo-Confucian learning and self-cultivation receive the influence of the Buddhist model of sudden and gradual enlightenment?

Within the breadth of Neo-Confucian learning and self-cultivation in addition to a distinction between quietude and activity,[3] there is also a fundamental though often subtle distinction drawn between what we might call effort and spontaneity. The Wang Yang-ming school expresses a fundamental confidence in humanity's innate knowledge, *liang-chih,* based upon their presupposition of the inherent nature of Principle, *li,* as the foundation of the mind itself. The result is confirmed in forms of praxis which suggest a greater reliability upon the spontaneous expression of an individual's true nature. On the other hand, the fundamental pedagogical tool of the Ch'eng-Chu school, the investigation of things, *ko-wu,* necessitates effort and discipline in order to acquire knowledge of

77

the basic principle within things as well as one's own nature. Thus, from the Ch'eng-Chu perspective, the major task of learning is the proper training and clarification of the mind that it might be employed to search for Principle. Effort is placed upon the cultivation of reverent seriousness, *ching*, to this end and the emphasis is upon the necessity of diligent effort and accompanying toil. There is an ease of learning and self-cultivation in the School of Mind that is not found in the extended process of learning recommended by the School of Principle.

These models of learning within Neo-Confucianism are suggestive of the sudden/gradual paradigm within Buddhism, particularly Ch'an Buddhism. There is, at least, a level of commonality of expression and the similarity could run much deeper. Neo-Confucians do not readily apply sudden/gradual nomenclature to their own modes of discourse. However, the pervasiveness of Buddhism in Chinese culture and thus the potential for broad intellectual as well as religious influence cannot be ignored.

To focus this very broad topic of the potential influence of a Buddhist paradigm within Neo-Confucianism I want to narrow the sights to a specific form of practice to be able to examine the practice itself within its Neo-Confucian context and adjudicate its potential impact from Buddhist sources. The practice that perhaps more than any other in Neo-Confucianism has been discussed as a clear indication of Buddhist influence, particularly Ch'an Buddhism, is the practice of meditation in its distinctive Neo-Confucian form, quiet-sitting. It speaks directly to the debate on Buddhist influence in Neo-Confucianism and also suggests the debate within Neo-Confucian circles between effort and spontaneity with its ramifications for the sudden/gradual controversy.

In general terms, the Chu Hsi school favored the practice of quiet-sitting while the Wang Yang-ming School felt it to be unneccessary and even potentially harmful as a practice. For Yang-ming and his followers, a person's sageliness was revealed within activity, reflecting the confidence in the innate knowledge to manifest itself of its own effort. A meditative regimen was not only secondary, but antithetical to the potential immediacy, *tang-hsia*, of the realization of sagehood. For the Chu Hsi school, particularly during the Ming dynasty, meditation was combined with other forms of learning and self-cultivation and viewed as beneficial to the gradual realization of sagehood. I am intentionally using the terms *sudden* and *gradual* here to indicate the potential perimeters within the Neo-Confucian context. The question that remains is the degree to which it is appropriate to employ sudden/gradual nomenclature as descriptive of the practice of quiet-sitting and thus, in turn, the nature of Neo-Confucian learning.

Mind Cultivation and Quiet-Sitting During the Sung Dynasty

The practice of quiet-sitting is discussed by a number of Sung Neo-Confucians, but certainly two of the names most frequently associated with the practice are those of Lo Tsung-yen (1072-1135)[4] and Li T'ung (1088-1158).[5] Both are students of Ch'eng I and Li T'ung is one of the teachers of Chu Hsi. In fact, Chu Hsi appears to have learned of quiet-sitting primarily from Li T'ung. The object of quiet-sitting as Lo Tsung-yen taught it to Li T'ung and in turn Li T'ung taught it to Chu Hsi was far more than a simple complement to reading and study. It was nothing less than a form of practice that was capable of penetrating to the very core of one's nature. Lo Tsung-yen says of the practice, "In quiet-sitting one observes happiness, anger, sorrow and joy before they are manifest [*wei-fa*] and have assumed material form [*ch'i-hsiang*]."[6] According to the *Sung-Yüan hsüeh-an, The Records of the Sung and Yüan Scholars,* Lo received this teaching from Ch'eng Hao rather than Ch'eng I,[7] although speculating upon a secret and esoteric transmission as Forke has suggested is probably not necessary.[8] Li T'ung, in turn, taught Chu Hsi that the practice of quiet-sitting revealed the Principle of Heaven, *T'ien-li,* in the unmanifest mind, *wei-fa.* Chu Hsi was young when he received the teaching of Li T'ung and because of other major influences upon him, he was never fully swayed to quiet-sitting as a method to reveal the Principle of Heaven in the mind.[9] Chu Hsi expressed in verse his ideal of quietude, but this in turn was criticized and as a result he came to be far more cautious of the practice of quiet-sitting.

> Holding firm to the recluse life resting in the empty valley,
> The wind and moonlight over a stream demand of man his attention,
> For the clouds their responsibility[10] rests with furrowing and unfurrowing,
> Yet ten-thousand ages the azure mountains are just azure.[11]

Hu Wu-feng (1105-1155) described Chu Hsi's verse as possessing substance, but having no function and thereby running the risk of lapsing into quietude. He countered Chu Hsi's verse by composing a verse of his own that was to suggest the importance of both substance and function.

> The recluse is partial towards the azure mountains' loveliness,
> This is because the azure of the azure mountains never grows old.
> Clouds come out of the mountains and rain in Heaven and Earth,
> Having once been washed, the mountains are even more lovely.[12]

As the verses suggest, Chu Hsi seems almost nostalgic for the simple life of the rustic and expresses a certain sense of appreciation for the fact that nature left to itself is all that is needed. The contrast to this bucolic scene is the rigor of learning and the necessity of perfecting human nature. There seem almost echoes of Hsün Tzu's metaphor of the blue of the indigo plant[13] in Hu Wu-feng's response. For Hu, the clouds over the mountains perform a function and a responsibility. They cleanse the mountains and, as a result, the loveliness of the mountains is even more apparent. The ramifications for learning and self-cultivation are obvious: quietude has little or no place in the rigors of learning and self-cultivation.

Hu, unlike Li T'ung, thought that the Principle of Heaven could only be realized in the active or manifest capacity of the mind, *i-fa*.[14] For Wu-feng, a focus upon the unmanifest, *wei-fa*, differed little from the theory and practice of Ch'an Buddhism. Care was taken to ensure the preservation and nourishment of the unmanifest, but the focus of the attention was placed upon the manifest as the basis for learning. Hu Wu-feng was a major influence upon Chu Hsi through Wu-feng's disciple Chang Nan-hsien (1130-1180),[15] and Chu Hsi's eventual qualification upon the role of quiet-sitting may well indicate the degree of such influence.

Chu Hsi's successful synthesis of Neo-Confucianism appears to incorporate elements of quiet-sitting, but it did not retain the focus both Lo Tsung-yen and Li T'ung saw for practice. The degree to which Chu Hsi sees quiet-sitting as a part of a regimen of learning, summed up in the expression, "a half-day of quiet-sitting, a half-day of study," *pan-jih ching-tso pan-jih tu-shu*, is the degree to which the practice is subsumed within the context of a pedagogy of learning focused upon the investigation of things. It is not surprising, then, that for Chu Hsi, when too much emphasis was placed upon quiet-sitting, when it became a practice as an end unto itself, and not simply a subsidiary element in the investigation of things and the cultivation of reverent seriousness, it ran the risk of becoming a Buddhist practice.[16]

There certainly exist other and varied perspectives on quiet-sitting during the Sung,[17] but in the same way in which Chou Tun-i's teaching of the "mastering of quietude," *chu-ching*, was thought potentially suspicious of Taoist or Buddhist inclinations and thus not given a prominent place in Chu Hsi's synthesis, so, too, with quiet-sitting. As a practice, it can be helpful, but it must be used in tandem with other forms of learning. In a sense, quiet-sitting was useful for Chu Hsi to the degree that it remained focused upon the active component of learning, the manifest mind, and it was suspicious and potentially harmful to the extent that it became a practice exploratory of the unmanifest mind.

At least one tentative conclusion that can be drawn from Sung materials would suggest that quiet-sitting was not the sole prerogative of the Ch'eng-Chu school. A good deal of the reason may simply be that "orthodox" Neo-Confucianism is only in the process of being defined[18] and orthodoxy itself covers a range of interpretation from state orthodoxy to the individual not unlike the Ming experience,[19] although less obvious. However, the fact that Ch'eng I and Ch'eng Hao as well as Chu Hsi and Lu Hsiang-shan all practiced quiet-sitting suggests a flexibility in the practice that permits it to adapt to varying points of view. The heart of the Goose Lake Temple debate between

Chu Hsi and Lu Hsiang-shan did not revolve around the practice of quiet-sitting. At the same time, however, "book learning" versus "immediate experience" is not irrelevant to the practice. Chu Hsi's refocusing of Li T'ung's emphasis in quiet-sitting may be reflected in the apparent "sudden/gradual" distinction between Chu Hsi and Lu Hsiang-shan. However, as Tu Wei-ming reminds us, the sudden/gradual elements may be quite secondary.

> Underlying the difference, however, is more than the conflict between sudden enlightenment and gradual enlightenment. It is also the conflict between the perception of mind as the authentic manifestation of principle and thus the ultimate ground as well as the actual faculty of self-realization, and the perception of mind as the synthesis of human nature and human feelings (a mixture of principle and material force) and thus the actual faculty but not the ultimate ground of self-realization.[20]

What does this say for the practice of quiet-sitting? At least as far as the Sung perception of the role of quiet-sitting is concerned, it appears capable of fitting into the context of Lu Hsiang-shan's immediate or sudden realization of the principle of the mind as well as Chu Hsi's gradual accumulation of knowledge of principle. *Sudden/gradual* remains a loose way of describing this essential difference. Its effectiveness as a paradigm, however, may be measured by its ability to suggest the inner dimensions of conflict felt by Wang Yang-ming in his attempt to come to grips with the Ch'eng-Chu learning and what becomes a commonly recognized Ch'eng-Chu form of practice—quiet-sitting.

Wang Yang-ming and the Decreasing Relevancy of Quiet-Sitting

The early life of Wang Yang-ming, as Tu Wei-ming has demonstrated, is frought with crisis when he is faced with the necessity of reformulating Chu Hsi's understanding of the investigation of things, *ko-wu*.[21] The resolution to the crisis is found in Yang-ming's formulation of the unity of knowledge and action, *chih-hsing ho-i*, which as Tu Wei-ming argues, is neither a rejection of the method of *ko-wu* nor even a minimizing of its importance, but simply a restoration of *ko-wu* to its original meaning from Wang's perspective.[22] At root is a profound philosophical difference between Chu Hsi and Wang Yang-ming. For Chu Hsi principle is acquired from external sources in a gradual process, but as Yang-ming came painfully to recognize through his own practices, such external sources need not be easily accrued to one's own self-realization. Thus, Yang-ming grapples with the Chu Hsi formulation of *ko-wu* and eventually reformulates it in his well-known focus on *ch'eng-i*, sincerity of intention, with the presupposition of the immanental nature of Principle.

Within the context of the development of Yang-ming's thought there is a change in focus in forms of self-cultivation. One such form of self-cultivation is quiet-sitting. Yang-ming continues to recommend the practice of quiet-sitting even after the formulation of *chih-hsing ho-i*, however, qualifications begin to be placed upon the practice. Note, for example, the following passage from the *Ch'uan-hsi lu, Instructions for Practical Living*:

> The teacher said: "Formerly, when I stayed in Ch'u-chou, seeing that students were mostly occupied with intellectual explanations and debates on similarities and differences, which did them no good, I therefore taught them sitting in meditation. For a time they realized the situation a little bit [they saw the true Way] and achieved some immediate results. In time, however, they gradually developed the defect of fondness for tranquility and disgust with activity and degenerated into lifelessness like dry wood. Others purposely advocated abstruse and subtle theories to startle people. For this reason I have recently expounded only the doctrine of the extension of innate knowledge.[23]

Wang Yang-ming moves away from the practice of quiet-sitting as a central component to the process of self-cultivation and instead focuses his efforts upon the self-realization of the embodiment of Principle, *ts'un t'ien li*, and the gradual elimination of human desires, *ch'ü jen-yü*.[24] One wonders why, however, Yang-ming rejects the quiet-sitting model of self-cultivation. As Tu Wei-ming has put it, "Why is quiet-sitting, a form of inner spiritual self-cultivation, not accepted as a highly desirable method of learning to become a sage? In other words, if the structure of the self is sufficient for the actualization of the inner sage, what else is needed to manifest what is inherent in human nature?"[25] Yang-ming would certainly seem to suggest the potential of quiet-sitting as a method for the realization of sagehood when he says in the *Ch'uan hsi-lu*, "If one's innate knowledge is clear, it will be alright to try to obtain truth through personal realization in a quiet place or to discover it through training and polishing in the actual affairs of life. The original substance of innate knowledge is neither tranquil nor active."[26] There is little doubt that the self is sufficient, at least metaphysically, to unfold the inner sage. The metaphysical nature of the individual is not the stumbling block. Neither is the setting; it can be a setting either of quietude or activity. However, this is predicated upon one condition—the clarification of the innate knowledge. The focus remains Yang-ming's reformulation of Chu Hsi's understanding of *ko-wu* and the priority rests with the process of self-actualization through self-rectification. As a result quiet-sitting becomes secondary, as it had for Chu Hsi, although obviously for very different reasons. For Chu Hsi and his synthesis of Neo-Confucianism the salient emphasis rests with *ko-wu* and a mind of reverent seriousness. Quiet-sitting is maintained as a practice, but is important essentially only to the degree that its role is supportive of *ko-wu* and *ching*. Yang-ming, on the other hand, in his reformulation of *ko-wu* as a substantiation of the immanental nature of Principle focuses upon a process of rectification as the existential confirmation of the individual's metaphysical nature. For both men quiet-sitting pursued as an end is filled with hazards. If put within the proper context it is acceptable but it still remains curiously secondary.

Yang-ming's seeming ambivalence toward quiet-sitting is echoed in divisions within the Yang-ming school. Lo Hung-hsien, for example, continues to advocate the use of quiet-sitting.[27] Wang Chi (1498-1583), Wang Ken (1483-1541), and members of the T'ai-chou school reject the practice outright as of no relation to the existential context that, from their perspective, provides the ground for the realization of sagehood.[28] While Yang-ming suggests that quiet-sitting can be useful, he certainly lessens its relevance to the cultivation and experience of sagehood. The liberal followers of Yang-ming only increase the irrelevancy of the practice of quiet-sitting to the existential context of sagehood. In the continued development of the Ch'eng-Chu tradition, however, quiet-sitting comes to occupy a prominent position.[29] It is as if Yang-ming's failure in the Chu Hsi learning and his own reformulation of *ko-wu* as well as his own decreasing focus upon quiet-sitting crystallized the relation between Ch'eng-Chu orthodoxy and the practice of quiet-sitting. Certainly for a number of post-Yang-ming members of the Ch'eng-Chu school quiet-sitting is of salient import to regimens of self-cultivation.

Late Ming Ch'eng-Chu Quiet-Sitting

The struggle represented by Yang-ming's attempt to reach sagehood is also present among Ch'eng-Chu followers during the Ming. The heightened sense of self-consciousness and corresponding genres of self-reflection and self-scrutiny have been commented upon at some length.[30] Numerous examples of Ch'eng-Chu interest in and articulation of the practice of quiet-sitting are found throughout the Ming.[31] Certainly two of the most thoroughgoing discussions of the role and practice of quiet-sitting come from the late Ming Tung-lin Academy members Ku Hsien-ch'eng and Kao P'an-lung.[32] For both Ku and Kao quiet-sitting is a major element in their neo-orthodoxy, an orthodoxy highly critical of the Wang Yang-ming learning, particularly the liberal followers of Yang-ming, yet in certain ways highly influenced by Yang-ming and his struggle with *ko-wu*.[33]

Quiet-sitting for Ku Hsien-ch'eng plays a major role in his self-cultivation. He is sensitive to its history, that is, the role it has played in the Ch'eng-Chu school and to the reservations and qualifications Chu Hsi had placed upon the practice. Ku's articulation of the practice suggests an attempt to synthesize various attitudes about the practice and from his own perspective to see a much greater role for quiet-sitting than Chu Hsi was either willing to allow or felt could be tolerated without running the risk of appearing either Buddhist or

Taoist. Part of the explanation for Ku's focus upon the practice of quiet-sitting is the position in which Ku held Chou Tun-i. From Ku's perspective, Chou was central to the Ch'eng-Chu tradition and not simply in terms of the recognized importance of Chou's cosmogony. Ku was particularly interested in Chou's teaching of the "mastering of quietude," *chu-ching*, a teaching that for Chu Hsi could lead dangerously in the direction of quietude. As Wing-tsit Chan has suggested, Chu Hsi's completion of Neo-Confucianism precluded a central position for Chou Tun-i's teaching of quietude.[34] To Ku Hsien-ch'eng, on the other hand, the quietistic imagery of man's true nature in Chou Tun-i's thought simply indicated the central role that could be assigned to quiet-sitting. Thus Ku says, "The quiescence advocated by Master Chou [Tun-i] which is doubtless deduced from the 'limitless' [*wu-chi*] is the final aim."[35] For Ku, quiet-sitting was to probe the depths of human nature. The idea that quiet-sitting was no more than a part of a regimen of study and learning, a view held by both Ch'eng I and Chu Hsi, was regarded by Ku as but a "preliminary exercise."[36] As we have already seen, quiet-sitting for Lo Tsung-yen and Li T'ung also involved an attempt to arrive at the roots of one's nature. Ku finds support for his own understanding of quiet-sitting in the Lo and Li tradition. He speaks of the method of quiet-sitting in some detail.

> If the mind has something to dwell on it stagnates; if it has nothing to dwell on it drifts. The state "antecedent to the activation of happiness, anger, sorrow and joy," of which Li T'ung speaks is just in the middle between having and not having something to dwell on. It offers an entrance to the interior. If one methodically and continuously [makes use of it], the life force [*ch'i*], after a while, gradually becomes calm and the mind settled, and [one can be] in this state when one is alone, when one is occupied, when one is with people, and even when happiness, anger, sorrow or joy suddenly overtakes us. When one is always and completely in this state antecedent to the activation [of the emotions], so that there is no distinction whatsoever between interior and exterior, quiescence and activity, then the preliminary phase becomes the final stage.[37]

For Ku, as for Li T'ung, the object of quiet-sitting is the direct experience of the unmanifest mind. Certainly for Ku, the direct experience of the unmanifest mind need not preclude an establishment of relation with the manifest mind, *i-fa*. In fact, from Ku's perspective self-cultivation may only be considered complete when *i-fa* and *wei-fa* are thought of as no longer two distinct realms; that is, "there is no distinction whatsoever between interior and exterior." Thus, for Ku, quiet-sitting does not stop with the calming and settling of the mind within a setting of quietude. The practice can only be considered successful at the point that interior and exterior or stillness and activity are regarded as a continuum, and this is the product of a lengthy process of learning and self-cultivation. A very similar perspective may be seen in Kao P'an-lung.

We have with Kao P'an-lung one of the most extensive records of the practice of quiet-sitting. Not only was quiet-sitting a frequent topic of letters, poems, and journals, but in addition Kao wrote two essays on the practice itself.[38] For Kao, quiet-sitting is a process that will result in the full understanding of one's nature, that is, the original substance, *pen-t'i*, of the nature. It is a practice that is pursued with diligence and earnestness, for it is seen as a method that will reveal the substance of the Principle of Heaven, *T'ien-li*, and thus the nature of sagehood. In many ways, this is reminiscent of the immanental nature of Principle Yang-ming struggled to realize and indicates a certain degree of influence of Yang-ming upon the late Ming neo-orthodoxy. We see this in Kao as well as other Ch'eng-Chu followers; Principle has become something interior, and, for Kao at least, if a person can quiet the activity of the mind, he will see the Principle that is the root of the mind itself, what Li T'ung referred to as the state antecedent to the arising of the emotions and what Kao himself paraphrases.

The actual moment of seeing into the nature is for Kao a sudden one, if I may use that phrase. Kao's description, as we have seen in the study of his autobiography,[39] is reminiscent of the classic accounts of enlightenment experiences. The experience itself is a sudden one, but it is a product of an agonizingly slow process of learning and self-cultivation in which moments of understanding, let alone self-confidence, are rare. It is precisely the toils of learning that become the agenda of Kao's autobiography. One might even argue that part of the purpose in writing an autobiography, as so many Ming figures did, was to summarize what, in fact, had been accomplished over the span of a life of learning.[40] Thus, even though there is a moment of sudden understanding, the regimen continues to suggest a gradual process of learning and self-cultivation.

As far as the method of quiet-sitting is concerned, Kao seems to downplay its discussion, focusing instead upon what he considers to be the naturalness of quietude itself. He advises that distracting thoughts are to be allowed to disperse of their own without force, or even more importantly, without the arising of any intention for their dispersal. Any thought of acting upon them only causes the ruination of quietude itself. Thus one proceeds by not proceeding in an intentional manner. The language suggests Ch'an Buddhism. One might also argue, however, that accepting Chou Tun-i's teaching of quietude establishes the philosophical priority of quietude and thus necessitates only a return to quietude, not an intentional pursuit.

Ideally, the state of quietude and that of activity ought to be one and the same. As we have already seen in Ku Hsien-ch'eng, dwelling in the unmanifest mind, stillness and activity are a continuum. Kao uses the phrase *p'ing-ch'ang* or *p'ing-p'ing ch'ang-ch'ang*, ordinary or ordinariness, to describe the essential state that precedes either quietude or activity and states that through the practice of quiet-sitting quietude and activity may be regarded as one.[41] The creation of this continuum of quietude and activity, the "ordinary," remains fundamentally for Kao a gradual process. Even with the partial acceptance of Yang-ming's struggle for innate knowledge, Kao still insists that quiet-sitting will not produce instantaneous results, but only gradually produce an understanding through great toil and effort. While for Chu Hsi, quiet-sitting was placed in a context of many forms of self-cultivation, for Ku and Kao quiet-sitting assumes an importance comparable to Lo Tsung-yen's and Li T'ung's understanding of the practice, although it is clearly part of a gradual learning process. We can see then that quiet-sitting is deeply reflective of the larger models of learning in Neo-Confucianism. In one fashion or another it seems to be primarily connected with the School of Principle rather than the School of Mind, and this, in turn, suggests its allegiance to gradual rather than sudden forms of learning. What meaning, however, do the terms sudden and gradual have in this context?

The Sudden/Gradual Paradigm

Sudden and *gradual* suggest at least something of the general context for the inner workings of the Neo-Confucian learning and self-cultivation process. As the practice of quiet-sitting itself indicates, however, such differences may remain largely superficial in sudden/gradual nomenclature in comparison to the breadth of the metaphysical dimensions of the problem. It is perhaps the case, however, that even the metaphysical dimensions of the problem remain only partially adumbrated until the Wang Yang-ming challenge to the Ch'eng-Chu orientation in learning. It is a challenge at the experiential level; Chu Hsi is tried and Chu Hsi is put aside. As a result, methods of practice such as quiet-sitting become more crystallized as part and parcel of Ch'eng-Chu orthodoxy, and in turn, opposition to such forms of practice becomes more articulate by those who reject the Ch'eng-Chu model.

What then of the potential impact of the Buddhist sudden/gradual paradigm? Let us return for a moment to the central focus of Yang-ming's reformulation of Chu Hsi's understanding of *ko-wu*, the unity of knowledge and action, *chih-hsing ho-i*. In summarizing Yang-ming's critique of Chu Hsi's *ko-wu*, Tu Wei-ming suggests that for Yang-ming *ko-wu* as it had been understood by Chu Hsi lacked urgency, "for it assumes that the process of self-realization is necessarily a gradual one."[42] On the other hand, *chih-hsing ho-i* suggests a certain immediacy in terms of the immanental nature of Principle and thus sagehood itself. If we follow this theme through the liberal followers of Yang-ming, the tendency becomes even more pronounced to focus upon the immediate response, *tang-hsia*, of the nature and thus the immediate or *sudden* realization of sagehood.

Are we, however, asking the right question when it is formulated in terms of sudden/gradual? In other words, is Yang-ming primarily concerned that he reformulate Chu Hsi's understanding of *ko-wu* away from a *gradual* accumulation of external principle toward the immediate or *sudden* realization of the innate knowledge and potential of sagehood? The answer would seem to suggest that sudden/gradual remain primarily adjectival, that is, they are qualifications upon the nominal substantive, and in this case the substantive is the basic formulation of human nature. That is not to say that sudden/gradual does not play a role, but simply that the role played may be rather more secondary. As such, it may well harken back echoes of the Buddhist paradigm, but at a level of consonance well below the threshold of sound influence.

To what degree is estimating the influence of the sudden/gradual paradigm in the neo-orthodox practice of quiet-sitting after Wang Yang-ming possible? Even though Ku Hsien-ch'eng and Kao P'an-lung engage in typical Neo-Confucian polemics against Buddhism,[43] a virtual requirement of the neo-orthodox school, there is yet a strong case to be made for cordial relations with Buddhists. For example, Kao has close ties with Te Ch'ing,[44] and one of Kao's writings on quiet-sitting was written while visiting a Buddhist monastery.[45] Such visits, which are relatively frequent in the case of Kao, certainly do not make Kao a Buddhist. On the other hand, such visits would seem to mitigate against Kao's seriousness in the often vituperative prose directed against Buddhists. Putting the discussions of quiet-sitting by Ku and Kao in this context, the issues they raise certainly appear to have their counterparts in Buddhist meditative praxis.

The question of a Buddhist model may be seen in several different areas: the relation between quietude and activity, the necessity of meditation to span both quietude and activity, and the sudden/gradual paradigm. The perspective they give to quiet-sitting implicitly speaks to the sudden/gradual issue. For both Ku and Kao, the practice of quiet-sitting leads toward the realization of sagehood; the mind gradually becomes calm with continued practice. With the calming of the mind the roots of the individual's sagely nature become clearer. Essentially, quiet-sitting is a gradual process of unfoldment and is indicative of the understanding of the gradual development of learning in general. On the other hand, for Ku and Kao, the liberal followers of the Yang-ming school, in particular the T'ai-chou school, represented the anathema of proper learning.[46] The reason was simple. Presupposing the immanental nature of Principle and thus suggesting a spontaneous expression of the sagely nature, the T'ai-chou followers deemed learning toilsome and discipline unnecessary. Such learning and discipline simply stood in the way of the spontaneous expression of the innate knowledge, *liang-chih*. Learning without structure and discipline was to the neo-orthodox followers the boat without a rudder, and its result was almost certainly great harm. As quiet-sitting became so prominently associated with the Ch'eng-Chu school in the late Ming and, in turn, was adamantly rejected by the liberal followers of the Yang-ming school, the practice takes on the character of gradual learning in contrast to the sudden learning of the radical wing of the School of Mind. Yet, at a deeper level, the contents of the traditions of Neo-Confucianism and Buddhism are remarkably different from each other. Can we assume that when a Neo-Confucian talks of quiet-sitting and, by implication, suggests either sudden or gradual learning, they have a Buddhist model in mind in any manner that would be judged significant?

The Relevancy of a Buddhist Paradigm

The tension felt over the practice of quiet-sitting within Neo-Confucianism raises some key questions for the assessment of the potential reflection of the Buddhist sudden/gradual paradigm in various modes of Chinese thought. First, the debate within Neo-Confucian forms of self-cultivation between what we have described as effort and spontaneity may be no closer to resolution by implementing a Buddhist model. One might argue that the issue at hand within the inner workings of Neo-Confucianism reflects a continuity between Neo-Confucianism and its own heritage in Classical Confucianism as, for example, reflected in the distinction between Mencius and Hsün Tzu or the *Ta-hsüeh* and the *Chung-yung*. If the issue is a central one to the classical tradition, then an argument for external impetus is at best only a secondary influence. As a preexisting structure of thought there may be little influence by the sudden/gradual paradigm per se, or at the very minimum it becomes increasingly difficult to measure. Another point can be made in this respect. Excluding Classical Confucianism as an impetus in the development of Neo-Confucianism is virtually impossible. On the other hand, however, suggesting that the development of Neo-Confucianism was not influenced to some degree from the cultural milieu from which it sprang is not easy. Thus, equally untenable is the suggestion that Buddhism plays no role at all.[47] One wonders, quite frankly, whether the actual character of the debate within Neo-Confucianism reveals echoes of either a Confucian or a Buddhist mode strongly enough to suggest varying degrees of consonance with the root paradigms.

A second question seems relevant. Is the application of sudden/gradual terminology to the inner workings of Neo-Confucianism a clear and consistent process that establishes an equivalency of meaning within both traditions? One aspect of the problem would seem to be the establishment of a consistent use of the sudden/gradual paradigm within the Buddhist context itself. My impression of the usage of sudden/gradual terminology in Buddhism has suggested a certain pejorative connotation. Gradual seems always to be what the other person represents, that is, "otherness," with its connotation of inferiority.[48] Essentially no one calls himself a member of the "lesser vehicle." Surely something other than a pejorative is intended, but does it possess a consistent usage? Consistency is not irrelevant, for if Neo-Confucianism is indeed influenced by the model, it would be assumed that there is enough consistency to create a model!

Depending again upon the actual nature of the debate within Buddhism, one could argue that the sudden enlightenment experiences of those Neo-Confucians who practiced quiet-sitting and define their self-cultivation within a meditative regimen gravitates against the application of the Buddhist paradigm in any meaningful manner. In such a case, sudden and gradual simply break down as meaningful distinctions. On the other hand, the distinction between the Ch'eng-Chu model of an extensive program of learning and the Yang-ming focus upon enlightenment embodied within ordinary existence may be all that is meant by the application of the Buddhist paradigm.

If indeed this is the level at which the paradigm is applicable and there exists a more than plausible model from within the tradition in terms of its own roots, then how are we to adjudicate the potential influence of either of these models? The focus must necessarily be upon the meaning of influence. In suggesting, for example, that broad intellectual and religious ramifications of a controversy exist within Buddhist circles, we are proposing a transfer of situation and in turn a translation of that situation to the degree that the given model is assimilated into a different context. Influence, or the transfer and translation of situation, implies several different types of relationship that might occur between the model and its different contexts. Avoiding spurious relations, either forms of mistranslation or overtranslation, the potential impact of transfer of paradigms can be expressed in several different modes.

Several terms describe modes of relationship among traditions though they often seem marred by imprecise or inconsistent usage. We have spoken of historical interrelationship, eclecticism, syncretism, or synthesis, and potentially each could explain the use of the sudden/gradual paradigm.[49] Essentially, the terms are arranged in ascending order of complexity of assimilation, at least insofar as there is an internal consciousness of the process of assimilation and an increasing attempt to deal with the model and its potential ramifications upon assimilation.

A historical interrelationship suggests contact between traditions and the borrowing of ideas and practices such that the given ideas and practices would be assimilated into the framework of a particular point of view with little attention to a restructuring of the truth claims of the initial and basic point of view. In fact, the assimilation of "outside" influences is thought of only as augmentation to assist or even reinforce the primary worldview. If we take the example of quiet-sitting, one might argue that a form of meditation is not part of the Classical Confucian tradition and is thus obviously of non-Confucian origin, either Buddhist or perhaps Taoist. Liu Ts'un-yan, in discussing Taoist self-cultivation during the Ming, suggests this by stating that the "Neo-Confucians merely invented a system of mental cultivation which the Confucians had never before possessed. . . . so they were obliged to adopt such a system of mystical practice from other religions and present it in respectable language taken from the Confucian Classics."[50] Quite apart from the difficulties Liu's point of view represents, it could certainly be concluded that the Sung Neo-Confucians primarily responsible for the formulation of quiet-sitting were influenced by a model of meditation whether Buddhist or Taoist. This does not suggest, however, that by adapting and practicing quiet-sitting the basic Neo-Confucian orientation has been altered in any significant manner. The critical issue in historical interrelationship is that borrowing and adaptation can take place but without any radical change or augmentation to the respective truth claims of the root tradition. Thus, in this particular case, the practice of meditation is borrowed and placed within a set of propositions that remain fundamentally Confucian, and the very object of the practice itself is the experiential verification of the truth claims. If this is the suitable framework for the sudden/gradual paradigm, it is suggestive of the common origin of processes of self-cultivation, but is attenuated at the level of truth claims.

An eclectic model is more complex, if only because the term itself implies not only complexity of relation, but a certain element of inconsistency as well.[51] The term *eclecticism* often suggests a pejorative judgment: to say someone is eclectic is to say that what he holds comes from different sources, and there is an internal inconsistency about the combination itself. Or it simply may mean that one does not understand how an individual holds the beliefs he holds.[52] If Neo-Confucianism is described as eclectic and quiet-sitting is regarded as an example of such eclecticism, the practice would be judged to find its origin in non-Confucian sources, but something more is involved. In addition to a practice from non-Confucian sources, eclecticism would imply that quiet-sitting would bring with it certain elements of the original setting that would not assimilate with Neo-Confucian truth claims. In terms of the sudden/gradual paradigm, eclecticism suggests that the Neo-Confucian finds the model attractive in itself, quite apart from whether it has correlates to the larger context of the Neo-Confucian worldview.

A syncretic model suggests yet another stage of assimilation.[53] If syncretism is not a misused form of historical interrelationship, but instead regarded as a separate phenomenon in which the participant is conscious of the truth-claims of the respective traditions, then a syncretic model would suggest a highly complex interrelationship. In the case of a true syncretism, quiet-sitting would carry with it a certain worldview and would be assimilated into Neo-Confucianism with a more obvious concern for its Buddhist or Taoist roots. Those who suggest that a Confucian cannot practice quiet-sitting without falling into Buddhism come close to this perspective. That is, the practice cannot be removed from its moorings: a simple historical borrowing of a practice does not explain syncretism. A conscious attempt must be made to reconcile potentially conflicting truth claims. In the case of the sudden/gradual paradigm, syncretism suggests that it is more than a model for processes of self-cultivation. It would be instead an attempt to deal with the truth claims the sudden/gradual model presupposes.

The final relation, a synthetic mode, suggests that truth claims rest not with the respective traditions whose practices and ideas are being assimilated, but rather in the assimilation itself. In other words, a new point of view is created claiming its own propositional truth value.[54] In this case, the combination of elements creates something categorically different. If this were to be applied to Neo-Confucianism, then the Neo-Confucian who practices quiet-sitting would have reached a new point of view precluding a label of Buddhist, but it also limits the usefulness of the designation Neo-Confucian.

It seems obvious that we are not dealing with a synthesis, for there is nothing posited that circumvents the perimeters of the respective traditions, unless one argues that something such as the T'ai-chou school represents a categorically different phenomenon.[55] In turn, a true syncretism seems ill-suited to describe the potential impact of the sudden/gradual paradigm, for the Neo-Confucian is not entertaining Buddhist truth-claims.[56] Eclecticism is, at best, a bad term. Suggesting that inconsistency is an appropriate designation whatever the roots of the given practice is difficult. Historical interrelationship seems at least at one level the most appropriate designation. Neo-Confucianism was influenced by Buddhism and such influence plays its role in developing and defining the continuing worldview bound by a certain set of truth claims that remain remarkably Confucian.

$\blacklozenge$ ——————————————— Chapter **VII**

Meditation and Ming Neo-Orthodoxy

For Kao P'an-lung, a member of the neo-orthodox[1] Tung-lin Academy, learning and self-cultivation involved the practice of quiet-sitting, *ching-tso*. Quiet-sitting, as we have seen, developed in the Ch'eng-Chu school as a practice supportive of both the disciplined, regulated and exhaustive search for *li*, principle, and the proper attitude of mind, *ching*, reverent seriousness.[2] As a contemplative form of practice, quiet-sitting was particularly suited to the changing focus of learning for the Ming Neo-Confucian, a focus shifting in the direction of the interiority of principle.[3] The role of self-examination and self-reflection, long distinguishing characteristics of Confucian cultivation, take on an added significance within the context of introspective investigation. Quiet-sitting provides a means for the advancement of learning through such self-examination and self-reflection.

Within the Ming experience of Neo-Confucianism the realization of sagehood stood as the goal toward which learning and self-cultivation were directed.[4] For Kao P'an-lung, too, sagehood is the aim of the learning and cultivation process. Kao's autobiography, *K'un-hsüeh chi*, begins with his resolve to pursue the attainment of the goal of sagehood.[5] The resolve indicates a reorientation and focusing of his own priorities. With sagehood clearly established as the proper aim, learning and self-cultivation can begin in earnest. Quiet-sitting is incorporated by Kao into the learning and self-cultivation schema. In describing the purpose of quiet-sitting, Kao states that through quiet-sitting the original substance, *pen-t'i*, of the true nature, *hsing*, will manifest itself and thus come to be understood.[6] Through understanding the true nature, one comes to understand the Way of Heaven. This is the ground upon which the individual fulfills his religious life. The degree to which this is a major form of self-cultivation corresponds to the importance of understanding the practice as a major element in the Confucian religious life. What follows is a close analysis of the characteristics, role, and expectation of quiet-sitting for Kao P'an-lung.

Isolation and Involvement:
The Tension of Contemplative Praxis

A persistent question in surveying Kao's writings on quiet-sitting is the degree to which a need was felt for withdrawal or isolation from familial and societal relations on the part of the individual engaged in quiet-sitting. Kao suggests that isolation or seclusion, *pi-kuan*, was to be part of the practice of quiet-sitting.[7] Such periods of isolation take several different forms. It can characterize nothing more than seeking out a quiet and perhaps secluded location to practice quiet-sitting, ameliorating the potential for distraction or disturbance, but suggesting no fundamental physical or emotional severing. On the other hand, more serious measures can also be implied. The withdrawal from family and friends can involve a greater physical isolation in terms of both length of time and location and may suggest varying degrees of emotional withdrawal or separation as necessary corollaries to the practice of quiet-sitting.[8] If the practice does involve the stringency of a thoroughgoing separation then quiet-sitting would have to be characterized not as a part of daily life,[9] but rather a radical break from it.

This is a question that is not foreign to philosophical dialogue within the tradition itself. The Wang Yang-ming school opposed the practice of quiet-sitting because there was no clear connection between the practice and what for them daily life ought to be. In a sense, quiet-sitting lacked relevancy for Wang Yang-ming because the practice did not appear to issue in moral action. From this perspective, quiet-sitting might help the individual to uncover his *hsing*, but it lacked the ability to extend the individual into his proper relation with humanity.[10] Yen Yüan (1635-1704), a not unrelated example, could undertake the practice of quiet-sitting for a number of years only eventually to relinquish it in dissatisfaction because as he characterized the problem, his self-cultivation ought to be defined in terms of what he could *do*, not what he could *be*.[11] For the follower of the Wang Yang-ming school the issue involved in quiet-sitting is a moral tension between the practice of self-cultivation in a form that suggests isolation and the goal of self-cultivation, the sage, a person distinguished by his commitment to, and involvement in, moral relationships.

Whether the issue can be presented in these terms for Kao P'an-lung is another question. He practiced quiet-sitting considering its very practice an act of engaging in the orthodox transmission of the Way, yet, at the same time, he defined the goals of his own neo-orthodoxy precisely in terms of involvement in the moral relations of society. The potential for tension between quiet-sitting and active involvement is either mitigated through a very qualified sense of isolation in the practice of quiet-sitting or the tension is not felt because within Kao's interpretation of Ch'eng-Chu orthodoxy the bifurcation and resulting tension is not real. There may be room, then, for a neo-orthodox rebuttal to the assessment by the Wang Yang-ming school that quiet-sitting is tangential to carrying out the task of the Confucian commitment.

The relation between quiet-sitting and other forms of self-cultivation is discussed by Kao in his autobiography. He alludes to Chu Hsi's broad schema, "a half day of quiet-sitting, a half day of study."[12] The phrase suggests the establishment of a strong emphasis upon comtemplative practice within the Ch'eng-Chu tradition. Rather than a fixed rule, however, scheduling one's day rigidly between the hours spent in meditation and those spent in study, a balance is sought between various activities of self-cultivation. One mode of self-cultivation was not to be pursued to the virtual exclusion of another. The general directive of Chu Hsi, which appears to be followed by Kao, does not encourage the separation of the practice of quiet-sitting from this larger context of learning and self-cultivation.

The question of quiet-sitting as a practice, which is not separated from broad learning, may have some bearing on the issue of the isolation or separation of the practitioner from his network of relations and responsibilities. The directive of Chu Hsi is suggestive of a necessary relational context for the pursuit of self-cultivation. It is true that it may not exclude all possibilities of withdrawal and isolation, for it would still seem quite possible that one might, so to speak, carry one's books with one! However, book learning need not suggest the rusticating and eremetic pedant. In fact quite the opposite may be more to the case. Book learning may imply, as Confucius himself seemed to suggest,[13] a pursuit to be shared or perhaps even fulfilled and perfected in relation with others. If quiet-sitting is a part of a broad cultivation process and if major elements of this process involve a relational context with other people, then Chu Hsi's schema of cultivation suggests necessary constraints upon the degree of isolation suitable in the practice of quiet-sitting.

An exemplification of Chu Hsi's general rule of a combination of quiet-sitting and study is found in Kao's travel diary of his journey to Chieh-yang, Kwangtung, in 1594, the *San-shih chi, Recollections of Three Seasons.*[14] Kao portrays his life in Chieh-yang as comprising various activities. There are the duties and responsibilities of his office,[15] but he also finds time to continue his pursuit of quiet-sitting and study. Whatever time there is beyond these tasks is according to Kao taken up with the instruction of students, correcting their compositions and attempting to rectify those areas where the students "had been lead astray by the modern discussions and had ventured to turn their backs on the standard commentaries."[16] Quiet-sitting in this context is integrated into a schedule of activity. Other than perhaps finding a quiet location for a few minutes in the course of the day, no indication is given of a withdrawal or separation from such activity as a necessary condition for the practice of quiet-sitting. Serving in office, instruction of the young, study, and quiet-sitting: the impression is that each serves its purpose as a means of learning within the Ch'eng-Chu tradition.

There are, however, contexts in which the dominant role within the self-cultivation matrix shifts to quiet-sitting and in these situations the question of isolation plays a larger role. Kao suggests in at least one passage a degree of severity marked by both physical and psychological strain. "Whether I was standing, sitting, eating or resting, these thoughts were continuously present [i.e., the methods of quiet-sitting]. At night I did not undress and only when I was weary to the bone did I fall asleep. Upon waking I returned to sitting, repeating and alternating these various methods of practice."[17] In the period Kao is discussing, other activities have been suspended and quiet-sitting is the focus of his attention. He suggests it is fortunate in fact that he is without normal affairs.[18] Even the balance between study and quiet-sitting appears abnegated though the practice is initially accompanied by study.[19] It is, in effect, sitting *sine qua non*. The practice is arduous, the hours long, the setting one of comparative isolation, sleep only a brief interlude at the point of exhaustion. Such a description is reminiscent of other systems of meditation, for example the Ch'an model of austere measures of meditative practice.[20] This passage appears unique, however, in the degree of severity displayed. There are clear reasons why the practice took on the level of arduousness with which it is characterized. The reasons unfold within the psychological and religious temperament of Kao himself. The journey upon which Kao speaks of his severe practices has many of the marks of extreme religious stress with its unequivocal urgency and commitment. Kao vows to allow himself only the length of time of this journey to reach an understanding of the original substance, *pen-t'i*, of his nature. "Making a thorough investigation, I realized that being totally ignorant of the Way, my mind and body had nothing to draw on. Thus I strongly affirmed, 'If I don't penetrate it on this trip, then my life will have been in vain.' "[21] He is uncompromising in the discipline he sets for himself and his practice of quiet-sitting bears this commitment.

The *Shan-chü k'o-ch'eng, An Agenda for Dwelling in the Mountains*, written in 1598 while Kao was staying in the Wu-lin Mountains,[22] illustrates an isolation from normal activities. It lacks the psychological and religious stress but suggests a more pronounced effort at isolation.

"At the fifth drum, wrapped in my blanket, I sit up with teeth chattering and spirits stiff. But I am content and collect myself together. As the sky begins to brighten I rest a little then rise. After I have washed up and rinsed my mouth out I light the fire and burn incense. I sit in silence and dally with the *I* [*Ching*]. After the morning meal I go out for a walk. Instruction is given to the young ones and I care for the flowers and trees. Then, entering the hall, my thoughts dwell on quietude and I study. After the noontime meal, I go for a short walk content and humming. [Then, however,] I am aware of an [inner] oppressive force [*hun-ch'i*] and I shut my eyes for a little rest. I sip tea, and burn incense and direct my thoughts to [what is] relaxed and then return to my studying. As the sun begins to decline and set, I sit cross-legged in meditation for the length of a single slender stick of incense. As the setting sun is held between the mountains, I go out to gaze upon the clouds and the scene and [then] to examine the trees the gardener has planted. The evening meal is plain and simple; a little wine brings contentment. Lighting the lantern my thoughts search and wander [through books]. When I am content and have stopped, I sit cross-legged on my bed till the moment of repose, then I sleep."[23]

The writing describes the events of a day spent in the mountains, or more specifically, the activities while visiting several mountain monasteries. It is a peaceful setting, a setting free of daily responsibilities and thus perhaps more conducive to meditation practices. Kao's actual practice of quiet-sitting itself is not at the exclusion of a number of other activities including even the teaching of children. The balance of activities in self-cultivation is maintained in this mountain setting. His sojourn in the mountains is, however, a break from his normal sphere of activity, and in that sense is a form of isolation. It is readily apparent, however, that whatever degree of isolation is involved is qualified; the time period involved is relatively brief, and it is followed by a return to family and societal affiliation and duties.

It appears that Kao felt that it was within the bounds of learning to set aside a certain amount of time, at most a several-day period, in order to pursue self-cultivation without distraction. In a short writing entitled *Fu-ch'i kuei, Rules for "Returning in Seven,"*[24] Kao suggests a period of seven days be set aside when extreme mental weariness is at hand. "When one's response to things has become weary, then one ought to settle oneself with quietude for seven days in order to obtain relief. . . . After the seventh day the spirit will be cleansed and illness gone."[25] Such a period of time would indeed represent a break from normal activities. The schedule itself is predicated upon the value of a period of isolation. At the same time, however, the isolation is of limited duration; once the seven-day period is completed, one returns to the daily course of activities and responsibilities. Ideally one returns refreshed in spirit and determination.

Isolation permitted Kao to establish himself in the right setting such that self-cultivation, particularly with its emphasis upon contemplative activity, could reestablish direction and goal. Such motivation lead to his retreats into the mountains and in addition to the building of a small hut, *Shui-chü*, the Water Dwelling. Concerning the building of the Water Dwelling Kao says, "In 1598 I built the Water Dwelling with the intention of practicing quiet-sitting and engaging in study there. After 1596 I had lost my parents, moved about, and saw my children getting married. Those years allowed me no peace. In the midst of these activities, I tried to continue my discipline but was only too well aware of the difficulties of transforming one's physical nature."[26] The activities Kao describes prevented the necessary focus on quiet-sitting and study. The proper surroundings were essential, thus he built a hut, a place for quiet reflection and meditation. Frequent references are found in Kao's writings to the time spent in the Water Dwelling either alone or with close friends pursuing quiet-sittting and study.[27]

The difficulties of self-cultivation and in particular the difficulties involved in gaining a sense of quietude are never underestimated by Kao. He sums up the toils of cultivation in the autobiography. "The Sages and the Worthies must have great spiritual capacity to enable them to master quietude in their ordinary daily lives. For the scholar whose spirit is deficient and whose physical nature is unstable several tens of years of effort are needed before quietude can be deeply established."[28]

Kao saw the need for an isolation from the daily activities in times of distraction and fatigue. Such periods of isolation indicate a qualified sense of separation from the world of activities and responsibilities. The isolation was of short duration; it was not marked by any sense of renunciation of relationships or responsibilities. The periods of isolation served in one sense to revive lagging spirits, a purpose by no means extraneous to reestablishing purpose and direction and renewing vigor in the task of learning and self-cultivation. Withdrawal for short periods of time also permitted the individual to focus his attention on quiet-sitting and study, but not at the risk of mitigating his primary responsibilities to a moral relation with other persons through the severing of the relation itself. For Kao, the ideal of self-cultivation and particularly its comtemplative model was difficult to emulate. Distractions, frustrations, responsibilities—each poses its difficulties in the pursuit of knowing the true nature. A brief respite from such difficulties does not suggest a model of renunciation as much as it suggests a renewed commitment to seeing the difficulties through.

Kao's use of isolation in effect serves the purpose of involvement through a renewed vigor brought to situations of responsibility. This is only a partial answer, however, to the Wang Yang-ming assessment of the practice of quiet-sitting. Kao's qualified sense of isolation may still involve a tension between self-cultivation and daily life. It is one thing to suggest that isolation serves the purpose of involvement, but it is an entirely different question to suggest a unity between self-cultivation and daily life.

"Method" in the Practice of Quiet-Sitting

We have seen a sense of qualified isolation in the practice of quiet-sitting, a degree to which Kao was willing to suggest that it was necessary to find a quiet and secluded location free from distraction in order to engage in quiet-sitting. Such an act of isolation might be for the length of a burning stick of incense or it might extend for several days. These are descriptions of conditions the creation of which are suitable to the practice of quiet-sitting, but they are not characterizations of the practice itself. An explication of the practice itself necessitates description of both the physical characteristics of the practice and the role of mind, that is, the direction and discipline under which the mind functions within the practice.

Remarkably little is said of the physical characteristics of the practice. A composite picture in general terms can be constructed from the various terse references made by Kao to the physical practice itself. Under most circumstances, Kao speaks of practicing quiet-sitting in association with Buddhist temples he visits, or in his own hut, the Water Dwelling.[29] A notable exception to this rule is the adaptability of the practice to Kao's various peregrinations, be it on board a boat or in a small inn.[30] The period spent in quiet-sitting is often described as either begun by or accompanied by the burning of one or more sticks of incense.[31] The burning of incense is the measure of time spent in quiet-sitting.

In describing the practice itself, Kao says little more than to indicate that the eyes were shut, that for purposes of the practice, one isolated oneself, *pi-kuan*, and that in general the cross-legged position of meditation, *fu-tso*, was employed.[32] These practices are in the context of a particular period of meditation and it cannot be said with certainty that such practices were all part of a standard form of meditation.

The *Fu-ch'i kuei*, which deals with an interval of time encompassing several days, suggests a number of procedural issues not indicated in the context of shorter periods of time. During an interval of several days of practice, Kao indicates that difficulties will be encountered with lethargy and laziness.[33] The remedy is found in periods of exercise together with moderation in eating and drinking integrated into the overall period of time set aside for self-cultivation. Such pursuits are descriptive, however, of the ideal circumstances surrounding and conducive to the practice rather than the nature of the practice itself.

One further aspect of the physical practice does elicit Kao's comments. The entry for the year 1600 in Kao's *nien-p'u*, chronological biography, includes a short passage taken from his diary, *jih-chi, Daily Records*. The subject of this passage is breath control, *t'iao-hsi*, a practice Chu Hsi had already commented upon.[34] Kao concluded for himself that it was a practice filled with potential dangers, easily becoming an object of attachment. Whatever minimal use had been made of breath control was discontinued.

The impression of the practice from the existing, yet laconic, references is on the whole a rather relaxed model of meditation. This does not minimize the degree of discipline and dedication with which the practice may be taken up, nor the severe forms of practice in times of psychological and religious anxiety. Indeed, there are conventions of practice to be sure; a quiet location, burning of incense, some concern with posture and the shutting of the eyes. Yet, there is no specific characteristic of the physical form of the practice that appears inextricably and irrevocably bound to the successful practice of quiet-sitting. Instead, it would appear that there is ground for modification and adaptability in the execution of the practice.

While the precise nature of the physical practice may be subject to personal and situational adaptation, it is an entirely different question whether the method and direction of mental discipline may be characterized in comparable terms. The initial impression may be of a similar level of adaptability in form, although it is perhaps misleading in the case of the mind component of the practice. Initially, a number of general rules are enunciated which govern the focus and direction of mental discipline. In both *Fu-ch'i kuei* and *K'un-hsüeh chi* Kao states that as a general guide one ought to follow the words of the Sages, a term by this point ubiquitous enough in meaning to include high antiquity and the masters of the Sung dynasty. "When first approaching quietude it is not known how to get a hold of it. Simply stick to the most important sayings of the Sages and Worthies and the beginning steps will unfold naturally."[35] Some more specific idea of *which* words of the Sages one is to follow is given in the *K'un-hsüeh chi.* "During quiet-sitting whenever I felt ill at ease, I would just follow the instructions of Ch'eng [I] and Chu [Hsi], taking up in turn: With sincerity and reverent seriousness consider quietude as fundamental; observe happiness, anger, sorrow and joy before they arise; sit in silence and purify the mind; realize for oneself the Principle of Heaven."[36]

Such phrases appear to serve as a general guide. They are to be held in mind and reflected upon, although it is unclear whether reflection upon these phrases is to precede and perhaps initiate the state of quietude or whether it is descriptive of the minds activity while in quietude. These various phrases are in a sense descriptions of the goal rather than the method itself. Suggesting that one ought to observe happiness, anger, sorrow, or joy before they have arisen does not tell one what to do in quiet-sitting in order to reach such a point of perception. Realizing for oneself *T'ien-li*, is descriptive of what ought to be the case under ideal circumstances, but not a practical guide to its realization. The mastering of quietude through reverent seriousness and sincerity might appear as an exception to this general rule of ambiguity, however, the degree to which these remain as unspecified goals suggests the same category of difficulty. The same may be said for the act of purifying the mind. The separation between the ideal and the reality is not bridged by the directive intended in the phrase itself.

The ambiguity of mental discipline within quiet-sitting is suggested by the negative terms employed to describe the method. There are to be no guidelines, no procedure, no intention, no attachment, no selfishness, no thought of a goal; in short it would appear that within the practice all conscious activity or direction is to cease. The effort made is to be *effortless* in the midst of quiet-sitting. "The rules for quiet-sitting are nothing more than this; arousing the mind to stately and constant clarity and not allowing one's aims to be set on anything. When the aims are no longer set on anything, the spirit of its own congeals together again. Do not wait for a particular procedure [*an-p'ai*]; there are no guidelines set forth and there should be no thought of the results."[37]

The same general view is elaborated in more detail in *Ching-tso shuo, A Discussion of Quiet-Sitting*:

> In considering the method for quiet-sitting, there is no need for any particular procedure [*an-p'ai*]. Just act in an ordinary fashion [*p'ing-p'ing ch'ang-ch'ang*] and let quietude come forth from silence. . . . In the midst of quietude false thoughts are not to be forcefully removed. Once the true substance [*chen-t'i*] manifests itself, false thoughts will disappear of their own accord. The dark forces cannot be forcefully removed either. When false thoughts disappear by themselves, dark forces will of themselves become clear. Simply recognize [*t'i-jen*] the original nature and the original form will again become clear. Neither attach yourself to a single intention nor to a single view; if only one thought is added, the original form is lost.[38]

In both contexts, Kao criticizes the idea of method or procedure in the exercise of mental discipline within quiet-sitting. The term *an-p'ai*, procedure, describes for Kao what appears as the incorporation of an exterior form in the practices of quiet-sitting. That which is conducive to the emergence of *hsing* and so in turn the converse of *an-p'ai* is what Kao calls "ordinariness" or "acting in an ordinary fashion," *p'ing-p'ing ch'ang-ch'ang* or *p'ing-ch'ang*. Its role is evident in Kao's elaboration of the concept.

> This idea of ordinary [*p'ing-ch'ang*] should not be taken lightly for it is the very substance of one's nature. If [the nature] is pure and clear and unencumbered by so much as a single thing then it can be called ordinary [*p'ing-ch'ang*]. The changes that took place before there were hexagrams are like this.[39] What is prior to "man at birth is quiet" is like this.[40] "Before the arising of happiness, anger, sorrow and joy" is also like this.[41] It is the naturalness of the Principle of Heaven, something that each should embody for himself to reach self-fulfillment.[42]

If the true nature is to emerge, it will emerge only in an attributeless context. *P'ing-ch'ang* is descriptive of the condition prior to the emergence of a person's feelings. When the motivations and intentions remain, the task of quiet-sitting is made more difficult. Kao gives a warning to this effect in the second essay written on quiet-sitting, *Ching-tso shuo-huo, A Later Discussion of Quiet-Sitting*, an essay whose intended purpose was to rectify and clarify issues raised by the first essay. "As soon as it [i.e., the unity of body and mind] is regarded as fundamental, there is the intention [*i*] to hold on to it. The intention is not one to be attached to either. When the mind is without affairs [*wu-shih*] it is called unified. When it is attached to an intention it is no longer unified. Yet not being attached to an intention can also be called an intention."[43]

The problem articulated by Kao is the relation of intention, *i*, to the creation of sources of attachment. Suggested is a causal relation; creating an object of intention and, in turn, becoming attached to it, gives rise to selfish motivations. Such selfish motivation is seen as the ruination of the content of quietude. "If there is within quietude even a slight mixture of selfish thought, it [i.e., quietude] cannot become straight."[44] In language reminiscent of Chuang Tzu, Kao suggests that even the possibility of remaining unattached to an intention can become a source of attachment as an attachment to the intention of nonattachment. In short, as long as intentions remain, so likewise the sources of attachment and thus encumbrances upon the quietude of the mind.

The alternative to ever-present intentions is *wu-shih*, not set on anything, and *wu-shih*, being without affairs, or "not busying the mind with anything."[45] To act in an ordinary fashion, *p'ing-ch'ang*, is to hold things lightly, without intention, without aim, without attachment. Kao speaks of the mind held in such fashion as both not set on anything and not busying the mind with anything. Such descriptions are suggestive of a certain sense of emptiness of mind[46] in which mind is portrayed as being void; void of intentions, void of aims, and void of attachments. What is left? Perhaps it is more suitable to ask exactly what it is that has been removed. What has been removed are the seeds of selfish motivation, what remains is one's true nature, identical in substance to *T'ien-li*. Emptiness in this sense does not suggest a void, but only the absence of inhibiting factors in the emergence of the true nature.

The Ch'eng-Chu distinction between the mind of Tao, *Tao-hsin*, and the mind of the ordinary person, *jen-hsin*,[47] is illustrative of the applicability of the concept emptiness to the content of quietude. The *Tao-hsin* as Principle of Heaven is in a yet unmanifest state, *wei-fa*. *Jen-hsin* dominated by habits and attachments is said to be manifest, *i-fa*. The practice of quiet-sitting, and thus the establishment of the mind in a state of quietude, suggests a cessation of the limitations of the *jen-hsin*. The mind may be said to be empty of the habituations of the ordinary mind. This only leaves the mind empty or open[48] to the manifestations of the *Tao-hsin*, the essence of the nature.

In the sense of emptiness, there is a certain quality of passivity suggested on the part of the participant. The impression created is of sitting virtually passive, and applying nothing of oneself, that is, ordinary mind, to the content of quietude. A passive quality is suggested in the reticence to act upon and remove what are called false thoughts during quiet-sitting.[49] The false thoughts are simply to subside by themselves. This appears to be predicated upon the belief that as the original substance emerges, false thoughts of their own desist. The role of the participant is to maintain a state of *wu-shih*, not busying the mind with things. Thus, while the field of the mind may still be occupied with false thoughts, these appear to be of little or no account if the mind is without sources of attachment. In other words, through being without affairs and not set on anything the ordinary mind clarifies itself to the point that the mind is open to and activated by *Tao-hsin*. Random false thoughts can come and go but they leave without the imposition of effort on the part of the individual. It is an inverse relation between the original substance and false thoughts; as one emerges the other fades away and the role of the individual appears quite passive.

In the broad spectrum of different models of self-cultivation within the Ch'eng-Chu school, Kao's focus appears to be in the direction of the quietude of Chou Tun-i rather than the reverent seriousness of Ch'eng I and Chu Hsi. Chou T'un-i's *chu-ching*, mastering of quietude, while suggestive of a certain quality of moral direction and guidance,[50] conveys in general the impression of a quiet-ism virtually devoid of effort or guidance. Ch'eng I's *chü-ching*, abiding in reverent seriousness, on the other hand, recognizes the need for such guidelines and direction to be given to the mind. De Bary has suggested that Kao has combined Chou Tun-i's element of quietism together with the Ch'eng I directive of abiding in reverent seriousness.[51] This would be a departure of Kao from his compatriot of the Tung-lin Academy, Ku Hsien-ch'eng, who followed far more closely a model of quietude suggestive of Chou Tun-i.[52] We have already seen that Kao describes the state of the mind in quietude in terms of *p'ing-p'ing ch'ang-ch'ang* by which is meant *wu-shih*, being without affairs, and *wu-shih*, not set on anything. This would follow Ku Hsien-ch'eng's understanding of quietude were it not for Kao's inclusion of reverent seriousness, sincerity, and goodness, in the content of quietude. At the conclusion of his first essay on quiet-sitting, Kao comments, "This [i.e., quietude] is none other than what is called reverent seriousness, none other than goodness and none other than sincerity."[53] Any sense of quietism or passivity ceases in the active moral context Kao ascribes to quietude. For Kao it is precisely within the emptiness of mind that the moral activism of the Ch'eng-Chu tradition is found.

The sense in which Kao's quietude and apparent passivity retains an element of direction and guidance, a moral directiveness, suggests that mental discipline involves a method. Over and above Kao's own claims that there are no real guidelines, no actual method, salient characteristics of a method emerge. The sense of *p'ing-ch'ang*, with its integral association to *wu-shih*, being without affairs, and *wu-shih*, not set on anything, define the method. Instead of the adaptable and flexible nature of the physical practice, mental discipline is consistently and intentionally to be a nonmethod. To vary the characteristics of this "nonmethod" would appear to reinforce only the activities of the ordinary mind, not quietude.

Within the emptiness of mind created in the practice of quiet-sitting a direction or guidance is maintained in terms of the moral activism of one's nature, the persistence of *T'ien-li*. This is sufficient grounds according to its adherents for preventing the practice from falling under the possible accusation of either a Taoist quietism or a Buddhist emptiness. The question that does remain, however, is the relationship that exists between quiet-sitting and the theory of mind of the Ch'eng-Chu school. Apart from the obvious criticism levelled against the practice by the School of Mind, on the basis of failing to meet the requirements of the unity of knowledge and action, the question persists as to whether quietude for Kao is suggestive of the activation of the moral mind in innate knowledge. The answer is found in Kao's understanding and explication of the major process of self-cultivation and learning maintained by the Ch'eng-Chu school, *ko-wu*, the investigation of things.

Investigation, Rectification, and Maintenance of Orthodoxy

The investigation of things, *ko-wu*, for Kao, as for other members of the Ch'eng-Chu school during the Ming,[54] shows marked differences from the general dictum promulgated by Chu Hsi, investigating the principles of things exhaustively. Such a process of investigation for Chu Hsi was broad based in content and involved both intellectual and ethical aims. For Kao, as for both Hu Chü-jen (1434-1484) and Wu Yü-pi (1391-1469) during the early Ming, there is a reinterpretation of the meaning and content of *ko-wu*. Sensing that the original intention of the investigative process may have lent itself to a search too broad in scope and thus extraneous to the concerns of understanding the true nature,[55] there is a general limit placed upon what legitimately ought to be investigated.

The process of investigation became in many ways synonymous with a form of introspection to a large degree contemplative in form. An inward-directed investigation appears to dominate either an external exhaustive investigation or even a balance between external and internal. To suggest that *ko-wu* is to be interpreted within the context of an introspective model necessitates a clarification of the process of introspection. Introspection may be suggestive of Wang Yang-ming's interpretation of *ko-wu* as rectification,[56] yet possible differences between introspection and rectification need to be explored if an independent Ch'eng-Chu position is to be maintained.

In late Ming figures such as Kao, a reaction against Wang Yang-ming's reformulation of the investigative process as rectification is found. While Kao attempts to criticize Wang Yang-ming and maintain his own ties with the Ch'eng-Chu tradition, at the same time, according to Huang Tsung-hsi (1610-1695), he reveals a position of interpretation very similar if not virtually identical to Wang Yang-ming.[57] Huang's comments are significant for they raise the same problem with *ko-wu*, as has been suggested with quietude, that is, the degree to which Kao is deeply influenced by the Wang Yang-ming teaching of innate knowledge.

> Kao's teaching is based on that of Ch'eng [I] and Chu [Hsi], thus the investigation of things is considered essential, and yet the investigation of things meant for Ch'eng and Chu that mind is the dominant force of each person while principle is scattered in all things. The preserving of mind and the exhausting of principle must both move forward together. Kao has said: "As soon as one gains the knowledge to 'search within the person,'[58] this truly is the investigation of things."[59] In a sense this is close to what Yang Chung-li[60] [1053-1135] has said: "If I reflect upon myself in sincerity then there is nothing in the world that is not me."[61] This is of course different from the premises of Ch'eng and Chu. Kao has also said that when the human mind is made manifest it is the Principle of Heaven.[62] Only in reaching the point of having no delusion can one reach principle.[63] This increasingly supports [Wang] Yang-ming's discussion of the extension of innate knowledge. Yet it is said by those who discuss innate knowledge that the extension of knowledge does not reside in the investigation of things. Thus [they regard] the function of the mind and heart to be mostly an expression of emotions and not as the natural [manifestation] of Heaven's Principle. This is indeed far from the highest good.
>
> My own category of the investigation of things is the investigation of the highest good. We consider the good to be fundamental, not knowledge. The "good" has no form or shape, and refers not to any particular good, which, when followed upon and when known to the utmost, becomes the highest good. When the extension of the innate knowledge is rectified this is the point at which one rests in the highest good. How is it possible to say that they are mutually apart?
>
> In summary, the extension of knowledge and the investigation of things cannot be spoken of in terms of that which precedes and that which follows. The investigation of things clearly explains the word "to extend." The investigation of things occurs within the process of extension. There is nothing which can be extended and not also investigated. If Kao speaks of an extension of knowledge that is not an investigation of things, then what thing is it that is being extended? If he means that fulfilling principle externally in affairs and things is investigation of things, then it is possible to speak of Yang-ming's extension of knowledge as not residing in the investigation of things. And yet if it is as Kao says, "When the human mind is manifest, it is this Principle of Heaven,"[64] then Yang-ming's extension of knowledge is clearly also the investigation of things. Kao's view of things requires little discussion. He wanted to differentiate himself from Yang-ming, but he only created obstacles for himself.[65]

Huang Tsung-hsi's analysis focuses upon several aspects of Kao's thought. First is Kao's transformation of the investigative process from an external to internal orientation. That there has been a change in the meaning of the investigation of things is predicated for Huang upon the view of *ko-wu* in Ch'eng-Chu orthodoxy as presupposing the bifurcation of mind and principle. Principle is understood to reside in both things and one's nature but not in mind. Mind,

the cognitive and volitional center of the individual, is responsible for the exhaustive search for principle. Importance is placed upon "preserving the mind," that
is, retaining its clarity particularly through reverent seriousness in order to
succeed in the exhaustive search for principle.

For Huang the focal point of the exhaustive search as it was understood in
the Ch'eng-Chu tradition was changed by Kao away from knowledge of external things in the direction of an inward search. The implications of such a
change seem to suggest for Huang, quite apart from Chu Hsi's own combination of intellectual and moral knowledge, the transformation from an intellectual knowledge of rational principle in things, to concern for knowledge of the
moral nature in a fashion suggestive of Wang Yang-ming.

From Huang's point of view, Kao's understanding of the relation between
mind and principle also represents a reinterpretation of the Ch'eng-Chu tradition. Huang quotes Kao as stating that mind contains principle, a statement
Kao reiterates on several occasions in his writings.[66] Regardless of the similarity of Kao's statement to Hu Chü-jen or Wu Yü-pi, thinkers who had incorporated the concept into Ch'eng-Chu orthodoxy, the concept is reminiscent of the
fundamental School of Mind position. For members of the Ch'eng-Chu school to
suggest that mind contains principle or further to establish the virtual identity
between mind and principle appears for Huang as a major departure from the
Ch'eng-Chu position of the separation of mind and principle.

Kao indicates that the point at which false thoughts disappear is concomi-
tant with the emergence of principle. This is predicated upon an interrelationship
of mind and principle. To remove the limitations, what in the *Shih-hsüeh che,
Illustrations of Learning,*[67] Kao calls the realm of thought, *nien,* is to permit mind
as principle to emerge. Analyzed in this manner there seems little difference
between Kao's position and Yang-ming's interpretation of *ko-wu* as rectification.

Huang finds Kao's understanding of the relationship between *ko-wu* and
chih-chih, extension of knowledge, untenable. For Huang the maintenance of a
difference between *ko-wu* and *chih-chih* is plausible only as long as *ko-wu* is
characterized as an external exhaustive search for principle. Redirecting the
focus of the investigation and, in turn, accepting the existence of principle in
mind suggests not separate stages but rather a process of rectification in which
investigation and extension proceed together. As far as Huang is concerned the
difference between Kao and Wang Yang-ming on the issue of *ko-wu* is nothing
more than a semantic one, a difference Huang would maintain that Kao falsely
views as substantive.

Huang Tsung-hsi's observations are perceptive as to the degree to which
the focus of Ming Ch'eng-Chu orthodoxy changed from the masters of the
Sung. Given the type of change that had taken place in such major elements of
the Ch'eng-Chu ideology, what for these men maintains their own sense of
orthodoxy? William Theodore De Bary has provided a number of senses to the

term *orthodoxy* and has suggested the continuation of an orthodoxy though often with a changing content.[68] Here the issue is simply the problem of *ko-wu* and the way in which Kao could employ the phrase suggesting its import for the cultivation process while at the same time maintaining a polemical and substantive position against Wang Yang-ming and the later developments of the Wang Yang-ming school. Although Huang Tsung-hsi saw little difference between Kao and Wang Yang-ming in terms of Kao's interpretation of *ko-wu*, Kao's own polemic against Wang Yang-ming would indicate that from Kao's perspective a difference was maintained. The basis of the difference as Kao understood it between himself and Wang Yang-ming is seminal to seeing the way in which Kao could regard himself as continuing Ch'eng-Chu tradition and his practice of quiet-sitting as the maintenance of orthodoxy.

In the *San-shih chi*, Kao discusses his understanding of the importance of *ko-wu*.[69] The passage involves a difference in interpretation with Li Ts'ai (ca. 1520-ca. 1606). Li Ts'ai is also mentioned by Kao in his autobiography, although no details are given of Li's teaching other than suggesting that Kao found his own point of view in line with Li.[70] When Li is mentioned in the *San-shih chi*, however, Kao disagrees with him. The nature of the disagreement is important for understanding Kao's position.

Li Ts'ai, a moderate follower of Wang Yang-ming, may be seen as trying to stem the influence of the T'ai-chou school.[71] His teaching, revolving around the interpretation of the cultivation schema of the *Great Learning*, emphasized what is termed *chih-hsiu*, the cultivation of resting, that is, resting in the highest good, *chih-shan*. It is within the context of the implications of this term that a subtle though significant difference can be seen between Kao and Li. The root of the difference may in turn be what separated Kao both from Li and from Wang Yang-ming in general. Kao first quotes part of Li Ts'ai's letter and then comments upon it.

> Chien-lo's letter had said . . . "The investigation, attainment [i.e., extension] and rectification are nothing more than the care and attention that is given to internal weaknesses and deficiencies and the creation of a constant 'resting.' When there is a constant 'resting,' then one is continuously cultivated, the mind continuously rectified, the intentions uninterruptedly sincere, knowledge in a state of unremitting attainment [i.e., extension], and things of their own accord investigated."
> . . . Through distinguishing between what lies within oneself and within others, investigating in great detail the polarity between righteousness and profit and right and wrong, and by penetrating above, discerning below, exhausting every haunt, attacking every den, the mind will be illuminated and [all things] thoroughly understood without so much as a speck of ambiguity or doubt in any hidden place that might create deception. Only then can one actually do good without any reluctance that might act as a restraint. And only then can one avoid evil actions without even the slightest desire to do such actions being a temptation. After following this

the intention becomes sincere, the mind rectified and the individual cultivated. This is how goodness becomes pure and perfect, and resting becomes genuine and firm. If this is not so, then it is not that there is no longing to stop the cultivation of desires, but that the natural endowment of material force and the worldly desires shackle and consign one to the ten-thousand beginnings. I am afraid that the individual will be unable to employ his own strength. Moreover, that the individual's cultivation is fundamental has been illustrated by the admonitions of the Sages of antiquity. Who is there who doesn't know this! [People have fallen short] because knowledge changes through the enticement of things and they are unable to examine themselves thoroughly. It is not that desires are able to bind people, but simply that knowledge is not capable of being attained. ... As to the sequence of the process, although it cannot be said that today [knowledge] is extended and the next day [the will] made sincere, yet the ensuing priorities have a significance and it is not correct to treat them in an undifferentiated manner. This does not exceed what the former Sages said long ago. Chien-lo considers himself to be in the direct line of transmission from Confucius and Tseng-[tzu], but I am afraid that he is definitely not.[72]

Kao's discussion of Li Ts'ai's letter illustrates his own mental reservations concerning Li's reliance upon *chih*, resting. For Kao the fundamental task is an arduous investigation so thorough that there is no possibility as to a lingering doubt of the difference between right and wrong. Only following a thorough investigation, *ko-wu*, and extension of knowledge, *chih-chih*, can one be assured of doing good and avoiding evil. Through such a process the intention has become sincere, *ch'eng-i*. Goodness or resting in goodness, *chih-shan*, emerges within the context of the progression of the stages of learning. Kao insists that the sense of priorities, that is, the sequence of stages, must be maintained. Without attention to the sequence and development of stages of learning, the emergence of *hsing* may falter.

From Kao's point of view, Li has diminished the importance of the steps of cultivation and learning. In reaching the point of resting, *chih*, the sequence and progression of stages of learning are of secondary concern. Instead Li suggests that the true nature will come forth of its own and from the point of rest moral activity will emerge. The method suggests spontaneity and a lack of concern as to the distractions and desires that might obfuscate the natural clarity of the true nature. For Kao this form of learning is insufficient to meet the needs of transforming the *ch'i*, material nature. There is no directing or guiding principle from Kao's perspective. Kao does not share Li's confidence that the true nature without guidance will emerge of its own and thus is not willing to relinquish the importance of the learning effort and discipline.

These differences with Li Ts'ai are suggestive of the relationship between Kao and Wang Yang-ming in their respective interpretations of the investigation of things. For Kao, there is the necessity of establishing the proper foundation and correct sequence of learning. The foundation must begin with the clarity of mind, a clarity distinguished by its one pointedness in reverent seriousness. The sequence in turn is initiated through the investigative process.

Kao can subscribe to the idea that principle is contained in mind and interpret *ko-wu* as contemplative introspection without accepting the spontaneous emergence of the true nature. While Kao has areas of interpretation that appear to move him within approximation of the School of Mind position, there is also the retention of a difference. Kao never relinquishes the element of discipline and control, essential elements for Kao in the unfolding sequence of learning and cultivation. For Kao, *ko-wu* establishes one in line with *Tien-li*, while the converse, that is, cultivating the spontaneous extension of the *liang-chih*, sets no absolute standards. Kao sees such an approach as frought with danger; there is no control or guiding principle directing one away from viewing any attitude or opinion as a manifestation of the *hsing*, an approach Kao chastises in the T'ai-chou school. A prevalent attitude amongst members of the T'ai-chou school, *tang-hsia*, the immediate response of the nature or "living in the immediate," was anathema to Kao. Seemingly lacking all standards of discipline, *tang-hsia* suggested the emergence of the good in spontaneous activity and attitudes. While an extreme development from Wang Yang-ming's innate moral activism found in the extension of *liang-chih*, the problem from Kao's perspective is a consistent one for the School of Mind.

The School of Mind recognizes the dynamic moral activity of the true nature, but for Kao they have failed to provide the basis for its emergence. There is no guidance, no discipline, no control provided. In short, the Wang Yang-ming school lacks the fundamental effort, *kung-fu*, moral guidance, to bring to fruition the emergence of the true nature. Through the retention of such moral effort Kao retains the distinction between himself and the Wang Yang-ming School. The degree to which the content of quietude is suggestive of the School of Mind interpretation of the activation of the moral mind can now be seen. Quietude for Kao, while negating the limitation of the ordinary mind, affirms the moral guidance of the *Tao-hsin*. The "method" of quiet-sitting maintains a discipline and moral guidance sufficient to suggest the maintenance of the Ch'eng-Chu tradition.

Quiet-Sitting and the Experience of Enlightenment

There are times according to Kao when a certain insight is gained while practicing quiet-sitting. Such insight may simply be a resolution to a difficulty encountered in the learning process, a quiet reflection followed by some measure of contentment.[73] On the other hand, there is also an experience far more penetrating and thoroughgoing, an experience in a fashion characterized as sudden, shattering, and all encompassing. Such experiences were referred to as *wu*, enlightenment, or *t'i-jen*, self-realization, and suggest for Kao, a point of insight at which a fundamental unity or oneness, was felt between self and the universe.[74]

Rather than an analysis of the enlightenment experience of Kao, an experience in many ways suggestive of a religious experience,[75] the question I would like to turn to here involves the relationship between the practice of quiet-sitting and the enlightenment experience. We need to be clear as to whether for Kao the experience of enlightenment is dependent upon quiet-sitting, that is, whether quiet-sitting is seen to be the foundation for the production of such experiences, and in turn whether quiet-sitting ought to culminate in such experiences.

The essential function of quiet-sitting for Kao was to assist in the understanding of the original substance of the true nature. The manner, however, in which the original substance was experienced seems to have some variation in Kao's writings. Such variation is an important consideration in Kao's understanding of the relationship between quiet-sitting and the experiences of enlightenment. It is apparent from several contexts that Kao in general disapproved of those who discussed their enlightenment experiences. He says in his autobiography that he had normally been critical of those who talked of their experience with great display.[76] He was critical, that is, until he had a similar experience himself. His criticism may not, however, have simply his own lack of experience, but rather that he recognized legitimate differences in the type of experiences people discussed. This point is adumbrated in the *San-shih chi*: "I knew that those scholars were wrong who upon catching a glimpse of a bit of brilliance considered that they had had an enlightenment."[77] Kao testifies to the same problem when in his autobiography he describes his own encounter with such moments of brilliance, fleeting though they might be. In describing a momentary insight that occurred in 1592, he states that he experienced the immediacy of *ch'eng*, sincerity or authenticity. For a moment, he says, he was aware that the immediate response, *tang-hsia*, of the nature was characterized by *ch'eng*.[78] "In that moment I felt rapturous, as if all fetters were cast off."[79] The experience is but a brief glimpse and appears to be neither permanent nor transforming in its effects.

Other such momentary experiences are recorded as having taken place on Kao's journey to Chieh-yang in the following year. In describing the rigorousness of his practice of quiet-sitting during a period in which most of his effort seems directed toward such practice, he suggests that such momentary insights occurred on occasion. "When the substance of the mind was clear and peaceful there was a sense of filling all Heaven and Earth, but it did not last."[80] Eventually on this same journey Kao experienced what he described as *wu*, enlightenment. It is an experience more thoroughgoing and more all-encompassing; it is an experience that had a lasting effect upon his life.[81] A substantial degree of aesthetic content to Kao's experience has been noted.[82] It might also be suggested that in addition to an aesthetic sensitivity, religious and ethical components are also present.[83]

A qualitative difference exists for Kao between what he has characterized as momentary insights and what stands as a substantive enlightenment experience. Such a distinction partially helps to explain Kao's criticism of those who would openly discuss such experiences. The suspicion would not be unwarranted from Kao's perspective that those so ready to discuss their experiences had only just superficially observed the original substance. Perhaps even more important, they lacked the proper method to integrate an enlightenment experience into the process of learning. In terms of the relationship that exists between the range of insight experience and self-cultivation, quiet-sitting plays a major role. Such experiences of insight seem to be in direct relation to the effort if not severity of the practice of quiet-sitting. If this is the case, then the enlightenment experience appears predicated upon the practice of quiet-sitting.

An important qualification must be added to the context of such experiences, however. The practice of quiet-sitting, as we have seen, is not to any substantial degree disassociated from other modes of learning. In various experiences of insight recorded in the autobiography the immediate context of the insight experience is a phrase read or remembered from a literary source, in one case the *Book of Changes*,[84] in another case the Ch'eng brothers.[85] This does not minimize the importance of the role of quiet-sitting for Kao in the insight experiences, but it does suggest a broader base of learning and as such puts the practice of quiet-sitting in a balance with other forms of learning. Thus, quiet-sitting does not have the exclusive and solitary relation to such experiences as might be suggested by the juxtaposition of the two. The dictum of one-half day of quiet-sitting and one-half day of study illustrates the balance of components in the learning process in relation to the insight experience.

A lingering question is the degree to which quiet-sitting as contemplative praxis was the major psychophysical catalyst in the production of the enlightenment experience. For Kao, the balance between quiet-sitting and other modes of learning appears to be maintained, although in periods of stress and dissatisfaction, there are signs of increased effort in quiet-sitting often more obvious than parallel increased effort in other modes of learning. It might be accurate to say that rather than quiet-sitting producing insight experiences, such experiences were the result of a range of activities of which quiet-sitting played a major role. If quiet-sitting or the range of activities of which quiet-sitting is a part produce insight experiences, then lacking such experiences the self-cultivation process would appear incomplete. The question is the degree to which the insight and enlightenment experiences were felt to be a necessary or perhaps anticipated part of the practice of quiet-sitting.

From Kao's various writings on quiet-sitting, the impression is created that the experience of enlightenment is not something toward which practice should be directed. Such experiences are not established as a conscious goal for self-cultivation. This does not necessarily eliminate the anticipatory element in the practice if there exists any parallel between Kao's discussion of enlightenment and method in quiet-sitting. His discussion of method suggests that there is to be no intentional method or goal established. The proscription of intentions could apply equally well to the discussion of enlightenment. The same problem is encountered. Establish enlightenment as something that ought to be sought after and the intention to seek after it has been created. This may help to explain why there is such reticence on the part of Kao to discuss enlightenment as a feature of self-cultivation even after he has accepted the occurrence of the experience as something "ordinary," *p'ing-ch'ang.*[86]

In describing enlightenment as something ordinary, however, the possibility is raised that the experience was something that not only could occur within the learning process, but perhaps in addition is something that ought to occur. While there could be no expectation of the experience within the "method" of quiet-sitting, at the same time its occurrence might be looked upon as something that rightfully ought to take place. It is difficult to be absolutely clear as to Kao's meaning in this respect. In concluding the *Ching-tso shuo-hou*, for example, Kao indicates that the process of acquiring quietude and an understanding of the true nature is a long and gradual one.[87] The meaning is perhaps that a sudden breakthrough need not be anticipated. In the *Shih-hsüeh che*, however, Kao indicates that after lengthy practice a sudden breakthrough should occur and that understanding will be readily at hand in such an experience.[88] Is this expectation for an enlightenment experience within the context of quiet-sitting? It is difficult to say. There certainly appears to be no regimentation of insight experiences into the context of self-cultivation. Such experiences do not seem to have been treated as a formal requirement or verification of successful practice. They could be accepted as an ordinary occurrence within self-cultivation, and it is perhaps not out of line to suggest that to a limited extent such experiences might have been an expectation within the paradigm of praxis.

To suggest that the experience of enlightenment is ordinary, *p'ing-ch'ang*, certainly indicates that it is viewed as a part of the cultivation or learning process. Yet even if there is expectation that such experiences ought to occur, the experience of enlightenment does not stand as the end point of the learning process. The experience counts for little if the learning process is not continued following any such experience. "With my own inferior endowment what use could an expansive insight be in the absence of such exertion?"[89]

Presumably the experience of enlightenment is an indication of the emergence of the true nature. Whether such emergence is permanent remains to be seen. It is certain at least that it is lasting enough for Kao to distinguish it from what he calls momentary insights and to say that it changed the orientation of his life. What is the nature of the learning that follows such an experience?

Perhaps the best answer is found in the statement Kao makes after describing his own enlightenment experience. "I ordinarily despised scholars who discussed enlightenment with grand display, but now I could see that it was something quite natural and realized that from now on it was suitable to apply my own efforts [*kung-fu*] to this end."[90] Enlightenment for Kao rather than a goal is only a prelude to the correct application of one's moral efforts.

The "Ordinariness" of Quietude and Activity

The enlightenment experience is not a goal, nor is it something that frees Kao from the world of involvement, activities, and responsibilities. Rather, it appears to permit Kao to carry forth his learning within the setting of involvements and responsibilities. When Kao states that his enlightenment experience puts him in the proper position to work on his moral effort, he is suggesting a close relationship between self-cultivation, particulary quiet-sitting, and such involvement in the world.

The relationship between quiet-sitting and activity, that is, the rapprochement of self-cultivation and involvement in the world, is discussed by Kao in the *Ching-tso shuo*.

> When the transition from quietude to activity is an ordinary one, the activity that emerges is pure. The time of quietude and activity are one, just as the time of activity and quietude are one. The reason that they are one is that they are both ordinary [*p'ing-ch'ang*]. Therefore it can be said that there is neither activity nor quietude. The essence of neither activity nor quietude can only be observed, however, by the student engaged in quiet-sitting. If quietude produces results, activity will certainly be productive; and [conversely] if activity is fruitful, quietude will have results. This is none other than goodness and none other than sincerity. It is the way of returning to one's nature.[91]

In the same sense in which Kao's experience of enlightenment is said to cement the ground for his *kung-fu*, moral effort, quietude is said to be the basis for carrying out activity. The focus of Kao's comments is upon the area of transition between quietude and activity. The movement from quietude to activity and activity to quietude is to be accomplished almost effortlessly if the relation between the two is properly understood.

Kao suggests that a fundamental unity exists between quietude and activity, a unity defined in terms of their common foundation in *p'ing-ch'ang*. Quietude and activity are both said to be ordinary; that is, they are ordinary or natural modes for the expression of the true nature. Once it is recognized that they are both "ordinary" occurrences then the distinctiveness of each is obviated, stressing instead the unity of the two in the nature of the individual. The burden of proof is placed by Kao upon the person engaged in quiet-sitting to realize the "ordinariness" and, thus, the unity of quietude and activity. With the recognition of their inherent unity, suggesting even the inappropriateness of labeling *p'ing-ch'ang* either quietude or activity, the difficulty of moving from one to the other is mitigated.

It is apparent from Kao's discussion of the relation between quietude and activity that the relation is not limited to quiet-sitting serving the purposes of involvement through an introspective examination and establishment of direction, goal, and commitment. Instead, the relationship is established in the unity of quietude and activity in the ordinariness of the nature. There is no bifurcation between them and, thus, for Kao no tension is suggested in the relationship of one to the other.

Learning for Kao does not confine itself to quietude, but instead is equally a part of the world of activities and responsibilities. The inner experience is incomplete without the expression of moral effort in daily life. From Kao's perspective the argument of the School of Mind against quiet-sitting fails to take into account the relation between quietude and activity. The practice of quiet-sitting for Kao is incomplete, or more specifically, it is not "ordinary," without an integration of knowledge and action. Such an integration of knowledge and action, firm in its maintenance of *ko-wu*, is different in method from Wang Yang-ming's innate knowledge. Such differences, however, do not lessen Kao's ability to establish a relationship between quietude and activity and thus integrate quiet-sitting and moral effort. If quiet-sitting were only involved with questions of "being" rather than questions of moral action, then it might be expected that Kao, as Yen Yüan, would have been dissatisfied with the potential of quiet-sitting for the realization of the learning process. Kao, however, saw more in the practice than the question of "being." Quiet-sitting probed both the roots, *pen-t'i*, of the nature and in addition issued forth in moral action, *kung-fu*. Quiet-sitting remains for Kao a process central to the task of unfolding the steps leading to the goal of sagehood. The stage for the realization of sagehood is the "ordinariness" of daily life.

CHAPTER **VIII**

The Problem of Suffering:
Christian and Confucian Dimensions

In a poem recorded in the *Shih-Ching* an unknown poet expresses his lamentations over his suffering in the world:

> O vast and distant Heaven,
> Who art called our parent,
> That without crime or offense
> I should suffer from disorder this great!
> The terrors of great Heaven are excessive,
> But indeed I have committed no crime.
> [The terrors of] great Heaven are very excessive,
> But indeed I have committed no offense.[1]

We feel directly the pain and suffering of the poet, the heartfelt feeling of an individual caught in the chaos and disorder of his age. His poem pleads for meaning in the world . . . a profound and deep religious meaning. The source of such meaning was expressed in the classical Chinese tradition in terms of *T'ien*, the absolute moral force of the universe for the later tradition and a potentially theistic supreme deity for the early tradition. It is Heaven that brings order and peace to the world and human society. It is Heaven that establishes the ruler through the Mandate of Heaven, *T'ien-ming*. The ruler is even called *T'ien-tzu*, the Son of Heaven. Yet the poet finds no such order or harmony in the world, but only chaos, disorder, and suffering. It seems random and capricious. It defies understanding, for the poet has committed no crime. Not unlike Job who, even with his friends' insistence upon his unrighteousness, maintained his own innocence,² the *Shih-Ching* poet sees himself as an innocent victim. He has committed neither crime nor offense and yet he suffers grievously. Why? Another poem in the *Shih-Ching* expresses a similar sentiment.

> Great and wide Heaven
> How is it you have contracted your kindness,
> Sending down death and famine,
> Destroying all through the kingdom?
>
> Compassionate Heaven, arrayed in terrors,
> How is it you exercise no forethought, no care?
> Let alone the criminals:
> They have suffered for their offense:
> But those who have no crime
> Are indiscriminately involved in ruin.³

The poem suggests that Heaven has been known for its kindness and its goodness. It has been responsible for the order the world possesses. It has shown its care and concern for the people. Now, however, Heaven responds with terror and all suffer. The righteous and the unrighteous fall together in ruin. And the reason for this? Surely Heaven is responding to the rulership of the kingdom. The Mandate of Heaven is in jeopardy as Heaven shows its wrath for the unrighteous ways of the ruler. But must this wrath and the suffering it brings involve the population at large, must it appear to be indiscriminate in those it touches? As with the first poem cited, this poem cries out as well for the seemingly indiscriminate and random nature of suffering. Those who have committed no crime are allowed to suffer and be destroyed. How is it that Heaven can allow this? What is it that the righteous have done that they too suffer. The words of Jeremiah seem not out of context. "Righteous art thou, O Lord, when I plead with thee: yet let me talk with thee of thy judgments: wherefore doth the way of the wicked prosper? Wherefore are all they happy that deal very treacherously?"⁴

These early poems provide an insight into the problem of suffering as it presented itself in the classical Chinese tradition. The poems articulate the major religious focus of the early worldview—the role of Heaven—and the disparity between the Way of Heaven and the suffering of humanity. This classical tradition is inherited, preserved, and developed by the Confucian tradition, and the role of Heaven remains a central and dominant concern to the evolving Confucian religious worldview. What of the question of suffering for the Confucians? What role does it play in the tradition and what meaning is given to suffering in major formulations of Confucian thought? The *Shih-Ching* poets seem to suggest suffering as the retribution of Heaven, and yet in the mystery of theodicy they wail their lament for those who suffer without offense. Is it ultimately the mere randomness and capriciousness of Heaven's ways? Heaven is known, however, for its ways of righteousness. Is suffering then ultimately an enigma, a central problem of existence seen as through a glass darkly, only partially adumbrated in a world of unrealized meanings? This is the stark reality of theodicy, the fact of the existence of suffering that Confucians must respond to just as religious persons everywhere.

Religion, Meaning, and Suffering

Suffering itself is a complex term. It has physical, psychological, and spiritual components. Although it may have cultural variants, it appears also to have a common and universal core. In a recent essay on suffering Jack Bemporad has offered the following definition:

> Suffering may be defined as the experience of organisms in situations that involve physical and mental pain, usually attended by a sense of loss, frustration and vulnerability to adverse effects. As a fact of sentient life, pain is a phenomenon concomitant to existence itself and yet, on the human level at least, it is one that is inextricably linked with the sense of one's individuality. As such, pain can only be defined subjectively, and because of its implications for the survival of the individual, the experience of pain provokes questions about the meaning of life itself.[5]

This can serve as a minimal definition to remind us of the association of suffering to pain and in turn the reaction of the individual to suffering in terms of raising basic questions about the meaning of life. As Bemporad goes on to say, much of the development of science and technology in the history of culture is associated with the attempt to eliminate or at least minimize the impact of suffering upon the individual and society. Science and technology are a panacea and yet suffering remains. Granted, that material culture cannot address all issues of suffering, it is religion that then becomes a focal point. This is a role that religion has traditionally played. Suffering remains a universal condition, and religion addresses the occurrence and meaning of suffering in a central way.

Religion itself is involved with meaning and purpose in the course of events and the nature of the universe. A universe that would confirm mere randomness and chance as its organizing principles may even be by definition nonreligious. As I have argued elsewhere, meaning and purpose are central to the definition of religion itself.[6] There must be a view of order and meaning— there is purpose and moral order in the world. And perhaps most significantly, all things must be for the best. What then is the meaning and purpose attributed to suffering? If all things are ultimately for the best, then do we assume that suffering is also for the best? In one fashion or another each religious tradition seems bound to address itself to this question and to try to provide some sense of meaning to the occurrence of suffering. Can we simply dismiss the connection and say that suffering lies outside of the sphere of meaning established by the religion itself? It seems awkward at best to suggest that the universe is ordered and meaningful except for that part of it which is not! And as dualistic theodicies will suggest, the status of evil, which is the source of suffering, is still established as part of the "meaning" of the world.

As religion establishes and maintains meaning and purpose in the universe, the occurrence of suffering must also be given meaning. The iniquities, the seeming capriciousness of events and the occurrence of suffering and tragedy, all must be given some semblance of meaning, some purpose. There is an attempt to put them in a larger context of religious meaning, to say that in the end all will be right, for it must be right. There may be little that can be said in the way of explanation, yet each and every event must by definition be part of the meaning and purpose of the world. Simply accepting the ineffable quality of the occurrence of suffering may in the end be all that can be hoped for. For some, such as Freud, this is precisely the problem with religion. As Freud says in this respect:

> The assertions made by religion that it could give protection and happiness to men, if they would only fulfill certain ethical obligations, were unworthy of belief. It seems not to be true that there is a power in the universe, which watches over the well-being of every individual with parental care and brings all his concerns to a happy ending. On the contrary, the destinies of man are incompatible with a universal principle of benevolence or with . . . a universal principle of justice. Earthquakes, floods, and fires do not differentiate between the good and devout men, and the sinner and unbeliever.[7]

Freud, in a sense, provides an answer to the poets of the *Shih-Ching* lamenting their fate of suffering. The answer, hardly a religious one, suggests that there is no reason behind the suffering of the just or even the unjust. There is just suffering, and it is purely random as to who suffers. There is no purpose behind it: it is, as one might say, just fate. As we have seen, however, the religious response remains to give comfort and care in the case of suffering and to provide meaning even if it is said ultimately to be lost in the mystery of God's will. Even there it remains a central part of the "meaning" of the world itself.

A Typology of Suffering—Judeo-Christian Models

Understanding of suffering can fall into several different categories. Bemporad's study of suffering highlights several forms of suffering found in

Judeo-Christian heritage.[8] In turn the comparative ethicist David Little has tried to create some working categories that might be applied across the lines of different religious traditions.[9] The categories I want to discuss are the product of both of these sources.

The first explanation of suffering is what might be called *retributive*. In speaking of retributive suffering, Little says, "Pain, injury, coercion and death may legitimately be considered as retribution or punishment for violations that themselves involve inflicting pain, injury, coercion or death."[10] This is obvious in the laws of society as protection against those who would abuse others. In the sphere of religion, it suggests punishment sent down upon those who are unrighteous or have committed transgressions. And in this sphere too there may be pain, injury, coercion and death as retribution. We see this expressed, for example, in Psalm 37:

> For the arms of the wicked shall be broken: but the Lord upholdeth the righteous . . .
> But the wicked shall perish and the enemies of the Lord shall be as fat of lambs: they shall consume; into smoke shall they consume away.[11]

A second explanation of suffering is *pedagogical*. It involves the suffering that occurs under the direction of instruction or discipline. In education, the process of learning involves toil and effort; it is a choice of a path taken that if it is to be pursued, must be pursued at the expense of other activities. Often this choice involves the denial of other activities and a struggle within learning itself. How much more is this true of the religious life. One takes upon oneself discipline and hardship. One dares in a sense to be uncomfortable and to suffer for a new-found goal. This experience of discomfort and suffering may in itself bring us to a new-found realization. We learn, as it were, from our hardships. Paul expresses this view of suffering in Romans: "And not only so, but we glory in tribulation also: knowing that tribulation worketh patience; and patience, experience; and experience, hope."[12] To suffer may also be offered to us as a form of discipline, a unique opportunity to establish one's faith and religious understanding. James tells us, for example, "My brethren, count it all joy when ye fall into diverse temptations; knowing this, that the trying of your faith worketh patience. But let patience have her perfect work, that ye may be perfect and entire, wanting nothing."[13]

A third explanation of suffering is what we might call *sacrificial suffering*. This speaks to the suffering involved in the sacrifice one makes for the religious worldview. It can involve merely the discomfort of pursuing something new and different in terms of social pressure and prejudice. Or, in turn, it can be a far more serious level of persecution for one's beliefs and practices, a continuance of suffering perpetuated through persecution. Ultimately, it may necessitate a recognition that one must even give up one's life to uphold a belief. The theme of sacrificial suffering plays a prominent role in the New Testament, particularly with the level of persecution that was a historical reality for the early Christian community. Matthew speaks, for example, of the suffering expected if one holds to the Christian beliefs. "Behold, I send you forth as sheep in the midst of wolves: be ye therefore wise as serpents and harmless as doves."[14] The ultimate form of sacrificial suffering is the giving up of one's life itself. Jesus' own death is of course an example as are the martyred deaths of members of the early Christian community, sharing themselves in the death of Jesus. There is an element here that is not necessarily negative, particularly as suffering is seen in redemptive terms. Thus, to suffer has redemptive meaning and as such can take on the character even of joy.[15]

A fourth explanation of suffering we might call the *suffering servant*. This is what Little has referred to as *vicarious* or *substitutive suffering*. It involves the substitution of one for another in which one assumes "pain, disablement, even death, for the sake of healing the ills or saving the life of someone else."[16] The suffering servant in Isaiah[17] is the *locus classicus* for this ideal, and whether it be nation or individual, the issue remains the burden of suffering endured for another. The distinctive role of Jesus within the Christian community focuses itself around this ideal of substitutive suffering. Jesus is the suffering servant. His death is a death for all of us from a Christian point of view. Much of the uniqueness of the Christian teaching is argued from this suffering servant motif, with the knowledge that Jesus' death was a substitute for the world's death and that through this death we all overcome death and suffering ourselves.

This is not in any way an exhaustive list of explanations of suffering, nor is this an attempt to fully account for suffering. Suffering remains complex and enigmatic. These are simply some of the possible strategies used by religious traditions to attempt to provide some meaning to suffering's occurrence. It would appear, in fact, that ultimately suffering is not fully accounted for by any category of meaning and the problem of theodicy remains at the very center of religious meaning.

Retributive Suffering

There is an attitude that pervades the writings of the classical Confucians relevant to the question of retributive suffering. It is the attitude expressed toward history. Not unlike the Deuteronomic historian, there is a sense of judgment upon kings. There were those who were virtuous and righteous, and there were those who were tyrants and villains. The righteous were said to follow the dictates (*ming*) of Heaven. They possessed the Mandate of Heaven (*Tien-ming*) and were truly *Tien-tzu*, Son of Heaven. In turn, those who turned their backs upon Heaven's ways were regarded as traitors to Heaven and their people alike.

Praise is heaped upon Yao, Shun, and Yü as sage emperors as well as the founders of the Chou dynasty, Kings Wen and Wu and the Duke of Chou. In turn, scorn is unabated for Chieh and Chou, the last kings of the Hsia and Shang dynasties respectively.

The connection to the problem of suffering is the nature of the reigns of the righteous and unrighteous alike. The sage kings brought peace and harmony. Those who violated the dictates of Heaven brought only suffering. This is the background to the poems of the *Shih-Ching* with which this chapter began. Suffering is directly related to the violation of the dictates of Heaven. To the poets of the *Shih-Ching*, Heaven is sending down its wrath, the so-called terrors of Heaven, because its ways have been violated. The only question for the poets is one of distribution. Why is it that all suffer, rather than just those who have committed offenses? There is no question as to the source of the suffering itself. It is Heaven and it is the retribution of Heaven that the poets are witnessing. This is retributive suffering, even though the poets are not so much accepting of the retribution as questioning its appropriateness. But can we make the same claim about the Confucian response? Can we say that the Confucians accept a retributive theory of suffering, seeing the terror and wrath of Heaven because of a violation of the Way of Heaven?

The status and role of Heaven is itself a complex problem in classical Confucian tradition, but it is quite apparent that there is little reference to a wrathful intent of Heaven in early Confucian texts. This does not deny Heaven a role in the affairs of the world, but that role is spoken to primarily in terms of good acts and deeds, not their counterpart. For example, the following passage from Mencius raises the question of the role of Heaven in the selection of the sage Kings.

> Wan Chang said, "Is it true that Yao gave the Empire to Shun?" "No," said Mencius. "The Emperor cannot give the Empire to another." "In that case who gave the Empire to Shun?" "Heaven gave it to him." "You say Heaven gave it to him. Does this mean that Heaven gave him detailed and minute instructions?" "No. Heaven does not speak but reveals itself through its acts and deeds."[18]

Heaven has selected Shun to rule. Shun is given to the people and the people accept him. This is taken as a demonstration of the actions of Heaven. Can we assume then that Heaven also gives to its people a tyrant and thus brings upon the people their suffering? This is not clear, for it appears that the mandate is given only to someone of virtue, someone who will carry out the Way of Heaven. The problem arises then not with Heaven giving the people a tyrant, for there would be no purpose to this, but rather that a particular ruler who has been given the mandate is unable to maintain it. Thus the problem is not Heaven's, but the ruler's. What then of the status of suffering itself? Perhaps the reason that there is no mention of Heaven being responsible for the suffering of the people is because Heaven is not responsible. This raises the intriguing question of the lack of omnipotence on the part of Heaven. It is the failed ruler who is ultimately at fault, for it is the failed rulership that brings the conditions of ruin upon the people, and Heaven can do little to remedy the situation other than take away the mandate. Mencius is frequent in his focus upon this dimension of suffering.[19]

What then of retributive suffering? Is Heaven sending down its wrath upon the people causing them to suffer? The Confucians do not make this argument, and in this respect they differ substantially from the earlier view that saw the potential retributive side of Heaven's ways. The category of retributive suffering seems to play little role in the Confucian formulation of the problem of suffering.

Pedagogical Suffering

A number of passages in Confucian writings would generally come under the category of pedagogical suffering. The learning process involves effort and there are hardships to be endured, as well as struggle and toil. This is pedagogical suffering. Such suffering itself can be the occasion for learning, particularly when it appears that the suffering is a trial to be overcome. There is one particular passage I want to focus upon in this respect, an intriguing discussion of the suffering undergone by sages of antiquity before they each were elevated to their positions of leadership and sagacity.

> Mencius said, "Shun rose from the fields; Fu Yüeh was raised to office from amongst the builders; Chiao Ke from amidst the fish and salt; Kuan Chung from the hands of the prison officer; Sun Shu-ao from the sea and Po-li Hsi from the market. That is why Heaven, when it is about to place a great burden upon a man, always first tests his resolution, exhausts his frame and makes him suffer starvation and hardship, frustrates his efforts so as to shake him from his mental lassitude, toughen his nature and make good his deficiencies. As a rule, a man can mend his ways only after he has made mistakes. It is only when a man is frustrated in mind and in his deliberations that he is able to innovate. It is only when his intentions become visible on his countenance and audible in his tone of voice that others can understand him. As a rule, a state without law-abiding families and reliable Gentlemen on the one hand, and, on the other, without the threat of foreign invasion, will perish. Only then do we learn the lesson that we survive in adversity and perish in ease and comfort."[20]

The passage itself suggests that a number of prominent persons from antiquity came from humble circumstances, and they were tested by Heaven before assuming their positions. Heaven puts the person in conditions of adversity to test and discipline the individual to a point where they will have the capacity for leadership and thus assume their rightful position. A great burden is placed upon the individual by Heaven. He must endure adversity and learn from his sufferings. This is pedagogical suffering. The latter part of the passage emphasizes the importance of this encounter with adversity, stressing that it is critical to the training and education of leadership. We learn, as Mencius emphasizes, in conditions of frustration, adversity and suffering. Out of these conditions are born creativity and innovation and the capacity for leadership. To see the shortcomings of pleasure, comfort, and ease and to endure adversity becomes the mark of the sage or culture hero.

Tu Wei-ming, who has discussed this passage in the context of understanding the role of suffering and pain within self-cultivation,[21] suggests the importance given to the human capacity for bearing the burden placed upon it by Heaven. He says in this respect:

> It is noteworthy, however, that the Mencian idea of the Heavenly burden, presumably the counterpart of God's calling, is basically a manifestation of human self-consciousness, even though the transcendent reference is implied. To put it simply, those who have succeeded in overcoming extreme odds have done so not because of divine intervention but because of their strong moral fabric. They learned the art of self-transcendence through physical and mental discipline, for their heightened self-awareness enabled them to bear the Heavenly burden themselves as a categorical imperative.[22]

Tu is certainly correct in stressing the importance placed upon the human capacity to overcome the burdens placed upon it. It is through the contact with adversity that this capacity for overcoming adversity becomes manifest. What is less clear, however, is the role of Heaven in this process. The overcoming of hardships is through the development of a strong moral character rather than "divine intervention," but this still does not rule out the role of Heaven in the process of confronting the individual with adversity itself. In this sense the parallel with the New Testament examples is worthwhile to examine. In both Romans and James, the conditions of adversity have been presented to man by God,[23] but in both cases it is not divine intervention that overcomes the adversity. It is human effort. If it were merely divine intervention, then there would be little to the pedagogical value of suffering and adversity. On the contrary, the pedagogical value lies precisely in the context being set for an individual to have to face and overcome adversity. Mencius seems to take a similar position, and one might well ask whether more could not be said of the role of Heaven itself in the establishment of these conditions that the individual through his effort overcomes. Here, I think, Tu may be too ready to dismiss the role of Heaven as an acting and intending high god. Tu says:

On the surface, Mencius seems to suggest that the reason that Heaven had placed a great burden on each of them is that they had already been chosen to perform the divine tasks. This interpretation, however, is quite foreign to the Mencian intention. For one thing, the idea of a willful Heaven deliberately choosing its own messengers to do things according to preconceived design does not at all feature prominently in the Confucian tradition.[24]

While Tu's comments represent the Neo-Confucian interpretation of Heaven and the Neo-Confucian interpretation of Mencius, there may be more traditional religious attitudes within the Mencian text. The status of Heaven in the Mencian text is not entirely clear. Its later monistic overlay is not adequate to account for usages by Mencius. Certain usages by Mencius suggest an active, intending, and willing high god far more theistic in structure than compatible with the later Neo-Confucian interpretation.[25] If there is some flexibility in the way that Heaven can be seen for Mencius, then the category of pedagogical suffering has even closer parallels with the way in which this form of suffering is used in other traditions, most notably the Christian. Neither God nor Heaven is rescuing the individual; they are instead providing the setting for adversity such that the individual can learn by his mistakes and can, through the development of the strength of his character, overcome any and all adversity.

Sacrificial Suffering

Sacrificial suffering focuses primarily upon the persecution one may have to endure for upholding one's beliefs and practices. In the setting of the New Testament, this is a prominent theme. The persecution of the early church community seemed only to bear witness to the life and death of Jesus himself. As the New Testament readily expresses, one can virtually anticipate persecution and suffering in a world hostile to the teaching of the new church. The early Christians are told to endure this persecution and to find in it virtue rather than penitence. The ultimate form of persecution was death itself, something the early church was also well acquainted with. Is there anything in the Confucian tradition that might correspond to this particular form of suffering?

Surprisingly, these ideals are not as foreign to Confucian thought and practice as might first be thought. They might not appear in precisely the same way, but a climate of these ideas exists within the tradition. At the most basic level, the historical reality of the early Confucians is not irrelevant. We think often of Confucius and Mencius traveling from state to state, advising the rulers of their day. We know, of course, that neither man was remarkably successful in these teaching efforts, and yet we neglect to think of the impact of this failure upon the men themselves and the disciples they gathered around them. Confucianism was not a popular teaching; no one wanted the advice they had to offer. The teachers and disciples represented a minority point of view. Did they suffer persecution for this minority point of view? At the minimum, we must recognize that there was a focus upon strengthening their resolve in the face of a world unwilling or unable to hear them. This resolution to overcome adverse conditions becomes a prominent feature of the teaching. We can hear this at times in the words of Confucius. "When under siege in K'uang, the Master said, 'With King Wen dead, is not culture [*wen*] invested here in me? If Heaven intends culture to be destroyed, those who come after me will not be able to have any part of it. If Heaven does not intend this culture to be destroyed, then what can the men of K'uang do to me!' "[26]

We think most often of this passage as representing Confucius' attitude toward Heaven, but there is also a sense here of carrying on the teaching and of knowing that the world itself has little interest. That the world's attitude does not quell the effort; if anything it only makes it stronger. After all, Heaven itself is behind the promulgation of these teachings, or at least that is the hope and faith. Confucius seems to admit the difficulty of his task and the adversity he endures. Yet even to the degree that one suffers, the resolution is firm. Such suffering must be accepted, dangers must be anticipated and not be a reason for discouragement or defeat. Confucius sacrifices himself for the furthering of these teachings, readily taking on discomfort and persecution in order to further those teachings that he believes have Heaven's favor as a way of remedying the ills of the world. The passage is focused upon physical dangers Confucius has encountered. Even these must be put aside in pursuit of the Way. The danger of death? The passage would indicate that no price is too great to pay for the promulgation of the Way.

Mencius addresses directly the question of death and its relation to the upholding of the teachings. "Life is what I want; dutifulness is also what I want. If I cannot have both, I would rather take dutifulness than life . . . . In other words, there are things a man wants more than life and there are also things he loathes more than death. This is an attitude not confined to the moral man but common to all men. The moral man simply never loses it."[27] Mencius is suggesting that there are times when the teaching of the Way stands in conflict with the ways of the world. A moral dilemma presents itself—does one abide by the teaching of the Way even though it may represent an unpopular and minority point of view or does one go along with the ways of the world? Obviously there is no choice, at least for Mencius. There are those individuals who would be willing to abide by the Way just as long as there was no danger, hardship, or suffering involved. But the point at which one may have to endure adversity and suffering for the upholding of these beliefs presents the dilemma. The dilemma is most acute at the point that the question is not just the choice between adversity in the following of the Way and the pleasures of the life of the world, but a choice that may involve death. This, however, is the cost for following the Way, that there may be those times when the risk of death must be taken for the promulgation of the Way, and there may be times as well when the promulgation of the Way results in death. This is the ultimate form of sacrificial suffering and one that the Confucian tradition is conscious of as a cost of following the Way.

This form of decision is not unknown in the history of Confucianism. We find biographies and records of many Confucians who sacrificed themselves rather than compromise the teaching of the Way. William Theodore de Bary, in his recent volume *Neo-Confucian Orthodoxy and the Learning of the Mind-and-Heart*, addresses this issue in discussing the rise of orthodoxy during the Sung and early Yüan periods. For de Bary the orthodox school struggles to survive and establish itself. During this period, the Neo-Confucians are what de Bary refers to as a "disadvantaged minority," paranoid for their very existence and fully conscious of the adversity and suffering necessary to endure for the teachings of the school to begin to emerge from complete obscurity. We tend to think of Ch'eng I, Ch'eng Hao, and Chu Hsi only with the hindsight of history and thus we place them comfortably in their positions as the patriarchs of the Neo-Confucian learning. Yet, as de Bary points out, "Ch'eng I, like his older brother, was a victim of intense persecution and died almost a martyr. Chu's sense of a special mission to uphold the Way was confirmed by his own experience of defamation and persecution for allegedly spreading 'false learning' [*wei-hsüeh*]."[28] One can also think of the later experiences of the members of the Tung-lin school and the persecutions they were subject to. Even the suicide of Kao P'an-lung must be seen in this light as an upholding of the teaching of the Way in the face of extreme adversity.[29] The historical records are filled with such accounts and attest to the degree to which Mencius' teaching was considered a foundation for moral decisionmaking and his recommendation to honor the Way more than life itself was a prescription for moral action. The upholding of this Way virtually necessitated encountering adversity. This was the sacrifice the individual made for the promulgation of the teaching of the Way.

The Suffering Servant

The suffering servant is most closely associated with its descriptions and presentation in Isaiah.

> Surely he has borne our griefs and carried our sorrows;
>   Yet we esteemed him stricken, smitten by God, and afflicted.
> But he was wounded for our transgressions,
>   he was bruised for our iniquities.
> Upon him was the chastisement that made us whole,
>   and with his stripes we are healed.

> All we like sheep have gone astray;
>   we have turned everyone to his own way;
> and the Lord has laid on him the iniquity of us all.[30]

The suffering servant is the one upon whom God has placed the burden of the world. As Isaiah goes on to say, "He bore the sin of many and made intercession for the transgressors."[31] The focus is the substitution of one for another, or in this case, one for the many. We have one who takes on the burden for all of us and who by his burden frees us all.

If one thinks in terms of comparative models for this image, the Confucian tradition is not the first to come to mind. Rather it is Buddhism and the role of the Bodhisattva. The Bodhisattva takes on the burden of the world and the sufferings of each person.

> All creatures are in pain . . . all suffer from bad and hindering karma . . . all that mass of pain and evil karma I take in my own body. . . . I take upon myself the burden of sorrow; I resolve to do so; I endure it all. I do not turn back or run away, I do not tremble. . . . I am not afraid, . . . nor do I despair. Assuredly I must bear the burdens of all beings . . . for I have resolved to save them all. I must set them all free, I must save the whole world from the forest of birth, old age, disease, and rebirth, from misfortune and sin, from the sound of birth and death, from the toils of heresy.[32]

Is there any comparable idea in Confucianism? There is a passage in the *Analects* that suggests at least something of the ideal of the suffering servant. "Tseng Tzu said, 'A Gentleman must be strong and resolute, for his burden is heavy and the road is long. He takes benevolence as his burden. Is that not heavy? Only with death does the road come to an end. Is that not long?' "[33] The passage suggests that the noble person takes on himself the learning and cultivation of goodness. That is his burden, and it is a heavy one. This would seem to have little to do with others, however, and certainly seems to have little to do with the burden of humanity. As Tu Wei-ming has pointed out, however, self-cultivation is not simply an issue of one's own humanity, for ultimately one's own humanity is only developed in relation to others. "Since humanity, in the Confucian perspective, can never be the private possession of a single individual, self-realization entails the task of bearing witness to that dimension of humanity which is communal and, in the ultimate sense, transcendent. The burden for the true Confucian scholar, then, is to learn to be fully human in such profundity and breadth that the Way itself can, as a result, be enlarged."[34] The man of goodness cultivates goodness not for himself, but for others. It is a communal act. It is ultimately for all humankind, and this is a burden he takes upon himself.

One might argue that the suffering he endures in the cultivation of goodness, the suffering of his burden, is a suffering not just for himself, but for all. This is not simply the act of taking on the responsibility for others. That is demonstrated in Mencius when in talking of the Sage Kings Yü and Chi he says, "Yü looked upon himself as responsible for anyone in the Empire who drowned; Chi looked upon himself as responsible for anyone in the Empire who starved."[35] There seems to be an additional quality in the passage from the *Analects*, a quality focused upon the taking on of the burden itself. The others do not have the burden. It is the man of goodness himself who bears this burden, and the suffering he experiences is not only for himself, but for the community and ultimately for all humankind. I am not sure we need or even can go all the way with the suffering servant motif. In its *locus classicus*, there is obviously a focus upon the action of God in relation to the suffering servant in a particular theological relationship. Whether there is any parallel with the standing of the person of goodness in relation to the dictates of Heaven is a subtle and complex question. Much of this depends, as in other arguments, upon the nature of Heaven for the early Confucians. As long as this remains unclear, the parallels can be pushed no further. There is, however, a curious hint of the suffering servant in this passage from the *Analects*, and that in itself is worthy of further discussion.

The Death of Yen Hui

One of the most poignant scenes of suffering in early Confucian writings is the death of Confucius' disciple Yen Hui recorded in the *Analects*. I want to look closely at Confucius' response to the death as a summary view of the way in which suffering, in this case Confucius's own, is dealt with and interpreted. Confucius' response to the death is recorded in several passages from the *Analects*. "When Yen Yüan died, the Master said, 'Alas! Heaven has bereft me! Heaven has bereft me!'"[36] Or further: "When Yen Yüan died, in weeping for him, the Master showed undue sorrow. His followers said, 'You are showing undue sorrow.' 'Am I? Yet if not for him, for whom should I show undue sorrow?'"[37] The death of Yen Hui was clearly an occasion for Confucius to suffer grievously. He is unrestrained in his emotions and his expression of grief as his disciples point out. There is no attempt to deny his grief. This in itself is an important response to suffering. Grief and mourning seem to be regarded as natural expressions of inner feelings. They are not to be hidden away. In turn, the loss of Yen Hui is also not to be denied. One does not move beyond tragedy by denying the tragedy. Instead it is accepted for what it is, a tragedy.

Confucius' own religious attitudes follow closely the classical traditions' focus upon Heaven as religious source and authority. It is thus appropriate for him to say that it is Heaven that has bereft him, for it is Heaven that has taken

Yen Hui away. There is little explanation given other than to suggest that Heaven is responsible for the allotment of life. "When Duke Ai asked which of his disciples was eager to learn, Confucius answered, 'There was one Yen Hui who was eager to learn. He did not vent his anger upon an innocent person, nor did he make the same mistake twice. Unfortunately his allotted span was a short one and he died.' "[28] Is there any attempt to question Heaven's allotment of life for Yen Hui? Is there a crying out that an injustice has been done? Confucius certainly cries out with grief and sorrow but not with bitterness. The Way of Heaven is to be accepted, and Heaven gave Yen Hui a short life span. Yet here is an example of someone whose entire character is that of righteousness, and he is taken away by Heaven. Does this not stir the basic question of theodicy? Does this not cause a crying out of the unrighteousness of Heaven? Confucius' only response is to accept the Way of Heaven. He differs from the poets of the *Shih-Ching* by accepting rather than questioning the dictates of Heaven. It does not prevent him from pouring out the feeling of loss he has suffered, but it does prevent either an acceptance of the retribution of Heaven or ultimately a denial of Heaven's dictates. Yen Hui was not taken away as retribution, nor was he taken away because of the inadequacy of Heaven's dictates. He was taken away as part of the Way of Heaven, even though it surpasses our comprehension to understand why. This quality of the ultimate enigma of Heaven's dictates is spoken to when Confucius says, "It is Destiny [i.e., the will of Heaven] if the Way prevails; it is equally Destiny of Heaven if the Way falls into disuse."[39] In a very fundamental sense it is beyond our capacity to understand why the Way should perish, but if it does, then even that is part of the Way of Heaven, as mysterious as it seems.

Suffering is thus accepted as a fact of existence. There is no attempt made to deny it or to explain it away, to make it any less a real or vital part of existence. Heaven is ultimately seen as the source of the turn of events in our lives. The dictates of Heaven prevail whether in prosperity or adversity. Yen Hui's allotment of life is short. There is no fault, there is no blame: it is simply beyond human understanding. And this is part of the fact of suffering—that it may not have an explanation. The noble person or the sage understands this and commits himself to helping others even when circumstances dictate that the meaning of events occurring defy explanation. This attitude is perhaps best summarized in Confucius' comments about Heaven. "The Master said, 'What does Heaven ever say? Yet there are the four seasons going around and there are the hundred things coming into being. What does Heaven ever say?' "[40] One does not expect an explanation from Heaven. One simply accepts events as they occur, recognizing they are part of the Way of Heaven. The noble person is able to accept this; the petty person demands an explanation. Adversity for the noble person is not put aside; it is overcome.

The Confucian Response to Suffering

Some of suffering can be explained, as we have seen, and the tradition avails itself of pedagogical and sacrificial suffering as well as at least a margin of substitutive suffering. The actual explanation of the cause of suffering remains, however, beyond description. It is the dictates of Heaven, not a capricious and random dictate, but one ultimately lost in mystery and beyond the comprehension of the human mind. The noble person, the one who has developed his Heaven endowed moral nature, understands this ultimate sense of mystery and accepts it.

There is nothing unusual about this explanation, or lack of explanation, for the cause of suffering. There is also nothing unusual about the religious person responding to suffering with an understanding that in some way it has meaning and purpose although there is no explanation of its cause. We can cite certain specific types of suffering, as we have done, and in some sense these at times may serve as an explanation for suffering. They tend, however, not to be used in that way. They may be offered as one explanation of suffering, but it is just one explanation and there may be other interpretations. In other words, when a cause of suffering is suggested it can often be not one, but a combination or a choice and the theological implications are often left to the individual to decipher. The actual cause defies explanation. It must have a purpose, that much is basic to the nature of religion and a religious worldview, but beyond that it may be a matter of the individual and his own inner understanding. It is for this reason that theodicy has remained as a central problem for any religious tradition.

The response to suffering does not stop, however, with the recognition that its ultimate explanation is lost in the mystery of God's Will or in the ineffable Way of Heaven. For the Confucian, as for any religious person, there is in addition to the need to come to understand suffering, an equal need to help others in their understanding and overcoming of suffering. The noble person, as we have seen, is one who has come to understand the Way of Heaven, and thereby accept the Way of Heaven, although these two are not necessarily simultaneous as Confucius' autobiographical note in the *Analects* illustrates.[41] The noble person's moral nature commits him to helping others to develop their own moral nature and to understand the dictates of Heaven. His moral nature commits him as well to helping those in need and easing the burden and the pain of those who suffer.

Confucius speaks to this form of moral action as a responsibility of the moral person.

> Tzu-lu asked about the gentleman. The Master said, "He cultivates himself and thereby achieves reverence!" "Is that all?" "He cultivates himself and thereby brings

peace and security to his fellow men!" "Is that all?" "He cultivates himself and thereby brings peace and security to the people. Even Yao and Shun would have found the task of bringing peace and security to the people taxing!"[42]

Waley translates the phrase "brings peace and security" as "to ease the lot."[43] He cultivates the capacity to "ease the lot" of the people as a whole. This is the moral commitment of the noble person, and while the occurrence of suffering may ultimately remain a mystery, the response of the noble person addresses directly the need to ease the lot of suffering.

Mencius makes this even more explicit with his discussion of the basis upon which humankind responds to suffering, the goodness of human nature. The *locus classicus* of such discussions is the famous example of the response to seeing the child about to fall into the well and summed up in the axiom, "No man is devoid of a heart sensitive to the suffering of others."[44] For Mencius, every human being should respond to the potential tragedy of a child about to fall into a well in the same way. One puts forth all effort to rescue the child. And it is for no other reason than to prevent the suffering that would otherwise occur. If one does not respond in this way, one lacks the basic and defining nature of humanity. The central component for Mencius is the "heart sensitive to the suffering of others," the heart that cannot bear to see the suffering of others.

This same point is made in a discussion between Mencius and King Hsüan of Ch'i concerning an ox being led off to sacrificial slaughter. The king, so it is recounted, cannot bear to see the animal suffer and so asks that the ox be spared. When asked whether the ceremony itself should be cancelled the king responds by suggesting that a sheep be substituted. To the people, the king appeared to grudge the cost of the ceremony and therefore substituted a smaller animal. The king says to Mencius that this is not the case, but rather, "It was simply because I could not bear to see it shrink with fear, like an innocent man going to the place of execution, that I used a lamb instead."[45] Yet there is the problem of why he was unwilling to see the ox go off to sacrifice while willingly ordering a sheep in its place. Mencius has an explanation for this. "It is the way of the benevolent man. You saw the ox but not the lamb. The attitude of a gentleman towards animals is this: once having seen them alive, he cannot bear to see them die, and once having heard their cry he cannot bear to eat their flesh . . . ."[46]

The argument returns then to the principle point, the heart that cannot bear to see the suffering of others, and in this case the centrality of this to a moral response by the ruler. Mencius ends by bringing the argument around to the king's relationship to his people, suggesting that a king that would have such a sensitive heart to animals surely could not at the same time ignore the sufferings of his people. The one who truly possesses a heart that cannot bear to see the suffering of others will exclude no one in his attempt to eliminate the suffering of the world.

The heart that cannot bear to see the suffering of others continues as a moral imperative for most of the Confucian tradition. The later Neo-Confucians see this as the foundation for moral action in a world they see united in a great moral vision. Heaven is the unifying structure of the world and the cosmos; each and every thing shares in it and in turn all are unified by its presence. The heart that cannot bear to see the suffering of others becomes the central moral response to a world seen in its unity, a unity of all Heaven and earth through moral virtue, the common Heaven endowed nature. As Ch'eng Hao puts it, making *jen* or goodness the unifying virtue: "The man of *jen* regards Heaven and earth and all things as one body. To him there is nothing that is not himself. Since he has recognized all things as himself, can there be any limit to his humanity? . . . Therefore to be charitable and to assist all things is the foundation of the sage."[47] Working to eliminate suffering is inherent in the very foundation of the sage's wisdom, the vision of the unity of all things. This vision is also found in the *Hsi-ming, Western Inscription*, of Chang Tsai. The first section of the work outlines this vision and its moral responsibilities.

> Heaven is my father and earth is my mother, and even such a small creature as I finds an intimate place in their midst. Therefore that which extends throughout the universe I regard as my body and that which directs the universe I consider as my own nature. All people are my brothers and sisters, and all things are my companions . . . Respect the aged—this is the way to treat them as elders should be treated. Show affection toward the orphaned and weak—this is the way to treat them as the young should be treated . . . Even those who are tried and infirm, crippled or sick, those who have no brothers or children, wives or husbands, are all my brothers who are in distress and have no one to turn to.[48]

This passage, one of the most famous in Neo-Confucian literature, is very specific in its response to suffering. It is a logical extension of the Neo-Confucian vision of the universe as unified through moral principle. Mencius' teaching of the heart that cannot bear to see the suffering of others pervades Chang Tsai's thinking, and other Neo-Confucians as well. Wang Yang-ming speaks of forming one body with others. "Only when I love my brother, the brother of others, and the brothers of all men can my humanity really form one body with my brother, the brothers of others, and the brothers of all men."[49] Through this vision of unity we have the basis for moral action, and that action is to serve all persons, to initiate caring and compassion to overcome people's suffering.

This represents the Confucian response to suffering. There is no attempt, as we have seen, to question the reality of suffering. It is real just as the world itself is real. Suffering is simply part of the nature of human existence. The Confucian responds to this with caring and compassion, building from the foundation of a shared moral nature endowed in us by Heaven and seeing humanity's moral responsibility as defined within the attempt to overcome adversity even when the ultimate explanation of such adversity remains beyond the grasp of human comprehension. Suffering's reason remains elusive, yet one acts with commitment and tenacity to overcome sufferings' effects. Such action is the reaction of a religious person confronting the enigma of suffering.

The question can still be raised as to whether there is anything about this response to suffering that is in fact religious. In other words, is it not possible to argue that while suffering remains a central problem in the definition of religion and every tradition struggles with its interpretation, the fact that it plays so small a role in Confucianism is an indication once again that Confucianism has little about it that is actually religious. One might suggest that we are dealing with little more than a sense of fate, one of the possible translations of *ming*, and thus the dictates of Heaven, *T'ien-ming*, is more properly understood as Fate, with little or no implication of a religious purpose or goal. In this case, Confucius' response to Yen Hui's death is simply one of recognizing and accepting fate. Fate takes place in inexplicable fashion over and above the rationality of humanistic teachings in the world. Why should there be any religious interpretation added? It is just fate.

We look to a tradition such as Christianity, and we see a central place given to the problem of suffering, not in terms of explication of cause, but recognition of the occurrence of suffering. It is not a matter of fate, but tied directly to religious meaning in the tradition. In turn we see in Christianity a clearly developed soteriology and eschatology. Through providing a soteriological and eschatological meaning to life, it can be argued that Christianity provides a religious basis for the problem of suffering. While Confucianism does not share a Christian eschatology, placing the suffering of Jesus in a specific soteriological context, a remarkable parallel is seen in the acceptance of the reality of suffering and the moral commitment to its overcoming. Is this enough, however, to provide suffering with religious meaning in Confucianism? The missing element is the religious basis of the tradition and there are still those who would argue against giving to Confucianism a soteriology, let alone an eschatology. I have argued for the religious basis of the tradition precisely upon the grounds of a existence of a Confucian soteriology, that is, the recognition of the Way of Heaven as an Absolute and the provision for the ultimate transformation of humanity.[50] It is through this soteriological capacity that the religious dimensions of the tradition can be understood and in turn it is on these grounds that the problem of suffering can be seen as first and foremost a problem in *religious* understanding.

An element of eschatology may not be entirely absent from the inner working of Confucianism. It is not impossible that Confucianism is sensitive to a redemptive capacity of suffering, particularly as it is expressed as a burden taken on for the benefit of all humankind in which, to use Tu Wei-ming's phrase, the individual becomes a cocreator with the universe itself.[51] Becoming a cocreator with the universe has potential eschatological meaning, and while I would not want to go too far with the term itself, there are intriguing questions of the appropriateness of disucssing an endpoint within a Confucian worldview. To become a cocreator with the universe has a quality of immortality about it not often thought of in terms of Confucian discourse and suggests an endpoint potentially fulfilling of the soteriological goal. Within this context the Confucian understanding of suffering is the recognition of a *religious* problem and the meaning brought to bear upon suffering is a *religious* response.

Modernity and Religion:
A Contemporary Confucian Response

In speaking of the process of modernization, Robert Bellah has said that, "Modernization, whatever else it involves, is always a moral and religious problem. If it has sometimes been hailed as an exhilarating challenge to create new values and meanings, it has also often been feared as a threat to an existing pattern of values and meanings. In either case the personal and social forces called into play have been powerful."[1] Summarizing his findings on the relationship of religion and modernization, Bellah makes several points relevant to a discussion of Confucianism and the modern world. First, "modernization inevitably disturbs the preexisting structure of meaning and motivation in any society where it seriously gets under way."[2] This raises the inevitable question of the nature of Confucianism in the current age as well as any future growth. Second, according to Bellah, "in premodern societies religion plays an important role in propagating meaningful orientation toward the world and in regulating personal feelings and contributes directly and indirectly to individual stability and social stability."[3] We can see the importance of this statement in terms of the role played by the Confucian tradition historically and until recent times throughout East Asia. The question involves the transformation of societies in successful process of modernization and the effects of such processes upon the life and integrity of the tradition itself. Third, Bellah comments that "various religious groups have led the way to modern social and cultural forms, opposed the development of those forms, or gradually adjusted to them, but it has been impossible for religion to remain entirely indifferent to modernization."[4] An obvious yet critical point, suggesting the range of differences in the response to modernization and readily bringing to mind the variety of ideological responses to modernization found in the modern history of East Asia.

John F. Wilson, in his recent article on modernity and religion, has outlined five specific responses of religion to the forces of modernization.[5] One response is what he calls, "advocacy of new religious ideas or the claim to new insights into ancient religious traditions."[6] The focus is upon the "new," but in order to understand the old. Here one deals with a religious tradition that attempts to link itself directly to an old or early tradition. A second response, according to Wilson, is the "self-conscious accommodation of religious traditions to modern society, often in very explicit terms."[7] It is an embracing of modernity and an open adaptation. Science and technology have become simply a part of the world with which religion deals and the discoveries of the world are part of what religion provides meaning for and accommodates itself to.

A third response, according to Wilson, is not the open adaptation of modernity, but rather "the determined attempt to preserve the continuing tradition, albeit self-consciously within limits posed by the new framework."[8] It is an adaptation in the face of necessity, recognizing the growing pressures for adaptation. A fourth response is simply to refuse to adapt, even by necessity, and instead to reject any new meanings. This response is what he calls "strident reassertion of presumed tradition in a condensed, purified or even reductionist form."[9] This is what we frequently identify as fundamentalism today, an element that plays a part of virtually all major religious traditions. As Wilson says, "In this perspective, fundamentalisms, as the simultaneous reduction and enhancement of particular traditions, are no less than modernism determined by the modern culture that they so stridently reject."[10] A final form of response according to Wilson is the creation of a completely new tradition. The various examples for each of these categories could be listed at some length. That is not our purpose, but rather to present an overview to better understand Confucianism in the modern world as a religious tradition struggling with certain of the issues of modernity.

What of the terms modernity or modernization? Are they simply the response of each generation of its own time, to the changes and transformations of a given generation? Are we in a sense as guilty as our forefathers of seeing our own time as one of significant new change or is our age of sufficient transformation substantially different from previous generations? Wilson concludes his article by supporting the degree to which the concept of modernity has a legitimate use for our generation.

> When taken together, the concepts of modernity and religion identify a broad range of religious responses to intense and self-conscious social change in the contemporary world. What is uniquely modern is not the particular religious responses to change per se but their variety, intensity and duration in the contemporary world. Crucial is the insight that religion is not so much threatened by modernity as challenged by it.[11]

Modernity is a legitimate category to reflect the profound level of change taking place in world cultures and religion's response to this reflects a level of breadth, seriousness, and intensity that can be expected to produce profound changes in the nature of religious traditions. How does this affect our understanding of Confucianism and, in turn, how might we expect to understand a Confucian response to these forces of modernity?

Whither the Contemporary Confucian Response?

The Confucian response to the forces of modernization is a long and complex historical process. It begins at least in the nineteenth century and follows through the explosive events of the history of the Far East since that time. My purpose here is not to summarize this process, but rather to present two examples of contemporary Confucian response. One is Tu Wei-ming, the other is Okada Takehiko. This is not intended as an in-depth study of either Tu or Okada, but instead an opportunity to refer to statements each has made relevant to the question of the role of Confucianism in contemporary Asia, and the future of Confucianism both in Asia and the world.

There is an assumption on the part of both Tu and Okada that Confucianism is far from a strictly historical phenomenon as some have chosen to describe it. It remains for both of them a living point of view and a potentially vital perspective for the future of East Asia and the world as a whole. Part of what makes the reflections of Tu and Okada so relevant is that they are first and foremost viewed as scholars of the tradition, but in turn they are themselves part of the Confucian heritage and reflect upon the role of the traditon for themselves and their generation, which is of course our own generation. Thus, we have a contemporary Confucian response, knowledgeable of the history of the tradition and committed to exploring the meaning of Confucianism for the present age as well as the future.

The entire issue of a contemporary response has recently been put in a creative mode of interpretation by Tu in his essay "Toward a Third Epoch of Confucian Humanism: A Background Understanding."[12] Tu argues that the last several decades have witnessed an extraordinary revitalization and resignification of Confucian humanism. This, he suggests, will provide the foundation for what he calls the third epoch of Confucian humanism. Instead of the Levensonian response suggesting the ultimate inability of Confucianism to survive the vicissitudes and upheaval of modern society, Tu argues for the vitality of a new-found creativity. To many, Confucianism is at most of interest and importance only as a historical object of study, as that which one studies in order to understand the background to the processes of modernization in East Asia. Tu states that students of modern Asia still, "take it for granted that the incongruity between Confucian traditionalism and rational scientific modernism is so clear-cut that the rise of modernity in China entails the demise of the Confucian tradition."[13] The same response might be found in terms of Korea and Japan, although Tu's comments are focused specifically upon China. Tu cites various responses that have sought to challenge this form of interpretation— William Theodore de Bary's studies of Neo-Confucianism, Thomas Metzger's interpretation of the tradition, even sociological studies of the economic development of the so-called post-Confucian states. Yet each of these still deals with a tradition of the past, not its effect upon the present or potential future growth. What can be said of the tradition as it is at present or its potential for future growth?

Is Joseph Levenson ultimately right that there really is no Confucian tradition left and the final proof is that the discussion of modern Confucianism is in fact a discussion of history? Levenson in the end could only lament the future; Tu, by contrast, suggests the approach of the third epoch—the role of Ch'ien Mu and T'ang Chün-i with the growth of the New Asia College in Hong Kong as well as Mou Tsung-san, Hsü Fu-kuan, and Fang Tung-mei (Thome Fang). In speaking of these individuals he says,

> The real challenge to them is how a revived Confucian humanism might answer questions that science and democracy have raised. . . . In a deeper sense, these scholars perceive the challenge to be the formulation of a Confucian approach to the perennial human problems of the world: the creation of a new philosophical anthropology, a common creed for humanity as a whole. They are fully aware that concern for the survival of the Confucian tradition and for the continuity of traditional Chinese culture must be subsumed under a broader concern for the future of humankind.[14]

One of the important points made by Tu is that the contemporary study of Confucianism is for some a different agenda than that of intellectual history. For those individuals cited, and we would also have to include Tu Wei-ming himself, Confucianism is potentially a source of authentic meaning about the world: it is not simply the study of the history of the tradition. This would seem virtually unnecessary to say were it not for the fact that much of the way Confucianism is studied retains the historical perspective even when studying the modern period and suggests modernity only as a response to what Confucianism was, rather than holding the possibility of fruitful meanings within Confucianism now and in the future. To Tu Wei-ming, and he is not alone in this respect,[15] Confucianism possesses significance for the future to the degree that it can address questions raised by modernity, science, democracy, and technology.

Is the attitude of Tu Wei-ming a welcoming of adaptation, in Wilson's categories, or an accommodation by necessity? From the perspective offered by Tu, it would appear to be an open and welcomed adaptation. Are we, however, discussing the revitalization and resignification of the old symbolism, or is it an agenda for a thoroughly new point of view? To move beyond it is, of course, at a certain point to move beyond the symbolism that defines even the minimum perimeters of the tradition itself. It is critical to understand what can be eliminated and still retain the minimal meaning significant enough to warrant the continued identification of the tradition itself. Clearly, this is not a problem exclusive to Confucianism, but it is of paramount importance to any discussion of the future of Confucianism, or to use Tu's phrase, the third epoch of Confucian humanism. One can reanimate the old, or one can move beyond the old, and Tu seems to suggest both possibilities. He says, however, that the real challenge is the Confucian response to human problems, not just the problems of Chinese, Korean, or Japanese culture. The question is not so much the individual tradition as it is the survival of humankind itself. In summarizing this issue he says, "If the well being of humanity is its central concern, Confucian humanism in the third epoch cannot afford to be confined to East Asia cultures. A global perspective is needed to universalize its perennial concerns."[16] This is the challenge for Confucianism in the modern world as Tu Wei-ming sees it. Either Confucianism remains culture bound and faces a fate of moribundity or it adapts itself to those universal concerns of humanity and enters the global community whose focus is the future of humankind and the world itself.

The Voice of Okada Takehiko

Many of the same issues raised by Tu Wei-ming appear equally relevant to the role of Confucianism throughout East Asia. I turn to Japan as the second example of a contemporary response to Confucianism. Tu mentions in passing three figures whom he considers to be what he calls, "contemporary exemplars of the Confucian heritage:"[17] Wing-tsit Chan, T'ang Chun-i and Okada Takehiko. It is the last of these figures, Okada Takehiko, I want to discuss. Some of my recent work has permitted me the privilege of coming to know the writing of Okada, but perhaps more importantly, his life and thought in a personal way.[18]

The beginning of this work goes back some years now to my first trip to Japan. My own teacher, William Theodore de Bary, suggested that while in Japan I should try to meet Okada, not only because of his expertise in the field of Neo-Confucian studies, but because there was something else about Okada that he felt was important for me to see. I asked what this was, and he responded by saying that when one met Okada, one was meeting the living tradition face to face! With my own scholarly interest in the Confucian practice of quiet-sitting, I completed a draft translation of Okada's work on quiet-sitting, *Zazen to seiza*, and I met with Okada to discuss his work. I soon discovered exactly what de Bary was talking about! Only moments after meeting Okada, he turned to me and said, "I feel that the world is in tremendous moral and spiritual decline. What do you think can be done about it?"[19] This was not simply a question from a scholar of the tradition, this was a Confucian responding to the plight of his own generation.

As I have thought about this incident over the past several years, it has occurred to me that as scholars of the Confucian tradition we do not adequately allow for the contemporary voice of the tradition to be raised in anguish at its own age. Historically, we know that Confucians have almost unanimously responded to conditions of their own age. We all know the examples, in fact we study and teach them as part of the history of Confucianism—Ch'eng I's memorial to Emperor Jen-tsung, Ch'eng Hao on reform, Chang Tsai on land equalization, Chu Hsi on Wang An-shih's new laws. The examples could go on and on. What, however, of the contemporary Confucian; does he have a response to his own age?

Perhaps our first problem is simply to recognize that there are contemporary and living Confucians. It seems that in the way we study the tradition we are more interested in a contemporary Confucian's response to a historical problem than we are in allowing that Confucian to speak not as a scholar, but as a Confucian to issues of his own age. As Tu Wei-ming has suggested, if Confucianism is to approach its third epoch, then this dimension of response must be sought out and listened for, and I might add, with very sensitive ears. As scholars we must allow ourselves to ask different questions. Some may well feel that Confucian studies is strictly an academic discipline and that the object of this study is a historical subject. Does this mean that we analyze historically those figures who are near contemporaries and thereby in this fashion bring Confucian studies to the modern period? Clearly this is an important task, and I do not in any respect want to denigrate such scholarly work, but it remains a historical entity, not a contemporary manifestation. Do we not need the contemporary Confucian response itself even to the degree it potentially breaks from a specific cultural setting and assumes a role such as Tu Wei-ming suggests, addressing the perennial issues of humanity itself?

My own thinking about this problem came initially from meeting with Okada Takehiko and realizing I was totally unprepared to encounter the actual tradition as a lived and authentic point of view. I was prepared to meet Okada as a scholar of the tradition, but a lived point of view was different. This quality of the lived tradition is a far more difficult thing to capture and to illuminate. Okada's scholarly works are well-known and masterful, but his life as a Confucian—how does one explore it and discuss it?

When one looks to the scholarly works for some hint of personal perspective or self-reflective challenge to the modern age, little is found and what is there could easily be overlooked. The preface to *Zazen to seiza* is one such example. It says, in part:

> In these times, there is a worldly spirit in Japan. People look to go this way or that in a world that has been rapidly transformed. They seem to have many different viewpoints and do not know what is correct. They dispute with one another and act without consideration of others. I feel that little by little there will be a loss of the humanistic spirit and an unsteadiness in the subjective nature. If the humanistic spirit is lost and the subjective nature unsteady, then neither individual nor society can make a correct judgment or act in the correct way. What then does one do to restore man's nature and reestablish subjectivity?"[20]

His solution to this loss of the humanistic spirit and the subjective nature is the practice of meditation, either as *seiza*, quiet-sitting, or *kotsuza*, "just sitting." He says that it is these kinds of practices that will provide a means to solve the problems of the world in positive ways. The statements are tantalizing even in their very paucity. What does the loss of the humanistic spirit and subjective nature mean in a world dominated by science and technology? And how can contemplative practice operate within this contemporary context? Okada's initial statement decries the very pressure of modernization pinpointed by Bellah, a rapid transformation with no point of stability. Yet how easy it is to overlook this material, to look to a work such as *Zazen to Seiza* as simply a historical and scholarly study of Confucian contemplative practice, even though Okada intended it in a much different way.

The hermeneutical task before us seems quite clear—the text has a meaning, a very important part of that meaning is understanding and incorporating into our meaning of the text the meanings in the mind of the author of that text. How can a work such as *Zazen to Seiza* not be seen as a challenge to Confucianism in the modern age? For that matter, the hermeneutical task suggests that a work such as *Zazen to Seiza*, even as a historical study, has as its agenda what Tu Wei-ming refers to as the third epoch of Confucian humanism and its relation to a world dominated by science and technology.

Okada's Response to Modernity

To Okada, science and technology are a necessary part of our world. We cannot prevent or stop the continued development of science. In fact, quite the contrary, we must recognize the necessary role it plays in the development of the human community and the positive nature of its knowledge for the world. Okada's response is not to deny the role of science, nor for that matter is it an attempt to deprecate the benefits created by science or the dominant scientific worldview of the modern world. There is, nevertheless, a problem in terms of the development of a world dominated by a scientific worldview. The problem, from Okada's point of view, is what he calls an increased lack of respect for life. At first encounter, this may seem a strange way of distinguishing the modern from premodern periods. After all, is it not the case that much of scientific knowledge has benefited humankind and thus shown a greater respect for human life? Okada would not deny this, and he speaks of such benefits when he talks of the necessity of the continued development of science.

Okada, however, is referring to something different. He is referring to the degree to which the humanistic and subjective nature of humanity has little role to play in the course of development of a scientific worldview. To see the world dominated by a scientific worldview is to see, from Okada's point of view, a preclusion of ethical questions unless consciously learned and introduced. In the development of an empirical epistemology, nothing automatically calls our attention to the axiological, the ethical importance of the individual and his or her relation with others. This is what Okada refers to as the lack of respect for life. He says in this regard: "If we are going to make science totally responsive to the needs of the human community, we must let everyone— scientist and non-scientist alike—learn the importance of human life; it is essential to realize the importance of one's own life as well as the lives of others. We live in the same world together and mutual respect for life is a prerequisite."[21] The issue as he sees it is a rapidly transforming world focused primarily upon its scientific and technological achievements in which questions of value have taken a secondary role, if any role at all. What is good is measured primarily in terms of the success rate of scientific and technological breakthroughs and innovative developments. Ethics is judged at best secondary; value orientation is subsumed in humankind's own confidence that scientific and technological development are capable of the remaking and transformation of the world.

For many, of course, there is a basic incompatibility between a scientific worldview and Confucianism, the position argued by Levenson. To Okada, this is not only exaggerated, but fundamentally wrong. His argument, based upon his interpretation of Chu Hsi's concept of "total substance and great functioning," *ch'üan-t'i ta-yung*, suggests that because human nature and the laws of nature operate by the same principle there is a natural relationship between them.[22] As the laws of nature apply to human nature, so in turn do the laws of human nature apply to nature itself. This suggests the extension of the ethical nature of humanity to the nature of all things and thus the degree to which a human articulation of ethics is a part not simply of the human community, but of nature itself. As such, to develop nature by scientific and technological means only is incomplete to the degree it fails to recognize the need to incorporate the ethical nature of humanity as a part of nature itself and thus as a logical extension of the development of nature.

How then does one live authentically, to use Tu Wei-ming's phrase, in modern technological society? How does one live, from a Confucian point of view, with the pressures of technological society upon the individual? Can the Confucian sense of forming one body with all things become a force in modern society? Okada responds by reasserting the fundamental teachings of Confucianism and his own emphasis in learning upon self-cultivation and contemplative practice.

> The main purpose of Confucianism is to establish true humanity. No matter how far science has developed, the Confucian never loses sight of the development of humanity. Before any discussion of logic or rationality the Confucian focuses upon the importance of subjectivity. In our day-to-day lives we distinguish what goes on within us from the outside world, but we become trapped by the outside world and in this way we lose our humanity. Given this situation we should try to control that external world, but in practice this is a very difficult thing to do. The important issue is to establish one's own inner subjectivity within the mind.[23]

The argument goes on to emphasize the need for contemplative practice and the inner cultivation of the humanistic spirit and subjective nature, crucial ingredients in a reassertion of human values into the context of the modern world.

The model remains dominantly one of individual learning and self-cultivation. The solution to the pressures of modern society is a return to individual learning and self-cultivation such that a balance will be struck between the continued development of science and technology and a concern for respect for human life, the humanistic spirit. Is this any different from the *Great Learning* where ultimately political problems are first and foremost problems in the development of the moral nature? Okada's response when I asked him that question suggests, from the Confucian perspective, the timeless quality of the *Great Learning*. "Even in this time self-cultivation is still essential to the individual as it is spoken of in the *Great Learning*. One must be educated to the importance of self-cultivation and if each individual in each country were to begin the practice of self-cultivation then we would have no further problem. I think that Chu Hsi and Wang Yang-ming would agree with me on this."[24]

Human Nature and the Modern World

At the very center of Confucian teaching stands the theory of human nature. Mencius' theory of human nature stood as a central element of Confucian teaching throughout the history of the tradition. It is no different in terms of Confucian teaching today represented by Okada. Okada's teachings suggest a role for Confucianism in a world dominated by scientific and technological advancement, a role that suggests the balancing of such advancements with a sensitivity to respect for human life and to the promulgation of values that would initiate such respect. For Okada, such learning is a form of self-cultivation, a self-cultivation that is oriented toward contemplative practice as the principal means of restoring what he constantly describes as the humanist spirit and the subjective nature. But what are such practices grounded in and what is the basis for concluding that through self-cultivation this wellspring of humanistic spirit will emerge and that humankind will truly form one body in their mutual respect for each other? The basis is no different than Mencius arguing the primacy of the goodness of human nature and Okada upholds this perspective.

How does this belief accommodate itself to the world as we know it? Is it still realistic to speak of a theory such as the goodness of human nature, or are we swayed by the various socioscientific models of humankind that suggest the dominance of aggression, selfishness, and what Hsün Tzu called evil? Okada is, in fact, posing the same risk I discussed in Chapter I. It is a risk to accept the goodness of humanity and to say that real security will be found in establishing the world on the basis of this view of human nature rather than the false security of defending ourselves from the opposite view of human nature.

Okada admits that the evilness of people's actions and the world appears real. It is, in turn, difficult to substantiate the goodness of human nature. In a sense, there is no rational proof of such goodness, and thus it is a risk posed. We can fall back upon the common wisdom that were the nature of humankind not good, then there would be no one we could trust. Obviously, however, most of us do trust other people and therefore the belief in the goodness of human nature is at least vindicated. Such optimism, as we all know too well, can be as quickly dispelled through the daily news. For Okada, however, there is another important point. The goodness of human nature is not merely a conclusion of rational inquiry, but instead a product of deep inner experience. For Okada, the arguments for the goodness of human nature by Mencius and in opposition to the thinker Kao Tzu are not arguments as a means of rational demonstration of proof. They are rather more of the nature of insight into the question of human nature, inviting Kao Tzu to the same experience. For Okada, it is the experience of goodness that is the proof of goodness. Until this experience occurs, the belief in the goodness of human nature is a matter of faith, and as we have argued in the first chapter, involves risk taking.[25]

The ramifications of this approach to the issue of human nature and its relationship to the pressures of modernity are important. Okada is not arguing the irrelevancy of the traditional Confucian teaching on human nature. He is simply arguing the degree to which the classical argument for such goodness should not be contrasted with modern socioscientific methodologies for the construction of meanings of self. He is stating instead that this inner core of self is simply not available to the same format of scrutiny as engaged in by standard socioscientific techniques. This does not invalidate it, but suggests that modern methodologies have only dealt with a part of the self. Another part of the self is available, but only through means of introspective and meditative technique, and it is only from the latter that the true nature of human nature will reveal itself.

For Okada, the true understanding of human nature is the object of religion in the modern world, and this is the role for Confucianism as well. These are synonymous in Okada's mind, and only through the depth that a religious dimension can offer, will the true character of humankind be revealed. Without this perspective, in other words, in a world no longer offering religious depth, humankind cannot know its true character. Without this possibility of knowing the true character, it will build its world and meaning from the self-directed and self-centered motives that are a part of human consciousness, the *jen-hsin*, rather than the root and foundation of such consciousness, the *Tao-hsin*. Under these conditions the very survival of humankind is at risk.

The Role of Religion and the Future of Confucianism

Religion has the possibility of remedying this alienation of humankind from its own nature, but according to Okada the history of religions has not demonstrated the viability of all religious traditions to engage in this task.[26] According to Okada, religious traditions have their own strengths and weaknesses. There is no doubt that untold suffering and misery has been wrought in the name of particular religious traditions. As sources of bigotry and exclusiveness, some have not played a positive role. On the other hand, as sources of compassion and caring some have provided a means for human beings to care for themselves and others and to touch the innermost recesses of their own natures. This is the positive good that religion can play. It is not just a positive good for our generation and the world we have created, it is an imperative in our time.

To Okada, however, a particular religious tradition, whatever the tradition, is not the important issue. It is the degree to which religious concerns point to the ultimate dimension of human nature and reveal a nature that by its nature seeks to express its concern and care for other human beings. This is what Okada simply calls the necessity of respect for human life, and in turn what links Okada to Mencius' theory of the heart of commiseration. I asked Okada whether in the way he expressed himself it would be more appropriate to talk of religious values or the religious dimension rather than a particular religious tradition or system. It seemed that his concern for the role of religion focused upon its capacity to express this respect for human life rather than any specific teaching, creed or doctrine.[27] His answer concurred, but only to a degree. He suggested that his ideas were probably not compatible with particular traditions, for his real focus was the largest level of respect for human life as a complement to the continued development of the modern scientific worldview.

His qualification on my statement, however, suggests the degree to which he feels Confucianism as a tradition is better-suited to this task than other traditions.

Confucianism, from Okada's point of view, is better-suited to this task because its focus has always been upon humankind. It is in humankind that ultimate meaning is to be found as a reflection of the Way of Heaven. It is the very foundation of the religious dimension of the tradition itself. This is not to deny a metaphysical absolute, but to suggest the unique way in which the tradition has focused this metaphysical absolute in terms of humanity itself. And, for Okada, this is a better starting point with the rapidly transforming scientific world we live in than a tradition that attempts to deny the ultimate existence of this world itself by focusing upon the sole reality of a transcendental world. To Okada, Confucianism's focus upon the concrete and real existence of the world has made it uniquely qualified to meet the issues of modernity. Its focus upon humankind, both with its ideal of goodness as well as its recognition of the reality of imperfection, does not differ markedly from the world of meaning we now inhabit with the demythologization of many traditional religious points of view and a dominance of humanistic learning more the product of the Enlightenment's freedom from religious roots than the Renaissance's religious foundation. What Confucianism can offer, from Okada's point of view, is a complement to the meaning of the world by providing a penetration into the depth of human understanding and human nature.[28]

Is this agenda, however, practical? Can one advocate a role for Confucianism in the waning years of the twentieth century when the name of the tradition still carries with it the baggage of the nineteenth century? How then does this third epoch begin? We have seen Tu Wei-ming's response to this in terms of the need of the tradition to address universal and perennial problems of humanity. Okada's answer is a very simple one and yet radical and innovative.

> We don't really need to have Confucianism as Confucianism in the future. All we need is the respect for human life and human dignity. In this country [i.e. Japan] if we were to advocate Confucianism today, there is very strong opposition; thus one's focus must remain upon the issue of respect for human life and human dignity, not the name of the tradition. If the name itself disappears in the future, that is all right, just so long as the issue of human dignity remains.[29]

In this statement, Okada is facing the challenge of modernity and is answering the critics who say Confucianism is a thing of the past. In Wilson's terms, what we see in Okada's response is not a recalcitrance to relate to modernity nor even an acting out of necessity alone. It is, like Tu Wei-ming's, a free and open accommodation. There is the clear recognition of the deep and profound changes the modern world has undergone and in turn the challenge this represents to a religious tradition. There is also the recognition that a defined tradition with its perimeters of doctrine and teaching may only be a vestige of the past when such teachings and doctrines stand in clear conflict with the modern scientific world view adopted by the world at large.

This is saying more certainly than Wilson intended by his first category of providing new insights into old traditions. There is certainly a recognition of the importance of the ancient teachings, but not as a static embodiment of authority. In other words, this is not a clarification of the new in order to reinstate the old. In turn, this does not correspond to Wilson's final category either, the creation of a new tradition, for the links to the past remain and the sense of the new is drawn without perimeters. Okada's conclusion resonates with a comment by Tu Wei-ming that, "concern for the survival of the Confucian tradition and for the continuity of traditional Chinese (and we might add— Japanese) culture must be subsumed under a broader concern for the future of humankind."[30] Okada seems, however, to carry the point even further. Not only is the issue the universal and perennial religious dimension of humankind. In this respect a specific name of a tradition, the religious burden of reification according to Wilfred Cantwell Smith,[31] only limits our vision. As a religion can adapt itself to any new and transformed meaning of the world, Okada is suggesting that the essential Confucian teaching does not need its own reification. Vitaly Rubin was certainly right when he observed that there has been a renaissance of Confucianism, what he refers to as the New Confucianism.[32] A mark of its creativity is the kind of thought we see in Tu Wei-ming and Okada Takehiko, suggesting that the third epoch is already underway, that it is open ended and its possibilities for growth virtually limitless.

Notes

Introduction

1. Wilfred C. Smith, *The Meaning and End of Religion* (New York: Harper and Row, 1978), pp. 1-14.

2. A few representative volumes that have dealt with the issue include: James Legge, *The Religions of China* (London: Hodder and Stoughton, 1880), Max Weber, *The Religion of China: Confucianism and Taoism* (New York: Free Press, 1951), C. K. Yang, *Religion in Chinese Society* (Berkeley: University of California Press, 1961), Julia Ching, *Confucianism and Christianity: A Comparative Study* (Tokyo: Kodansha International, 1977), Julia Ching and Hans Kung, *Christianity and Chinese Religions* (New York: Doubleday, 1989), Tu Wei-ming, *Humanity and Self-Cultivation: Essays in Confucian Thought* (Berkeley: Asian Humanities Press, 1979), Tu Wei-ming, *Confucian Thought: Selfhood as Creative Transformation* (Albany, N. Y.: SUNY Press, 1985), Rodney L. Taylor, *The Way of Heaven: An Introduction to the Confucian Religious Life* (Leiden: E. J. Brill, 1986).

3. Frederick Streng, *Understanding Religious Life, Third Edition* (Belmont, Calif.: Wadsworth, 1985), pp. 1-8.

4. See, for example, Okada Takehiko and the role of Kao P'an-lung he has outlined in the history of the Yamazaki Ansai School of Neo-Confucianism in Japan. R. L. Taylor, *The Confucian Way of Contemplation: Okada Takehiko and the Tradition of Quiet-Sitting* (Columbia, S. C.: University of South Carolina Press, 1988), pp. 123-137.

5. Taylor, *Confucian Way*, pp. 210-212.

Chapter I

1. See, for example, the way in which the background of Confucianism is presented in Wing-tsit Chan, *A Source Book in Chinese Philosophy* (Princeton N. J.: Princeton University Press, 1969), Ch. 1.

2. See Joachim Wach, *The Comparative Study of Religion* (New York: Columbia University Press, 1961), pp. 30-38.

3. Frederick J. Streng, *Understanding Religious Life, Third Edition* (Belmont, Calif.: Wadsworth, 1985), pp. 1-8.

4. Streng, *Understanding Religious Life*, p. 37.

5. This issue is discussed in Chapter III in terms of the text known as the *Ta-hsüeh* [*Great Learning*], one of the most important models for the learning process in the history of the Confucian tradition. The *Great Learning* identifies eight steps in the learning process and of the eight, the first five all refer to internal processes of learning.

6. This issue, summarized some years ago by C. K. Yang, remains a pressing problem in the study of Chinese culture. See C. K. Yang, *Religion in Chinese Society* (Berkeley: University of California Press, 1961), pp. 3-6.

7. David N. Keightley, "The Religious Commitment: Shang Theology and the Genesis of Chinese Political Culture," *History of Religions* 17, no. 3-4 (Feb.-May., 1978): 211-215.

8. Keightley, "Religious Commitment," p. 217.

9. Keightley, "Religious Commitment," p. 223.

10. Ibid.

11. Keightley, "Religious Commitment," p. 224.

12. Ibid.

13. For one interpretation of *te* and its relation to *T'ien* see Donald Munro, *The Concept of Man in Early China* (Stanford, Calif.: Stanford University Press, 1969), pp. 185-97. See also David L. Hall and Roger T. Ames, *Thinking Through Confucius* (Albany, N. Y.: SUNY Press, 1987), pp. 201-26.

14. A brief but excellent overview of *T'ien-ming* is found in K. C. Chang, *Art, Myth and Ritual: The Path to Political Authority in Ancient China* (Cambridge, Mass.: Harvard University Press,1983), pp. 33-35.

15. A lengthy interpretation of the exemplary person is given by Hall and Ames, *Thinking Through Confucius*, pp. 176-92.

16. *Analects*, 4:16, D. C. Lau (trans.), *Confucius: The Analects (Lun-yü)* (Middlesex: Penguin Books Ltd., 1979), p. 74.

17. *Analects*, 4:11, Lau., *Analects* p. 73. While following Lau generally, I have substituted several phrases in this passage.

18. *Analects*, 2:13, Lau, *Analects* p. 64.

19. *Analects*, 15:31, Lau, *Analects* p. 136.

20. *Analects*, 4:5, Lau, *Analects* p. 72.

21. The difficulty in the interpretation and translation of this term is discussed in Hall and Ames, *Thinking Through Confucius*, pp. 89-110.

22. *Analects*, 15:2.

23. *Analects*, 4:15.

24. *Analects*, 2:3, Lau, *Analects*, p. 63.

25. The most thorough study of shame in Chinese culture remains, Wolfram Eberhard, *Guilt and Sin in Traditional China* (Berkeley: University of California Press, 1971), pp. 1-4, 12-24. See also, however, the short discussion of shame in Hall and Ames, *Thinking Through Confucius*, pp. 173-176.

26. *Analects*, 12:19, Lau, *Analects*, pp. 115-16.

27. *Analects*, 12:7, Lau, *Analects*, p. 113.

28. *Analects*, 13:6, Lau, *Analects*, p. 119.

29. *Analects*, 15:5, Lau, *Analects*, p. 132.

30. Fingarette argues a similar characteristic, but in terms of the role of *li*, rites or propriety. See Herbert Fingarette, *Confucius: The Secular as Sacred* (New York: Harper and Row, 1972), pp. 1-17.

31. *Analects* 12:17, Lau, *Analects*, p. 115.

32. Further elaboration of the relation between these terms can be found in Hall and Ames, *Thinking Through Confucius*, pp. 156-68.

33. *Analects*, 15:13, Lau, *Analects*, p. 134.

34. See, for example, *Analects* 13:10, 14:37, 9:5.

35. *Analects*, 15:9, Lau, *Analects*, p. 133.

36. Mencius 1A:1, D. C. Lau (trans.), *Mencius* (Middlesex: Penguin Books Ltd., 1970), p. 49.

37. *Mencius*, 4A:9, Lau, *Mencius*, pp. 121-22.

38. *Mencius*, 1A:5, Lau, *Mencius*, p. 53.

39. *Mencius*, 1A:7, Lau, *Mencius*, p. 58.

40. *Mencius*, 6A:2.

41. *Mencius*, 2A:6.

42. Ibid.

43. *Mencius*, 2A:6, Lau, *Mencius*, p. 82.

Chapter II

1. See, for example, William Theodore de Bary (ed.), *The Unfolding of Neo-Confucianism* (New York: Columbia University Press, 1975); Tu Wei-ming *Humanity and Self-Cultivation: Essays in Confucian Thought* (Berkeley: Asian Humanities Press, 1979); Rodney L. Taylor, *The Cultivation of Sagehood as a Religious Goal in Neo-Confucianism: A Study of Selected Writings of Kao P'an-lung (1562-1626)* (Missoula, Mont.: Scholar's Press/American Academy of Religion, 1978).

2. *Shuo-wen chieh-tzu ku-lin* (Taipei, 1977) Vol. 9, p. 1986.

3. Ibid.

4. Bernhard Karlgren, *Grammata Serica Recensa* (Stockholm: Museum of Far Eastern Antiquities, 1964), p. 222.

5. William G. Boltz, "The Religious and Philosophical Significance of the 'Hsiang-erh' Lao Tzu in the Light of the Ma-Wang-Tui Silk Manuscripts," *Bulletin of the School of Oriental and African Studies* 45, Part 1 (1982): 101-02.

6. *Shuo-wen chieh-tzu ku-lin*, Vol. 9, p. 1086.

7. Few studies have been written on the nature of scripture in Chinese Buddhist sources. See Roger Corless, "The Meaning of Ching (Sutra?) in Buddhist Chinese," *Journal of Chinese Philosophy* 3, No. 1 (Dec. 1975): 67-72; and Miriam Levering, "Scripture and Its Reception: A Buddhist Case," in *Rethinking Scripture: Essays from a Comparative Perspective*, ed. Miriam Levering (Albany: SUNY Press, 1989), pp. 58-101.

8. *Shuo-wen chieh-tzu ku-lin*, Vol. 10, p. 527.

9. Karlgren, *Grammata*, pp. 219-20.

10. *Analects* 8:8 D. C. Lau (trans.) *Confucius: The Analects (Lun-yü)* (Middlesex: Penguin Books Ltd., 1979), p. 93.

11. *Analects*, 6:27 Lau, *Analects*, p. 85. (Changed *gentleman* to *noble person*.)

12. *Analects*, 17:9 Lau, *Analects*, p. 145.

13. *Analects* 2:2 Lau, *Analects*, p. 63.

14. *Mencius*, 6B:3.

15. *Mencius*, 7B:3.

16. Quoted in Fung Yu-lan *A History of Chinese Philosophy, Vol. I, The Period of the Philosophers* (trans. Derk Bodde) (Princeton, N. J.: Princeton University Press, 1952), p. 400.

17. Quoted in Fung, *History of Chinese Philosophy*, pp. 401-02.

18. John K. Shryock, *The Origin and Development of the State Cult of Confucius* (no. 1: American Historical Association, 1932; reprint edition, New York: Paragon Reprint Corp., 1966), p. 41.

19. Shryock, *State Cult*, p. 70.

20. See Shryock, *State Cult*, Chap. 3, for an excellent summary of this development.

21. See the translation of this material in Fung, *History of Chinese Philosophy*, pp. 44-45.

22. Wing-tsit Chan (trans.), *Reflections on Things at Hand, The Neo-Confucian Anthology Compiled by Chu Hsi and Lü Tsu-ch'ien* (New York: Columbia University Press, 1967), p. 104.

23. See Sam D. Gill, "Nonliterate Traditions and Holy Books: Toward a New Model," in *The Holy Book in Comparative Perspective*, eds. Frederick M. Denny and Rodney L. Taylor (Columbia, S.C.: University of South Carolina Press, 1985), pp. 224-39.

24. See Frederick M. Denny and Rodney L. Taylor, "Introduction," in *The Holy Book in Comparative Perspective*, pp. 1-9.

25. See Wing-tsit Chan, "Chu Hsi's Completion of Neo-Confucianism," in *Études Song— Sung Studies, In Memoriam Étienne Balazs*, ed. Françoise Aubin, ser. II, no. 1 (1973): 82.

26. Ibid.

27. Chan, "Completion," p. 83.

28. Ibid.

29. While the *Chin-ssu lu* contains one chapter considered essential to the Neo-Confucian metaphysical system, the majority of the text deals with practical details in learning and self-cultivation. As a guide to the life of cultivation it is one of the most important works available in translation that exemplifies the Confucian religious life. For a complete translation see Chan, *Reflections*.

30. Chan, *Reflections*, p. 98.

31. Chan, *Reflections*, p. 97.

32. Chan, *Reflections*, p. 101.

33. Chan, "Completion," p. 85.

34. Ibid.

35. Ibid.

36. Chan, "Completion," pp. 85-86.

37. Chan, *Reflections*, p. 102.

38. Ibid.

39. Chan, *Reflections*, p. 103.

40. Ibid.

41. For general reading on the differences between the major schools see Wing-tsit Chan, *A Source Book in Chinese Philosophy* (Princeton, N. J.: Princeton University Press, 1963), Chaps. 33-35. For an excellent study of the School of Mind, see Tu Wei-ming, *Neo-Confucian Thought in Action: Wang Yang-ming's Youth (1472-1509)* (Berkeley: University of California Press, 1976).

42. Chan, *Source Book*, p. 580.

43. See William Theodore de Bary, *Neo-Confucian Orthodoxy and the Learning of the Mind-and-Heart* (New York: Columbia University Press, 1981), pp. 1-66.

44. De Bary, *Orthodoxy*, p. 17.

45. De Bary, "Some Common Tendencies in Neo-Confucianism," in *Confucianism in Action*, eds. David Nivison and Arthur Wright (Stanford, Calif.: Stanford University Press, 1959), pp. 34-35.

46. De Bary, *Orthodoxy*, p. 137.

47. Chan, *Reflections*, p. 35.

48. Chan, *Reflections*, p.83.

49. Chan, *Reflections*, p. 52.

50. Ibid.

51. The different dimensions of orthodoxy are summarized by William Theodore de Bary in *Principle and Practicality: Essays in Neo-Confucianism and Practical Learning*, eds. William Theodore de Bary and Irene Bloom (New York: Columbia University Press, 1979), pp. 16-17.

52. The seminal article on the life of learning and self-cultivation is William Theodore de Bary, "Neo-Confucian Cultivation and the Seventeenth-Century 'Enlightenment,'" in de Bary, *Unfolding*, pp. 141-216. See also Chap. VII herein.

53. I have found this to be reflected in autobiographical expression. See Chaps. IV and V herein and Rodney L. Taylor, "Journey Into Self: The Autobiographical Reflections of Hu Chih," *History of Religions* 21, No. 4 (May 1982): 321-38. An excellent study of the Confucian view of learning and maturation is found in Tu Wei-ming "The Confucian Perception of Adulthood," *Daedalus* 105, No. 2 (Spring 1976):113-27, reprinted in Tu, *Humanity*, pp. 35-56.

54. Chan, *Reflections*, p. 122.

55. Chan, *Reflections*, p. 121.

56. See Taylor, "Journey" and a comparative study of the autobiographies of Kao and Hu Chih, Rodney L. Taylor, "Acquiring A Point of View: Confucian Dimensions of Self-Reflection," *Monumenta Serica* 34 (1979-1980): 145-70.

Chapter III

1. James Hastings, *Encyclopaedia of Religion and Ethics* (New York: Charles Scribner's Sons, 1921), vol. 11, p. 51.

2. Tu Wei-ming, "The Confucian Sage: Exemplar of Personal Knowledge," in *Saints and Virtues*, ed. J. S. Hawley (Berkeley: University of California Press, 1987), pp.75-86.

3. Those who have examined the sage as a religious figure include William Theodore de Bary, "Neo-Confucian Cultivation and the Seventeenth-Century 'Enlightenment,' " in *The Unfolding of Neo-Confucianism*, ed. William Theodore de Bary (New York: Columbia University Press, 1975), pp. 141-216; Tu "The Confucian Sage"; Rodney L. Taylor, *The Cultivation of Sagehood as a Religious Goal in Neo-Confucianism: A Study of Selected Writings of Kao Pan-lung (1562-1626)* (Missoula, Mont.: Scholar's Press/American Academy of Religion, 1978); and Rodney L. Taylor, "Neo-Confucianism, Sagehood and the Religious Dimension," *Journal of Chinese Philosophy* 2, no. 4 (September 1975): 389-415. See also Robert C. Neville, *Soldier, Sage, Saint* (New York: Fordham University Press, 1978).

4. There have been two recent attempts to discuss sainthood as a category within the context of the history of religions: R. Kieckhefer and G. Bond (eds.), *Sainthood: Its Manifestations in World Religions* (Berkeley: University of California Press, 1988); and Hawley, *Saints and Virtues*.

5. The question of imitability and inimitability is well-developed by Kieckhefer and Bond. See "Afterword: Toward a Comparative Study of Sainthood," Kieckhefer and Bond, *Sainthood*, pp. 243-53. It appears to be implicit as well in Hawley's discussion of the saint's role as an example, both *of something* and *to someone*. See J. S. Hawley, "Introduction: Saints and Virtues," in Hawley, *Saints and Virtues*, pp. xiii-xviii

6. Tu, "The Confucian Sage," p. 85.

7. *Analects*, 7:1.

8. *Analects*, 7:34

9. See the discussion of the term *sage* in Chap. II herein.

10. *Analects*, 6:30, 14:42.

11. *Analects*, 8:19, 8:18, 8:21.

12. *Analects*, 8:20.

13. Hawley, *Saints and Virtues*, p. xiii.

14. *Mencius*, 2A:1, 2:B:9.

15. *Mencius*, 2A:2, 3B:9.

16. *Mencius*, 4A:2.

17. *Mencius*, 4A:1.

18. *Mencius*, 7B:25.

19. *Mencius*, 7A:24.

20. *Mencius*, 2B:9.

21. *Mencius*, 5B:1, 2A:2.

22. *Mencius*, 2B:1.

23. *Mencius*, 2A:7.

24. *Mencius*, 6A:7.

25. Ibid.

26. *Mencius*, 6B:2. As the passage explores the point, Mencius argues that nothing separates the ordinary person from the sage.

27. A thorough discussion of the relevance of the goal of sagehood to the Neo-Confucian may be found in both de Bary, "Neo-Confucian Cultivation," and Taylor, *Cultivation of Sagehood*.

28. See de Bary, "Neo-Confucian Cultivation," pp. 153-60 for a discussion of the *Chin-ssu lu*. For a translation of the *Chin-ssu lu*, see Wing-tsit Chan (trans.), *Reflections on Things at Hand: The Neo-Confucian Anthology Compiled by Chu Hsi and Lü Tsu-ch'ien* (New York: Columbia University Press, 1967).

29. Chan, *Reflections*, p. 35.

30. Chan, *Reflections*, p. 307.

31. Chan, *Reflections*, p. 308.

32. *Mencius*, 7A:1.

33. William Theodore de Bary, Wing-tsit Chan, and Burton Watson, *Sources of Chinese Tradition* (New York: Columbia University Press, 1960), p. 559.

34. A number of works have attempted to discuss and interpret mysticism. Two works that are sensitive to the frequent misuse and overuse of the term are: Steven T. Katz, *Mysticism and Religious Traditions* (Oxford: Oxford University Press, 1983); and Frits Staal, *Exploring Mysticism: A Methodological Essay* (Berkeley: University of California Press, 1975). The psychological character of mysticism is discussed by Abraham Maslow, *Religions, Values, and Peak Experiences* (New York: Penguin Books, 1976).

35. Two of the most famous of such experiences are those of Kao P'an-lung and Hu Chih as they are recorded in their autobiographical writings. Both are discussed in this volume, Kao P'an-lung in Chap. IV, and Hu Chih in Chap. V.

36. De Bary, *Sources of Chinese Tradition*, p. 515.

37. Chan, *Reflections*, pp. 74-75.

38. Chan, *Reflections*, p. 85.

39. One finds such expressions in the T'ai-chou school, perhaps the most radical of the followers of Wang Yang-ming. See, for example, William Theodore de Bary, "Individualism and Humanitarianism in Late Ming Thought," in *Self and Society in Ming Thought*, ed. William Theodore de Bary (New York: Columbia University Press, 1970), pp. 171-88.

40. My own research with Neo-Confucian religious autobiography has indicated that in the assessment process of the autobiography the individual concludes that the goal of sagehood is still far in the distance. Such autobiographies tend to end with some statement indicating not what has been accomplished but the distance that still separates the individual from his goal. See, for example, Rodney L. Taylor, "Acquiring a Point of View: Confucian Dimensions of Self-Reflection," *Monumenta Serica* 34 (1979-1980):145-70.

41. De Bary, "Neo-Confucian Cultivation," pp. 156-57.

42. Chan, *Reflections*, p. 299.

43. Chan, *Reflections*, pp. 305-06.

44. Chan, *Reflections*, p. 302.

45. Chan, *Reflections*, p. 303.

46. For a study of sainthood in Christianity, see Richard Kieckhefer, "Imitators of Christ: Sainthood in the Christian Tradition," Kieckhefer and Bond, *Sainthood*, pp. 1-42; and Peter Brown, "The Saint of Exemplar in Late Antiquity," Hawley, *Saints and Virtues*, pp. 3-14.

47. Donald Attwater, *The Penguin Dictionary of Saints* (Baltimore, Md.: Penguin Books, 1965), p. 7.

48. For a discussion of the saint in Islam, see Frederick M. Denny, "Prophet and *Wali*: Sainthood in Islam," in Kieckhefer and Bond, *Sainthood*, pp.69-97.

49. The philology of the term for *sage* is discussed in Chap. II.

50. G. van der Leeuw, *Religion in Essence and Manifestation* (New York: Harper and Row, 1963), p. 236.

51. Joachim Wach, *Sociology of Religion* (Chicago: University of Chicago Press, 1971), p. 358.

52. Ibid.

53. William James, *The Varieties of Religious Experience, A Study in Human Nature* (New York: Modern Library, 1929), pp. 254-69.

54. James, *Varieties*, pp. 266-67.

55. James, *Varieties*, p. 350.

56. Wach, *Sociology of Religion*, p. 358.

57. *Analects*, 8:21.

58. The image of the sage as both a teacher and learner is emphasized by Tu Wei-ming. See Tu, "The Confucian Sage," pp. 73-74.

59. I am indebted to Charles White, who in his capacity as the discussant on a panel where this paper was first presented (American Academy of Religion, San Francisco, December 1981), suggested that traditional models of the saint as he who is only quiet and passive limits the dimensions of sainthood.

60. *Analects*, 14:45.

61. *Analects*, 15:5.

62. *Analects*, 19:23.

Chapter IV

1. Roy Pascal, *Design and Truth in Autobiography* (Cambridge, Mass.: Harvard University Press, 1960), p. 9. Of the few critical studies of autobiography that exist, I find Pascal's to be particularly illuminating. See also James Olney, *Metaphors of Self: The Meaning of Autobiography* (Princeton, N. J.: Princeton University Press, 1972); and John Morris, *Versions of the Self: Studies in English Autobiography from John Bunyan to John Stuart Mill* (New York: Basic Books, 1966).

2. I am relying upon Shea's study of Woolman's *Journal*. See Daniel B. Shea, Jr., *Spiritual Autobiography in Early America* (Princeton, N. J.: Princeton University Press, 1968), pp. 45-84.

3. I take strong issue with Pascal's argument for the exclusive Western origin of autobiography (Pascal, *Design and Truth*, p. 80). Sixteenth- and seventeenth-century Chinese examples will be discussed here. The earlier history of autobiography in China is discussed in Wolfgang Bauer, "Icherleben und Autobiographie im Älteren China," *Heidelberger Jahrbücher 8* (1964): 12-40.

4. Kao P'an-lung, t. (*tzu*) Yün-ts'ung, t. Ts'un-chih, h. (*hao*) Ching-i, c.s. (*chin-shih*) 1589 See *Ming-shih* [*History of the Ming Dynasty*], Ssu-pu pei-yao ed. (Taipei, 1965) 243:9a-11a (*Ming-shih* hereafter *MS*, Ssu-pu pei-yao hereafter *SPPY*); Huang Tsung-hsi, *Ming-ju hsüeh-an* [*The Records of the Ming Scholars*] (Taipei, 1965), pp. 625-42 (hereafter *MJHA*); L. Carrington Goodrich and Chaoying Fang eds., *Dictionary of Ming*

Biography (New York: Columbia University Press, 1976), pp. 701-10 (hereafter *DMB*). Two additional sources not listed in *DMB*: William Theodore de Bary, "Neo-Confucian Cultivation and the Seventeenth-Century 'Enlightenment,'" in *The Unfolding of Neo-Confucianism*, ed. William Theodore de Bary (New York: Columbia University Press, 1975), pp. 178-88; Rodney L. Taylor, "Neo-Confucianism, Sagehood and the Religious Dimension," *Journal of Chinese Philosophy* 2, no 4 (1975): 389-415. Kao's own writings are found in *Kao-tzu i-shu* [*Literary Remains of Master Kao*], ed. Ch'en Lung-cheng, 1876 reprint edition (hereafter *KTIS*); *Kao-tzu ch'üan-shu* [*Complete Works of Master Kao*]; ed. Hua Hsi-min, 1742 ed.; *Kao-tzu wei-k'o-kao* [*Unpublished Manuscripts of Master Kao*], Rare Book Collection of the Peking National Library, reel no. 793, Library of Congress, Washington, D.C. The most complete biographies are *Kao Chung-hsien kung nien-p'u* [*Chronological Biography of Kao Chung-hsien*], ed. Hua Yün-ch'eng, appendix to *KTIS* (hereafter *nien p'u*); Yeh Mao-ts'ai, *Hsing-chuang* [*Annals of Conduct*], *Tung-lin shu yüan-chih* [*Records of the Tung-lin Academy*], ed. Hsü Hsien, 1881 edition, 7:47b-59b.

5. See de Bary, "Neo-Confucian Cultivation," pp. 141-216; also see William Theodore de Bary, "Introduction" and "Individualism and Humanitarianism in Late Ming Thought," in *Self and Society in Ming Thought*, ed. William Theodore de Bary (New York: Columbia University Press, 1970), pp. 1-38, 145-247.

6. See de Bary, "Neo-Confucian Cultivation," pp. 194-207, A number of trends of Ming thought have been summarized in William Theodore de Bary, "The Ming Project and Ming Thought," *Ming Studies* 2 (Spring 1976): 19-25.

7. See Burton Watson (trans.), *The Old Man Who Does as He Pleases: Selections From the Poetry and Prose of Lu Yu* (New York: Columbia University Press, 1973). The travel journal is not used by Lu Yu as an occasion for philosophical discussion. Kao's *San-shih chi* [*Recollections of Three Seasons*], *KTIS*, 10:25b-48a, is in sharp contrast to Lu Yu's journal on this point.

8. There appears to be no one term for *autobiography*. Two frequently used are *chi*, record or recollection, and *nien-p'u*, chronological biography, although strictly speaking neither need be autobiographical. There are some ninety autobiographical *nien-p'u* during the Ming dynasty alone. See Richard Howard, "Modern Chinese Biographical Writing," *Journal of Asian Studies* 21, no. 4 (1962): 468. Given various titles employed for autobiography, this should be some indication of its popularity.

9. Bauer, "Icherleben und Autobiographie," pp. 12-40.

10. Quoted in Pascal, *Design and Truth*, pp. 18-19.

11. Kao P'an-lung, *K'un-hsüeh chi*, [*Recollections of the Toils of Learning*], *KTIS*, 313b-18a (hereafter *KHC*); Hu Chih, *K'un-hsüeh chi*, *MJHA*, pp. 221-24.

12. *Analects*, 16:9.

13. Hu Chih, t. Cheng-fu, h. I-chü, h. Lu-shan, c.s. 1556. See *MJHA*, pp. 216-28; *DMB*, pp. 624-25.

14. Lo Hung-hsien, t. Ta-fu, h. Nien-an, c.s. 1529. See *MS*, 283:9b-10b; *MJHA*, pp. 157-78; *DMB*, pp. 980-84.

15. See Pei-yi Wu, "The Spiritual Autobiography of Te-ch'ing," in de Bary, *Unfolding*, pp. 67-92.

16. Te Ch'ing begins his autobiography with recollections of childhood. This may be due to the particular importance he placed on the relation with his mother during his formative years (Wu, "Spiritual Autobiography," pp. 68-72).

17. Hua Yün-ch'eng, t. Ju-li, h. Feng-ch'ao, c.s. 1622. See *MS*, 258:2b-5b; *MJHA*, p. 669; Heinrich Busch, "The Tung-lin Academy and Its Political and Philosophical Significance" (Ph.D. diss., Columbia University, 1954), pp. 207-08, also published in *Monumenta Serica* 14 (1949-1955): 1-163.

18. Yeh Mao-ts'ai, t. Ts'an-chih, h. Yüan-shih, c.s. 1589. See *MS*, 231:13a-b; *MJHA*, pp. 660-61; Busch, "Tung-lin," pp. 229-30.

19. Li Fu-yang, t. Tsung-ch'eng, h. Yüan-ch'ung, c.s. 1583. See *Tung-lin lieh-ch'uan* [*Biographies of the Tung-lin*], ed. Ch'en Ting, 1711 ed., 21:18a.

20. Ku Hsien-ch'eng, t. Shu-shih, h. Ching-yang, c.s. 1580. See *MS*, 231:1a-3b; *MJHA*, pp. 614-25; *DMB*, pp. 736-44; Busch, "Tung-lin," pp. 7-28, 106-76; Charles Hucker, "The Tung-lin Movement of the Late Ming Period," in *Chinese Thought and Institutions*, ed. John Fairbank (Chicago: University of Chicago Press, 1964), pp. 132-62.

21. After giving family background, both biographies describe events early in Kao's childhood (*nien-p'u*, 2b; *hsing-chuang*, 48b).

22. Tu Wei-ming, "The Confucian Perception of Adulthood," *Daedalus* 105, no. 2 (Spring 1976): 115.

23. For a definition and discussion of the religious dimension of the tradition, see "Introduction" herein.

24. The question of the relation of ethics and religion in the Confucian tradition has yet to be fully explored. Kupperman's suggestion that the role of ethics is similar in both religious thought and Confucian thought is one attempt. See Joel J. Kupperman, "Confucius and the Nature of Religious Ethics," *Philosophy East and West* 21, no. 2 (April 1971): 189-94. The kind of approach taken by Little and Twiss, differentiating moral and religious action guides (MAGs and RAGs) may shed further light on the Confucian context of the problem even if it indicates an interdependence of guides. See David Little and Sumner B. Twiss, Jr., "Basic Terms in the Study of Religious Ethics" in *Religion and Morality: A Collection of Essays*, eds. Gene Outka and John P. Reeder, Jr. (Garden City, N.Y.: Anchor Books, 1973), pp. 35-77. Such an interdependence is suggested, though in different terms, by Chung-ying Cheng. See Chung-ying Cheng, "Dialectic of Confucian Morality and Metaphysics of Man," *Philosophy East and West* 21, no. 2 (April 1971): 114-18.

25. *KHC*, 14a.

26. Ibid.

27. *KHC*, 14a-b.

28. Lu Ts'ui-ming, t. Ku-ch'iao, a follower of Ch'en Hsien-chang. See *Hsin-hui hsien-chih* [*Gazetteer of Hsin-hui*], ed. Lin Hsing-chang and Huang P'ei-fang (Taipei, 1966), p. 259.

29. Wu Chih-yüan, t. Tzu-wang, h. Ch'ü-an. See *Chia-shan hsien-chih* [*Gazetteer of Chia-shan*], 1894 ed., 20:2b.

30. *KHC*, 14b. Part of Kao's crisis involves a recognition that he is not able to appreciate adequately the beauty of the scenery. The relation of aesthetic sensitivity and self-cultivation suggests an important unexplored area of Neo-Confucian thought.

31. *KHC*, 15a.

32. See Chap. VII herein. For more detailed studies of Neo-Confucian meditation, see Okada Takehiko, *Zazen to seiza* [*Buddhist and Confucian Meditation*] (Tokyo, 1972); Rodney L. Taylor, *The Confucian Way of Contemplation: Okada Takehiko and the Tradition of Quiet-Sitting* (Columbia, S.C.: University of South Carolina, 1988).

33. See *KHC*, 15b-16a, for the full context of Kao's enlightenment experience. De Bary has analyzed Neo-Confucian enlightenment in "Neo-Confucian Cultivation."

34. *Analects*, 7:15.

35. Ch'eng I and Ch'eng Hao, *Erh-Ch'eng ch'üan-shu* [*The Complete Works of the Two Ch'eng Brothers*], *SPPY* ed., 6:3a.

36. The "Great Transformation" is the cycle of increase and decrease of *yin* and *yang* in the four seasons.

37. The "six points" refer to the four compass points combined with the zenith and nadir.

38. There is a previous contact with Buddhist institutions (*KHC*, 14a; *hsing-chuang*, 49b). Apparently, however, this is the first effort to study Buddhism.

39. Arguments against Buddhism are found in *I-tuan pien* [*Criticism of Heterodoxy*], *KTIS*, 2:52a-54a.

40. *KHC*, 16b.

41. Ibid.

42. *KHC*, 16b-17a.

43. *KHC*, 17a. The passages suggest spontaneousness and effort.

44. *KHC*, 17b.

45. Kao's work on the *Great Learning* includes three writings, all in *KTIS*: *Ku-pen ta-hsüeh t'i-tz'u* [*Introduction to the Old Version of the Great Learning*], 3:1a-2b; *Ta-hsüeh shou-chang yüeh-i* [*The First Chapter of the Great Learning Narrowly Defined*], 3:2b-4a; *Ta-hsüeh shou-chang kuang-i* [*General Interpretations of the First Chapter of the Great Learning*], 3:4a-12b. In the *Ku-pen ta-hsüeh t'i-tz'u* Kao discusses the controversy over the interpretation and rearrangement of the text. He states that the problems of this text had weighed upon him for many years (*KTIS*, 3:1a). This was apparently written in 1611 (*nien-p'u*, 15a), the point at which his doubts were resolved.

46. Kao was recalled in 1621. He asked for and was granted retirement in 1623, only to be recalled again in 1624. Through the hostility of the eunuch Wei Chung-hsien, Kao was soon removed from his position as censor-in-chief in a general purge of Tung-lin men, a purge that lasted into 1626 when, in April, Kao took his own life by drowning rather than face arrest and torture (see *MS*, 243:10a-b; *MJHA*, p. 625; *DMB*, pp. 704-8; Busch, "Tung-lin," pp. 50-95; Hucker, "Tung-lin Movement," pp. 153-56).

47. *Ta-hsüeh huo-wen* [*Questions and Answers on the Great Learning*]; *Chu-tzu i-shu* [*The Literary Remains of Master Chu*], undated ed., vol. 2.

48. Kao seems to have paraphrased the text of the *Ta-hsüeh huo-wen*. This passage is also found in the *Chin-ssu lu* [*Reflections on Things at Hand*]. See Wing-tsit Chan (trans.), *Reflections on Things at Hand, The Neo-Confucian Anthology Compiled by Chu Hsi and Lü Tsu-ch'ien* (New York: Columbia University Press, 1967), p. 133. In the *Chin-ssu lu*, the passage is assigned to Ch'eng I-ch'uan not to Chu Hsi.

49. The phrase *a square inch of space* means one particular spot.

50. This phrase is found in both the *Hsiao-hsüeh* [*Elementary Learning*] and the *Chin-ssu lu*. In the *Hsiao-hsüeh*, the passage is assigned to Ch'eng Ming-tao (*Hsiao-hsüeh chi-chu* [*The Hsiao-hsüeh with Collected Commentaries*], ed. Ch'en Hsüan, *SPPY* ed., 5:17a). In the *Chin-ssu lu* Ch'eng I-ch'uan is credited with the saying (Chan, *Reflections*, p. 137).

51. As the translation of the title *Hsiao-hsüeh* indicates, the work was intended primarily for young people.

52. *Hsiao-hsüeh chi-chu*, 5:17a. The passage Kao quotes as an explanation of the term *ch'iang-tzu*, bodily frame, is the commentary to the statement that initially mystifies Kao, "The mind must be retained within the bodily frame."

53. Lo Mao-chung, t. Chih-an, *KTIS*, 8a:63-64b.

54. Li Ts'ai, t. Meng-ch'eng, h. Chien-lo, c.s. 1562. Li's cultivation stressed *chih-hsiu*, the cultivation of the point of rest (see *MS*, 227:3b-4b; *MJHA*, pp. 293-310; *DMB*, pp. 874-77).

55. *Chih-pen*, knowing the root, is from the *Great Learning*. See James Legge, *The Chinese Classics, Vol. I, Confucian Analects, the Great Learning and the Doctrine of the Mean* (Oxford: Clarendon Press, 1893), p. 365.

56. The mourning is for Kao's foster parents. His foster mother died in 1584 (*nien-p'u*, 3b), while his foster father died in the seventh month of 1589 after Kao's completion of the *chin-shih* degree (*nien-p'u*, 4b-5a).

57. Kao presents himself in 1592 rather than immediately after the completion of the *chin-shih* degree because of the three-year mourning for his foster parents.

58. The appointment that Kao receives is as a *hsing-jen*, emissary, in the sixth month of 1592 (*nien-p'u*, 5b; *hsing-chuang*, 49a).

59. Chao-t'ien kung, a Taoist temple located in Chiang-ning (Kiangsu). It was used for the practice and instruction of officials in court ceremony and ritual.

60. It is difficult to judge from the passage whether there is a separation in time between the quiet-sitting and the sentence that begins, "Suddenly I thought of the sentence . . . ." The chronological biography assumes that there is no break between the two: "One day he had been quiet-sitting a lengthy time and suddenly he thought of the sentence . . . ." (*nien-p'u*, 6b).

61. The passage occurs in the *Book of Changes*, SPPY ed., 1:2b.

62. Kao's part in the struggle between the so-called pure critics and the Grand Secretariat led to his banishment. In the triennial personal evaluation of 1593, the pure critics, in a dominant position, removed sympathizers with the grand secretaries. The positions were soon reversed, however, with the grand secretaries revenging their loss through the removal of the pure critics. When Kao returned from an official trip to Nanking in late 1593, he denounced the recent purge of a number of his close friends. The result was his own demotion (see *MS*, 243:9b; *MJHA*, p. 625; *DMB*, pp. 702, 738-39).

63. The Ch'ien-t'ang River flowing close to Hangchow (Chekiang).

64. The Liu-ho Tower on the bank of the Ch'ien-t'ang River.

65. For identification of these phrases, see Okada, *Zazen to seiza*, p. 106 (Taylor, *Confucian Way*, p. 130.)

66. *Mencius*, 2A:2. See D. C. Lau (trans.), *Mencius*, (Middlesex: Penguin Books Ltd., 1970), p. 77.

67. *Pu-chu*, a standard Buddhist phrase for nonattachment.

68. *Analects*, 7:15. Legge translates the passage: "With coarse rice to eat, with water to drink, and my bended arm for a pillow; I have still joy in the midst of these things . . . ." (Legge, *Chinese Classics*, p. 200).

69. Ch'eng Hao and Ch'eng I, *Erh-Ch'eng ch'üan-shu*, 6:3a.

70. See footnote 36.

71. See footnote 37.

72. The "Limitless Ultimate" or the "Ultimateless" is the beginning point of the "Diagram of the Supreme Ultimate," Chou Tun-i's cosmogony.

73. Two short writings by Kao in *KTIS* concern the Water Dwelling: *Shui-chü chi* [*Recollections of the Water Dwelling*], 10:48b-49a, and *K'o-lou chi* [*Recollections of the Suitable Loft*], 10:49a-50a.

74. Kao's mother and father were both seventy years old in 1596. His father died in the third month and his mother died in the seventh month of that year (*nien-p'u*, 11b).

75. This may well refer to the *Hsiao-hsüeh* of Chu Hsi.

76. An allusion to *Analects*, 16:9.

77. *Mencius*, 3A:5. *Locus classicus, Shu-ching*. See James Legge, *The Chinese Classics, Vol. III, The Shoo King or the Book of Historical Documents* (Oxford: Clarendon Press, 1893), p. 252.

78. *Locus classicus* of the phrase seems to be *Shih-Ching* (Mao number 239). See James Legge, *The Chinese Classics, Vol. IV, The She King or Book of Poetry* (Oxford: Clarendon Press, 1893), p. 445. The *Doctrine of the Mean* quotes this ode (Legge, *The Chinese Classics, Vol. I*, pp. 391-93).

79. *Mencius*, 2A:2. I have followed the rendering of D. C. Lau: "You must work at it and never let it leave your mind" (Lau, *Mencius*, p. 78).

80. *Mencius*, 2A:2.

81. For the years between 1607 and 1611, the *nien-p'u* records that Kao took part in several meetings and traveled to at least one academy. Aside from these brief incidents, nothing further for these years is recorded (*nien-p'u*, 3b-15a).

82. The reference seems to be to the *Ku-pen ta-hsüeh* [*Old Version of the Great Learning*] recorded in the chronological biography for 1611 (*nien-p'u*, 15a), a work found in *KTIS* under the title *Ku-pen ta-hsüeh t'i-tz'u*.

83. The 1876 edition of the *KTIS* has *t'ien-ti*, "Heaven and Earth," rather than *t'ien-li*, "Principle of Heaven." I have followed *MJHA*, p. 626.

Chapter V

1. A prominent figure in this respect, and one I will return to is Lin Chao-en. See Liu Ts'un-yan, "Lin Chao-en (1517-1598), The Master of Three Teachings," *T'oung Pao* 53 (1967): 253-278; Judith Berling, "The Uniting of the Ways: The Syncretic Thought of Lin Chao-en (1517-1598)," Ph.D. diss., Columbia University, 1976 published as *The Syncretic Religion of Lin Chao-en* (New York: Columbia University Press, 1980); and Judith Berling, "Paths of Convergence: Interactions of Inner Alchemy Taoism and Neo-Confucianism," *Journal of Chinese Philosophy* 6, no. 2 (June 1979): 123-47.

2. See Liu Ts'un-yan, "Taoist Self-Cultivation in Ming Thought," in *Self and Society in Ming Thought*, ed. William Theodore de Bary (New York: Columbia University Press, 1970), pp. 291-330; Pei-yi Wu, "The Spiritual Autobiography of Te-ch'ing," in *The Unfolding of Neo-Confucianism*, ed. William Theodore de Bary (New York: Columbia University Press, 1975), pp. 67-92; and Sung-peng Hsü, *A Buddhist Leader in Ming China: The Life and Thought of Han-shan Te-ch'ing (1546-1623)* (University Park, Penn.: Pennsylvania State University Press, 1979).

3. Note, for example, the discussion of the relationship between Buddhism and Confucianism in Araki Kengo, *Bukkyo to Jukyo* [*Buddhism and Confucianism*], (Kyoto, 1963).

4. Hu Chih, t. Cheng-fu, h. I-chü, h. Lu-shan, c.s. 1556. See Jung Chao-tsu, *Ming-tai ssu-hsiang shih* [*History of Ming Thought*], (Taipei, 1969), pp. 206-18; Huang Tsung-hsi, *Ming-ju hsüeh-an* [*The Records of the Ming Scholars*], (Taipei, *1965*), Chap. 22 (hereafter cited as *MJHA*); L. Carrington Goodrich and Chaoying Fang, eds., *Dictionary of Ming Biography* (New York: Columbia University Press, 1976), pp. 624-25 (hereafter cited as *DMB*).

5. Wang Shou-jen, t. Po-an, h. Yang-ming, c.s. 1499. See *DMB*, pp. 1408-16.

6. For a discussion of sagehood see Chap. III. In addition, see William Theodore de Bary, "Neo-Confucian Cultivation and the Seventeenth-Century 'Enlightenment,'" in de Bary, *Unfolding* pp. 141-216; Rodney L. Taylor, *The Cultivation of Sagehood as a Religious Goal in Neo-Confucianism: A Study of Selected Writings of Kao P'an-lung (1562-1626)* (Missoula, Mont.: Scholar's Press/American Academy of Religion, 1978); Rodney L. Taylor, "Neo-Confucianism, Sagehood and the Religious Dimension," *Journal of Chinese Philosophy* 2, no. 4 (1975): 389-415.

7. On Ming autobiography, see Chap. IV. See also Pei-yi Wu, "Spiritual Autobiography," a study of the autobiography of Te Ch'ing.

8. Hu Chih, *K'un-hsüeh chi,* [*Recollections of the Toils of Learning*], appendix to *Heng-lu ching-she hsü-kao*, ed. Kuo Tzu-chang, 1902 edition; also found in *MJHA* 22: 6a-10b (hereafter cited as *KHC*).

9. Ou-yang Te, t. Ch'ung-i, h. Nan-yeh, c.s. 1523. *DMB*, pp. 1102-04. See *KHC*, 6b.

10. *KHC*, 7a.

11. *KHC*, 6b.

12. *Analects*, 2:4.

13. Lo Hung-hsien, t. Ta-fu, h. Nien-an, c.s. 1529. *DMB*, pp. 980-84. *KHC*, 7a.

14. See Chap. VII and also Rodney L. Taylor, *The Confucian Way of Contemplation: Okada Takehiko and The Tradition of Quiet-Sitting* (Columbia, S.C.: University of South Carolina, 1988).

15. *KHC*, 7a.

16. *MJHA*, 22/1a. See also Keng Ting-hsiang, *Keng T'ien-t'ai hsien-sheng wen-chi* [*Collecton of Literary Works of Keng Ting-hsiang*], (Taipei, 1970), p. 1228.

17. Jung Chao-tsu identifies Teng as a Buddhist (Jung Chao-tsu, *Ming-tai ssu-hsiang shih*, p. 206.

18. *KHC*, 7b.

19. Ibid.

20. Ibid.

21. Ibid.

22. Ibid.

23. Ibid.

24. Ibid.

25. Frits Staal, *Exploring Mysticism: A Methodological Essay* (Berkeley: University of California Press, 1975), pp. 168-89.

26. *KHC*, 7b.

27. Ibid.

28. Ibid.

29. Ibid. See also Keng Ting-hsiang's biography of Hu, *Keng T'ien-t'ai hsien-sheng wen chi*, p. 1229.

30. *MJHA*, 22/1b; Jung Chao-tsu, *Ming-tai ssu-hsiang shih*, pp. 209-11.

31. Ch'ien Tê-hung, t. Hung-fu, h. Hsü-shan, c.s. 1532. *DMB*, pp. 241-44.

32. *KHC*, 7b.

33. Ibid.

34. *KHC*, 8a.

35. See Abraham Maslow, *Religions, Values, and Peak Experiences* (New York: Penguin Books, 1976), pp. 59-68.

36. *Mencius*, 7A:4

37. *Erh-Ch'eng i-shu* [*Surviving Works of the Two Ch'eng Brothers*], 2A/3a-b in *Erh-Ch'eng ch'üan-shu*, [*The Complete Works of the Two Ch'eng Brothers*], SPPY edition, (Taipei, 1969).

38. *Hsiang-shan ch'üan-chi*, [*The Complete Works of Lu Hsiang-shan*], SPPY edition, (Taipei, 1970) 22:5a.

39. *KHC*, 8a.

40. Ibid.

41. Ibid.

42. Ibid.

43. Ibid.

44. Ibid.

45. Ibid.

46. *KHC*, 8b.

47. See *KHC*, 9a-b.

48. *KHC*, 10b.

49. *The Compact Edition of the Oxford English Dictionary, Vol. II* (Oxford: Oxford University Press, 1971), p. 3210.

50. Robert D. Baird, *Category Formation and the History of Religions* (The Hague: Mouton, 1971), p. 147.

51. Ibid.

52. Ibid.

53. Ibid.

54. The claim for nonpropositional truth has been argued at length by Wilfred Cantwell Smith in his *The Meaning and End of Religion* (New York: Harper and Row, 1962), however, a serious critique of his position has been offered by Ninian Smart, *The Philosophy of Religion* (New York: Random House, 1970), pp. 126-27.

55. Baird, *Category Formation*, p. 147.

56. Baird, *Category Formation*, p. 145.

57. *MJHA*, 22/1a.

58. Maslow, *Religions, Values, and Peak Experiences*, pp. 59-68.

59. Lin Chao-en, t. Mou-hsün, h. Lung-chiang. *DMB*, pp. 912-15.

60. Berling has worked out a rather interesting scheme of historical types of syncretism and has argued for the syncretic nature of Lin Chao-en's thought. Syncretism appears to me to be primarily a problem in philosophy of religion, and I see no clear attention to the issue of sorting truth claims from practice. As such, I would have to

interpret Berling's types of syncretism as forms of interaction between traditions that do not go beyond what we have described as historical interrelationships of various kinds. There may be reasons for addressing these as examples of syncretism, particularly at a popular level, but if it is used too widely as an interpretation it will only serve to diminish the potential for the specialized use of the term in incidents where it does apply. See Berling, *The Syncretic Religion*, chaps. 1-3.

61. Note, for example, Alicia Matsunaga, *The Buddhist Philosophy of Assimilation: The Historical Development of the Honji-Suijaku Theory* (Tokyo, 1969).

Chapter VI

1. Okada Takehiko, *Zazen to seiza* [*Buddhist and Confucian Meditation*], (Tokyo, 1972), p. 95. See translation in Rodney L. Taylor, *The Confucian Way of Contemplation: Okada Takehiko and the Tradition of Quiet-Sitting* (Columbia, S.C.: University of South Carolina, 1988), p. 121.

2. Ibid.

3. See Chap. II and the role of quietude and activity in the figure of the sage.

4. On Lo Tsung-yen, see Huang Tsung-hsi, *Sung-Yüan hsüeh-an* [*The Records of the Sung and Yüan Scholars*], (Taipei, 1975), 10:58-65.

5. On Li T'ung, see Huang, *Sung-Yüan hsüeh-an*, 10:65-79.

6. Huang, *Sung-Yüan hsüeh-an*, 10:63.

7. Huang, *Sung-Yüan hsüeh-an*, 10:64.

8. Alfred Forke, *Geschichte der neueren chinesischen Philosophie* (Hamburg: Friederichen, DeGruyter and Co., 1938), pp. 156-63.

9. Okada, *Zazen to seiza*, p. 118. Taylor, *Confucian Way*, p. 140. See also, Huang, *Sung-Yüan hsüeh-an*, 10:72.

10. The term *responsibility, i-jen*, suggests the responsibility of holding office and assuming one's rightful duty. Used in this way, it reinforces Chu Hsi's own sense of the eremitic ideal in the present poem.

11. The verse is quoted in Okada, *Zazen to seiza*, pp. 118-19. See also Conrad Schirokauer, "Chu Hsi and Hu Hung," in *Chu Hsi and Neo-Confucianism*, ed. Wing-tsit Chan (Honolulu: University of Hawaii Press, 1986), pp. 480-502.

12. Quoted in Okada, *Zazen to seiza*, p. 119, Taylor, *Confucian Way*, p. 140.

13. Hsün-tzu, 1:1.

14. Okada, *Zazen to seiza*, p. 119, Taylor, *Confucian Way*, p. 141.

15. Tu Wei-ming, *Humanity and Self-Cultivation: Essays in Confucian Thought* (Berkeley: Asian Humanities Press, 1979), p. 129.

16. Okada, *Zazen to seiza*, p. 123, Taylor, *Confucian Way*, pp. 143-44.

17. Note, for example, Lu Hsiang-shan's practice of quiet-sitting. See Siu-chi Huang, *Lu Hsiang-shan: A Twelfth Century Chinese Idealist Philosopher* (New Haven, Conn.: American Oriental Society, 1944), pp. 69-70.

18. See Wing-tsit Chan's seminal article on the role played by Chu Hsi in the formation of Neo-Confucianism. Wing-tsit Chan, "Chu Hsi's Completion of Neo-Confucianism," in *Études Song—Sung Studies: In Memoriam Étienne Balazs*, ed. Françoise Aubin, ser. II, no. 1 (1973), pp. 59-90.

19. On the range of meanings to orthodoxy during the Ming see William Theodore de Bary, "Introduction," in *Principle and Practicality: Essays in Neo-Confucianism and Practical Learning*, eds. William Theodore de Bary and Irene Bloom (New York: Columbia University Press, 1976), pp. 16-17.

20. Tu, *Essays*, p. 130.

21. Tu Wei-ming, *Neo-Confucian Thought in Action: Wang Yang-ming's Youth (1472-1509)* (Berkeley: University of California Press, 1963), p. 217.

22. Tu, *Essays*, p. 146.

23. Wing-tsit Chan (trans.), *Instructions for Practical Living and Other Neo-Confucian Writings by Wang Yang-ming* (New York: Columbia University Press, 1963), p. 217.

24. Okada, *Zazen to seiza*, p. 91, Taylor, *Confucian Way*, p. 118 and Tu, *Essays*, p. 149.

25. Tu, *Essays*, p. 149.

26. Chan, *Instructions*, p. 217.

27. See L. Carrington Goodrich and Chaoying Fang (eds.), *Dictionary of Ming Biography 1368-1644* (hereafter cited as *DMB*.) (New York: Columbia University Press, 1976), pp. 980-84.

28. This is exemplified in William Theodore de Bary, "Introduction," in *The Unfolding of Neo-Confucianism*, ed. William Theodore de Bary (New York: Columbia University Press, 1975), pp. 18-19. A further discussion is found in William Theodore de Bary, "Neo-Confucian Cultivation and the Seventeenth-Century 'Enlightenment,' " in de Bary, *Unfolding*, pp. 194-99. See also, Tu, *Essays*, pp. 149-54.

29. See Heinrich Busch, "The Tung-lin Academy and its Political and Philosophical Significance" (Ph.D. diss., Columbia University, 1945). (Page references refer to the dissertation.) Also published in *Monumenta Serica* 14 (1949-1955): 1-163. See also Rodney L. Taylor, *The Cultivation of Sagehood as a Religious Goal in Neo-Confucianism: A Study of Selected Writings of Kao P'an-lung (1562-1626)* (Missoula, Mont.: Scholar's Press/American Academy of Religion, 1978), pp. 78-88, 187-202.

30. See William Theodore de Bary, "Individualism and Humanitarianism in Late Ming Thought," in *Self and Society in Ming Thought*, ed. William Theodore de Bary (New York: Columbia University Press, 1970), pp. 145-247.

31. See Chap. VII.

32. Busch, "Tung-lin," pp. 168-74, 178-88; on Ku see *DMB*, pp. 736-44; on Kao see *DMB*, pp. 701-10.

33. See Taylor, *Cultivation of Sagehood*, pp. 47-58.

34. Chan, "Chu Hsi's Completion," p. 63.

35. Busch, "Tung-lin," p. 174.

36. *Chung-yung*, 1:4.

37. Busch, "Tung-lin," p. 174, with some minor word changes.

38. See Chap. VII.

39. See Chap. IV.

40. The theme is developed in Rodney L. Taylor, "Acquiring a Point of View: Confucian Dimensions of Self-Reflection," *Monumenta Serica* 34 (1979-1980): 145-70.

41. See Chap. VII where the dimensions of these terms are explored.

42. Tu, *Essays*, p. 145.

43. See Busch, "Tung-lin," pp. 126-34. Kao wrote a refutation of Buddhism titled *I-tuan pien* [*Criticism of Heterodoxy*] See *Kao-tzu i-shu*, [*Literary Remains of Master*

Kao], ed. Ch'en Lung-cheng, 1876 reprint edition, 3:51b-54a; a partial translation is contained in Rodney L. Taylor, *Cultivation of Sagehood*, p. 21.

44. See Pei-yi Wu, "The Spiritual Autobiography of Te-ch'ing," *Unfolding*, pp. 83-84.

45. See, for example, *Shan-chü k'o-ch'eng [An Agenda for Dwelling in the Mountains]*, *Kao-tzu i-shu* 3:18a, translated in Taylor, *Cultivation of Sagehood*, pp. 195-96.

46. See, for example, Busch, "Tung-lin," pp. 110-25 where the attacks on Wang Yang-ming followers are discussed in some detail.

47. Okada cautions against value judgments in this question. "In general terms those who are in a position of defending Buddhism have a tendency to criticize the Chu Hsi learning and the Yang-ming learning as a remolded and renovated Zen, particularly the Yang-ming learning. Chu Hsi and Yang-ming were critical of Zen Buddhism in general, but when you speak of it from the position of Buddhism, their arguments are said to be taken from Zen Buddhism itself." (Okada, *Zazen to seiza* p. 95, Taylor, *Confucian Way*, p. 121.)

48. Strenski raises some basic philosophical issues involved in attempting to define and explicate the sudden/gradual categories and goes on to suggest an intriguing solution based upon the predominance of a prior epistemological model in meditational practice. "Typically, it is facilely assumed that this problem is merely a *factual* matter about temporal duration. . . . What could have been the possible interest for the early Buddhist in saying that enlightenment was to be attained gradually?" See Ivan Strenski, "Gradual Enlightenment, Sudden Enlightenment and Empiricism," *Philosophy East and West* 30, no. 1 (Jan. 1980), pp. 3-4.

49. See Chap. V for a close analysis of these terms.

50. Liu Ts'un-yan, "Taoist Self-Cultivation in Ming Thought," in de Bary, *Self and Society*, p. 312.

51. The term remains primarily as description of what others do or believe and to this degree it often becomes a value judgment.

52. The manner in which the beliefs remain misunderstood with the application of the term eclecticism suggests the quite spurious nature of the term itself.

53. See Chap. V where syncretism is fully explored.

54. Robert Baird has suggested that the term *synthesis* might be applied to an implied unity but is more concerned with its potential self-contradictory claim than the creation of a new position with correspondingly new truth claims as I argue. See Robert Baird, *Category Formation and the History of Religions* (The Hague: Mouton, 1971), p. 147.

55. See Thomas A. Metzger, *Escape From Predicament: Neo-Confucianism and China's Evolving Political Culture* (New York: Columbia University Press, 1977), pp. 52-53.

56. See Chap. V on the technical nature of syncretism.

Chapter VII

1. On the use of the term *neo-orthodox*, see William Theodore de Bary, "Neo-Confucian Cultivation and the Seventeenth-Century 'Enlightenment,' " in *The Unfolding of Neo-Confucianism*, ed. William Theodore de Bary (New York: Columbia University Press, 1975), p. 180 and also Rodney L. Taylor, "Neo-Confucianism, Sagehood and the Religious Dimension," *Journal of Chinese Philosophy*, 2, no. 4 (September 1975): 393.

2. See Chap. VI where the overview of quiet-sitting is presented.

3. William Theodore de Bary, "Introduction," de Bary, *Unfolding*, pp. 13-15.

4. For a discussion of the degree to which sagehood may be spoken of as a religious goal, see Taylor, "Neo-Confucianism, Sagehood," pp. 389-415.

5. Kao P'an-lung, *K'un-hsüeh chi* [*Recollections of the Toils of Learning*], (hereafter referred to as *KHC*), found in *Kao-tzu i-shu* [*Literary Remains of Kao P'an-lung*], Ch'en Lung-cheng (1585-1645) ed., 1876 ed., 3:13b. (hereafter referred to as *KTIS*). For more details, see *Kao Chung-hsien kung nien-p'u* [*Chronological Biography of Kao P'an-lung*], Hua Yün-ch'eng (d. 1648) edition, appendix to *KTIS*, 15b (hereafter referred to as *nien-p'u*).

6. *KHC*, 14a.

7. *nien p'u*, 12a.

8. *Shui-chü chi* [*Recollections of the Water Dwelling*], *KTIS* 10:48b-49a and *K'o-lou chi* [*Recollections of the Suitable Loft*], *KTIS* 10:49a-50a and *KHC* 15a, exemplify varying degrees of seclusion.

9. de Bary, "Neo-Confucian Cultivation," p. 172.

10. This includes Wang Yang-ming, Wang Chi (1498-1583) and others. See de Bary, "Introduction," p. 17.

11. Tu Wei-ming warns against overstressing the connection between Yen and Wang Yang-ming. While they shared a concern for the relationship between knowledge and moral activism, there were substantial differences in the sources of such knowledge for each man. Their similarity is striking, however, in their criticism of quiet-sitting. Tu Wei-ming, "Yen Yüan: From Inner Experience to Lived Concreteness," de Bary, *Unfolding*, pp. 511-41.

12. *KHC*, 15a.

13. *Analects*, 1:1.

14. *San-shih chi, KTIS* 10:25b-48a (hereafter referred to as *SSC*).

15. Kao was demoted to the lowly post of supernumerary jail warden. Huang Tsung-hsi, *Ming-ju hsüeh-an* [*The Records of the Ming Scholars*] (Taipei, 1965), p. 625 (hereafter referred to as *MJHA*).

16. *SSC*, 35b.

17. *KHC*, 15a.

18. Ibid.

19. Ibid.

20. The Neo-Confucian retention of principle, *li*, is suggestive, however, of one major area of difference.

21. *KHC*, 14b-15a.

22. According to the chronological biography Kao visited the T'ao-kuang, Huang-lung, and Ti-chiu Temples in the Wu-lin Mountains. See *nien-p'u*, 12a.

23. *Shan-chü k'o-ch'eng* [*An Agenda for Dwelling in the Mountains*], *KTIS* 3:18a.

24. While sojourning in the Wu-lin Mountains in 1598, Kao wrote *Fu-ch'i kuei* [*Rules for "Returning in Seven"*] describing the schedule for a period of seclusion (*nien-p'u*, 12a).

25. *FCK*, 18b-19a.

26. *KHC*, 16a.

27. The entry for 1600 in the chronological biography records that Kao was practicing quiet-sitting with Wu Tzu-wang and several others in the *Shui-chü*, Water Dwelling, (*nien-p'u*, 12b).

28. *KHC*, 16b.

29. *Shui-chü chi*, 48b-49a.

30. *KHC*, 15a-b.

31. *Shan-chü k'o-ch'eng*, 18a

32. *Nien-p'u*, 12a.

33. *FCK*, 19a.

34. *Nien-p'u*, 12b-13a. Chu Hsi, *T'iao-hsi chen* [*An Exhortation on the Regulation of the Breath*]. See *Chu-tzu ta-ch'üan* [*Complete Literary Works of Master Chu*], *Ssu-pu pei-yao* ed. (Shanghai, n.d.), Vol. 7, 85:6a (*Ssu-pu pei-yao* hereafter referred to as *SPPY*).

35. *FCK*, 18b-19a.

36. *KHC*,15a.

37. *FCK*, 18b.

38. *Ching-tso shuo* [*A Discussion of Quiet-Sitting*], *KTIS*, 3:19b-20b (hereafter referred to as *CTS*). Written in 1613 (*nien-p'u*, 15b).

39. Before there were hexagrams, i.e., undifferentiated change.

40. *Li Chi, Yüeh Chi, 1:1:11.*

41. *Chung-yung*, 1:4.

42. *CTS*, 20a.

43. *Ching-tso shuo-huo* [*A Later Discussion of Quiet-Sitting*], following *KTIS*, 1746 edition. *KTIS*, 1876 edition, title reads *Shu ching-tso shuo-huo* [*A Later Note to the Discussion of Quiet-Sitting*], *KTIS*, 3:21a. Written in 1615.

44. From Kao's correspondence with Wu Tzu-wang, *KTIS*, 8a:54a.

45. De Bary, "Neo-Confucian Cultivation," p. 185.

46. See de Bary's discussion of the Neo-Confucian concept of emptiness, "Neo-Confucian Cultivation," pp. 184-85.

47. T'ang Chun-i, "The Development of the Concept of Moral Mind from Wang Yang-ming to Wang Chi," in *Self and Society in Ming Thought*, ed. William Theodore de Bary (New York: Columbia University Press, 1970), pp. 93-97.

48. The ramifications of "openness" are discussed by de Bary, "Neo-Confucian Cultivation," pp. 186-87.

49. *CTS*, 20a.

50. De Bary, "Neo-Confucian Cultivation," p. 174.

51. De Bary, "Neo-Confucian Cultivation," p. 181.

52. Busch, "Tung-lin," pp. 172-74.

53. *CTS*, 20b.

54. Wing-tsit Chan, "The Ch'eng-Chu School of Early Ming," in de Bary, *Self and Society*, pp. 29-51.

55. See de Bary's discussion of burden of culture. William Theodore de Bary, "Introduction," in de Bary, *Self and Society*, pp. 8-12.

56. Jung Chao-tsu, *Ming-tai ssu-hsiang shih* [*History of Ming Thought*] (Taipei, 1969), pp. 305-07.

57. *MJHA*, p. 627.

58. *Mencius*, 2A:7, 4A:4.

59. *KTIS*, 1:1b.

60. Yang Shih, t. Chung-li, c.s. 1076, *Sung-shih* [*History of the Sung Dynasty*], *SPPY* (Taipei, 1965), pp. 4b-7b.

61. Source not identified.
62. *KTIS*, 1:5a.
63. The rest of this passage is unidentified as a quote from Kao.
64. *KTIS*, 1:5a.
65. *MJHA*, p. 627. This passage is included in a slightly different translation in Huang Tsung-hsi's biography of Kao P'an-lung found in Huang Tsung-hsi, *The Records of Ming Scholars by Huang Tsung-hsi*, trans. and ed. Julia Ching (Honolulu: University of Hawaii Press, 1987), p. 240.
66. *KTIS*, 8a:54a, 1:5a.
67. *Shih-hsüeh che* [*Illustrations of Learning*], *KTIS*, 3:21b.
68. The meanings of orthodoxy are discussed by de Bary in "Introduction," de Bary, *Unfolding*, pp. 1-37.
69. *SSC*, 31b-32b. See also *SSC*, 42a-b.
70. *KHC*, 14a.
71. L. Carrington Goodrich, Chao-ying Fang (eds.), *Dictionary of Ming Biography* (New York: Columbia University Press, 1976), pp. 874-77. For Huang Tsung-hsi's comments, see *MJHA*, pp. 293-94.
72. *SSC*, 31b-32b.
73. *Shan-chü k'o-ch'eng*, 18a.
74. *KHC*,15b-16a.
75. Taylor, "Neo-Confucianism, Sagehood," pp. 398-403.
76. *KHC*, 16a.
77. *SSC*, 37a.
78. *KHC*, 14a. Kao appears to be able to employ the term *tang-hsia* within the context of the maintenance of orthodoxy.
79. Ibid.
80. *KHC*, 15a.
81. *KHC*, 16b.
82. De Bary, "Neo-Confucian Cultivation," pp. 178-84.
83. De Bary, "Neo-Confucian Cultivation," p. 173, Taylor, "Neo-Confucianism, Sagehood," pp. 395-403.
84. *KHC*, 14a.
85. *KHC*, 15b.
86. *KHC*, 16a.
87. *Ching-tso shuo-huo*, 21a.
88. *Shih-hsüeh che*, 21b.
89. *KHC*, 16b.
90. *KHC*, 16a.
91. *CTS*, 20a-b.

Chapter VIII

1. James Legge, *The Chinese Classics, Vol. IV, The She King or the Book of Poetry* (Oxford: Clarendon Press, 1893), p. 340.

2. For example, Job 8.

3. Legge, *Chinese Classics*, pp. 325-26.

4. Jeremiah 12:1.

5. Jack Bemporad, "Suffering," in *The Encyclopedia of Religion*, ed. Mircea Eliade (New York: Macmillan, 1987), vol. 14, p. 99.

6. Rodney L. Taylor, "Compassion, Caring and the Religious Response to Suffering," in, *They Shall Not Hurt: Human Suffering and Human Caring*, eds. Rodney L. Taylor and Jean Watson (Boulder: Colorado Associated University Press, 1989), pp. 11-32.

7. Quoted in John Bowker, *Problems of Suffering in Religions of the World* (Cambridge: Cambridge University Press, 1970), pp. 1-2.

8. Bemporad, pp. 101-03.

9. David Little, "Human Suffering in a Comparative Perspective." In Taylor and Watson, *They Shall Not Hurt*, pp. 53-71.

10. Ibid.

11. Psalm 37:17, 20.

12. Romans 5:3-4.

13. James 1:2-4.

14. Matthew 10:17.

15. I am thankful to Langdon Gilkey for suggesting this feature of the Christian response to suffering.

16. Little, "Human Suffering," p. 60.

17. Isaiah 53:4-6.

18. *Mencius* 5A:5, D.C. Lau (trans.), *Mencius*, (Middlesex: Penguin Books Ltd., 1970), p. 143.

19. See *Mencius*, 1A:3,4,5; 1B:6,12; 2A:1.

20. *Mencius* 6B:15, Lau, *Mencius*, p. 181.

21. Tu Wei-ming, "Pain and Suffering in Confucian Self-Cultivation," *Philosophy East and West* 34, no. 4 (October 1984): 379-88.

22. Tu, "Pain and Suffering," p. 380.

23. Romans 5:3-4; James 1:2-4

24. Tu, "Pain and Suffering," p. 380.

25. See Vincent Y. C. Shih, "Metaphysical Tendencies in Mencius," *Philosophy East and West* 12, no. 4 (January 1963): 319-41.

26. *Analects*, 9:5, D. C. Lau (trans.), *Confucius: The Analects (Lun-yü)* (Middlesex: Penguin Books Ltd., 1979), p. 96.

27. *Mencius*, 6A:10, Lau, *Mencius*, p. 166.

28. William Theodore de Bary, *Neo-Confucian Orthodoxy and the Learning of the Mind-and-Heart* (New York: Columbia University Press, 1981), p. 15.

29. See Rodney L. Taylor, *The Cultivation of Sagehood as a Religious Goal in Neo-Confucianism: A Study of Selected Writings of Kao P'an-lung (1562-1626)* (Missoula, Mont.: Scholar's Press/American Academy of Religion, 1978), pp. 13-17.

30. Isaiah 53:4-6.

31. Isaiah 53:12.

32. William Theodore de Bary, *Sources of Indian Tradition* (New York: Columbia University Press, 1958), p. 161.

33. *Analects*, 8:7, Lau, *Analects*, p. 93.

34. Tu, "Pain and Suffering," p. 381.
35. *Mencius*, 4B:29, Lau, *Mencius*, pp. 134-135.
36. *Analects*, 11:9, Lau, *Analects*, p. 107.
37. *Analects*, 11:10, Lau, *Analects*, p. 107.
38. *Analects*, 6:3, Lau, *Analects*, p. 81.
39. *Analects*, 4:36, Lau, *Analects*, p. 130.
40. *Analects* 17:19, Lau, *Analects*, p. 146.
41. *Analects*, 2:4.
42. *Analects*, 12:45, Lau, *Analects*, p. 131.
43. Arthur Waley, *The Analects of Confucius* (New York: Vintage Books, 1938), pp. 191-92.
44. *Mencius*, 2A:6, Lau, *Mencius*, pp. 82-83.
45. *Mencius*, 1A:7, Lau, *Mencius*, p. 55.
46. Ibid.
47. Wing-tsit Chan (trans.), *A Source Book in Chinese Philosophy* (Princeton, N. J.: Princeton University Press, 1963), p. 530.
48. William Theodore de Bary, Wing-tsit Chan, and Burton Watson, *Sources of Chinese Tradition* (New York: Columbia University Press, 1960), p. 524.
49. Wing-tsit Chan (trans.), *Instructions for Practical Living and Other Neo-Confucian Writings of Wang Yang-ming* (New York: Columbia University Press, 1963), p. 273.
50. See the Introduction herein for a discussion of the definition of religion in Confucianism.
51. Tu Wei-ming, from a conversation at the Confucian Christian Conference, Hong Kong, 1988, pertaining to a Confucian soteriology and ways in which the immortality of the individual may be discussed within Confucianism.

Chapter IX

1. Robert Bellah, *Beyond Belief: Essays on Religion in a Post-Traditional World* (New York: Harper and Row, 1976), p. 64.
2. Bellah, *Beyond Belief*, p. 72.
3. Ibid.
4. Ibid.
5. John F. Wilson, "Modernity and Religion," in *The Encyclopedia of Religion*, ed. Mircea Eliade (New York: Macmillan, 1987), vol. 10, pp. 17-21.
6. Wilson, "Modernity," p. 21.
7. Ibid.
8. Ibid.
9. Ibid.
10. Ibid.
11. Wilson, "Modernity," pp. 21-22.
12. Tu Wei-ming, "Toward a Third Epoch of Confucian Humanism: A Background Understanding," in *Confucianism: The Dynamics of Tradition*, ed. Irene Eber (New York: Macmillan, 1986), pp. 3-21.

13. Tu, "Third Epoch," p. 5.

14. Tu, "Third Epoch,"p. 20.

15. Two recent conferences have demonstrated the degree to which Confucianism is viewed as an ongoing tradition: the International Symposium on Confucianism and the Modern World (Taipei, 1987), and the International Conference on Christianity and Confucianism in the World Today (Hong Kong, 1988).

16. Tu, "Third Epoch,"p. 21.

17. Tu, "Third Epoch,"p. 6.

18. Rodney L. Taylor, *The Confucian Way of Contemplation: Okada Takehiko and the Tradition of Quiet-Sitting* (Columbia, S.C.: University of South Carolina Press, 1988), pp. 7-10.

19. Taylor, *Confucian Way*, p. 8.

20. Taylor, *Confucian Way*, p. 77.

21. Taylor, *Confucian Way*, p. 199.

22. Taylor, *Confucian Way*, p. 200.

23. Taylor, *Confucian Way*, p. 204.

24. Taylor, *Confucian Way*, p. 209.

25. Taylor, *Confucian Way*, pp. 193-95.

26. Taylor, *Confucian Way*, p. 210.

27. Taylor, *Confucian Way*, pp. 211-12

28. Taylor, *Confucian Way*, p. 211.

29. Taylor, *Confucian Way*, p. 212.

30. Tu, "Third Epoch," p. 20.

31. Wilfred Cantwell Smith, *The Meaning and End of Religion* (New York: Harper and Row, 1978), in particular Chap. 2, pp. 25-50.

32. Vitaly Rubin, "Values of Confucianism," *Numen: International Review for the History of Religions* 28 (1981): 72. Referred to in Tu, "Third Epoch," p. 3.

Glossary of Chinese Characters

an-p'ai 安排

Araki Kengo 荒木見悟

Bukkyō to Jukyō 佛教と儒教

Chan Wing-tsit 陳榮捷

Chang Nan-hsien 張南軒

Chang Tsai 張載

Ch'en Hsüan 陳選

Ch'en Lung-cheng 陳籠正

Chen Te-hsiu 真德秀

chen-t'i 真體

Ch'en Ting 陳鼎

cheng (government) 政

cheng (rectification) 正

ch'eng (manifest) 呈

ch'eng (sincerity, authenticity) 誠

Ch'eng-Chu 程朱

Ch'eng Hao, Ming-tao 程顥，明道

Ch'eng I, I-ch'uan 程頤，伊川

ch'eng-i 誠意

chi 記

ch'i 氣

ch'i-hsiang 氣象

chi-jan 寂然

Chia-shan hsien-chih 嘉山縣志

ch'iang-tzu 腔子

chien-hsing 見性

Ch'ien Mu 錢穆

Ch'ien Te-hung, Hung-fu, Hsü-shan 錢德洪，洪甫，緒山

chih (resolve) 志

chih (resting) 止

chih (wisdom) 智

chih-chih 致知

chih-hsing ho-i 知行合一

chih-hsiu 止修

chih-pen 知本

chih-shan 至善

chin-shih 進士

Ch'in Shih Huang ti 秦始皇帝

Chin-ssu lu 近思錄

ching (classic) 經

ching (quietude) 静

ching (reverent seriousness) 敬

ching-tso 静坐

Ching-tso shuo 静坐說

Ching-tso shuo-hou 静坐說後

Chou Li 周禮

Chou Tun-i 周敦頤

chu-ching (mastering quietude) 主静

chü-ching (abiding in reverent seriousness) 居敬

Chu Hsi 朱熹

ch'ü jen-yü 去人欲

Chu-tzu i-shu 朱子遺書

Chu-tzu ta-ch'üan 朱子大全

Ch'uan-hsi lu 傳習綠

Ch'üan-t'i ta-yung 全體大用

Ch'un Ch'iu 春秋

chün-tzu 君子

chung 忠

Chung-yung 中庸

erh 耳

Erh-Ch'eng ch'uan-shu 二程全書

Erh-Ch'eng i-shu 二程遺書

Erh-ya 爾雅

Fan Chung-yen 范仲淹

Fang Tung-mei 方東美

Fu-ch'i kuei 復七規

fu-tso 趺坐

Heng-lu ching-she hsü-kao 衡盧精舍續稿

honji-suijaku 本地垂迹

Hsi-ch'uan t'ung-lun 繫傳通論

Hsi-ming 西銘

Hsiang-shan ch'üan-chi 象山全集

Hsiao-ching 孝經

Hsiao-hsüeh 小學

Hsiao-hsüeh chi-chu 小學集注

hsiao-jen 小人

hsin (faith) 信

hsin (mind) 心

hsin-hsüeh ("new" learning) 新學

hsin-hsüeh (School of Mind) 心學

Hsin-hui hsien-chih 新會縣志

hsing 性

hsing-chuang 行狀   hsing-jen 行人

hsing-t'i 性體   Hsü Fu-kuan 徐復觀

Hsü Heng 許衡   Hsü Hsien 許獻

Hsün-tzu 荀子

Hu Chih, Cheng-fu, I-chü, Lu-shan 胡直，正甫，宜舉，　廬山

Hu Chü-jen 胡居仁   Hu Wu-feng 胡五峰

Hua Hsi-min 華希閔

Hua Yün-ch'eng, Ju-li, Feng-ch'ao 華允誠，汝立，鳳超

Huang P'ei-fang 黃培芳   Huang Tsung-hsi 黃宗羲

hun-ch'i 昏氣   i (intention) 意

i (righteousness, rightness) 義   I Ching 易經

i-fa 已發   i-jen 一任

I-tuan pien 異端辨   jen 仁

jen-hsin 人心   jih-chi 日記

Jung Chao-tsu 容肇祖   kami 神

Kao Chung-hsien kung nien-p'u 高忠憲公年譜

Kao P'an-lung, Yün-ts'ung, Ts'un-chih, Ching-i 高攀籠，雲從，存之，景逸

Kao-tzu ch'üan-shu 高子全書   Kao-tzu i-shu 高子遺書

Kao-tzu wei-k'o-kao 高子未刻稿

Keng T'ien-t'ai hsien-sheng wen-chi 耿天台先生文集

Keng Ting-hsiang 耿定向   K'o-lou chi 可樓集

ko-wu 格物   kotsuza 兀坐

Ku Hsien-ch'eng, Shu-shih, Ching-yang 顧憲成，叔時，涇陽

Ku-liang chuan 穀梁傳

Ku-pen ta-hsüeh t'i-tz'u 古本大學題詞

K'un-hsüeh chi 困學記   kung-fu 工夫

Kung-yang chuan 公羊傳   Kuo Tzu-chang 郭子章

li (distance measurement) 里   li (principle) 理

li (profit) 利   li (rites, propriety) 禮

Li Chi 禮記   Li Chi, Yueh-chi 禮記，樂記

Li Fu-yang, Tsung-ch'eng, Yüan-ch'ung 李復陽，宗誠，元冲

li-hsüeh 理學

Li Ts'ai, Meng-ch'eng, Chien-lo 李材，孟誠，見羅

Li T'ung 李侗   liang chih 良知

Lin Chao-en, Mao-hsün, Lung-chiang 林兆恩, 懋勛, 籠江

Lin Hsing-chang 林星章

Lo Hung-hsien, Ta-fu, Nien-an 羅洪先, 達夫, 念菴

Lo Mao-chung, Chih-an 羅懋忠, 止菴　　Lo Tsung-yen 羅從彥

Lu Hsiang-shan 陸象山

Lu Ts'ui-ming, Ku-ch'iao 陸粹明, 古樵　Lu Yu 陸游

Lun-yü 論語　　　　　　　　　Meng-tzu 孟子

ming 命　　　　　　　　　　　Ming-ju hsüeh-an 明儒學案

Ming-shih 明史

Ming-tai ssu-hsiang shih 明代思想史　Mou Tsung-san 牟宗三

nien 念　　　　　　　　　　　nien-p'u 年譜

Okada Takehiko 岡田武彦　　　　Ou-yang hsiu 歐陽修

Ou-yang Te, Ch'ung-i, Nan-yeh 歐陽德, 崇一, 南野

pan-jih ching-tso pan-jih tu-shu 半日静坐半日讀書

pen-t'i 本體　　　　　　　　　pi-kuan 閉關

p'ing-ch'ang 平常　　　　　　　pu-chu 不著

san-chiao ho-i 三教合一　　　　　San-shih chi 三時記

seiza 静坐

Shan-chü k'o-ch'eng 山居課程

sheng 聖

sheng-jen 聖人

Shih chi 史記

Shih Ching 詩經

shih-hsin 實信

shih-hsüeh 實學

Shih-hsüeh che 示學者

shu 恕

Shu Ching 書經

Shu ching-tso shuo-hou 書静坐説後

shui-chü 水居

Shui-chü chi 水居記

Shuo-wen 説文

Shuo-wen chieh-tzu ku-lin 説文解字詁林

Ssu-ma Ch'ien 司馬遷

Ssu-pu pei-yao 四部備要

Sung-shih 宋史

Sung-Yüan hsüeh-an 宋元學案

Ta-hsüeh 大學

Ta-hsüeh huo-wen 大學或問

Ta-hsüeh shou-chang kuang-i 大學首章廣義

Ta-hsüeh shou-chang yüeh-i 大學首章約義

T'ai-chou 泰州

t'ai-hsüeh 太學

T'ang Chün-i 唐君毅

tang-hsia 當下

tao-hsin 道心

tao-t'ung 道統

te 德

Te Ch'ing 德清

Teng Tun-feng 鄧鈍峰

t'i 體

t'i-jen 體認

t'iao-hsi 調息

T'iao-hsi chen 調息箴

t'ien 天

t'ien-li 天理

t'ien-ming 天命

t'ien-ti 天地

t'ien-tzu 天子

t'ing 聽

ts'un t'ien-li 存天理

Tso-chuan 左傳

t'ung 通

Tung Chung-shu 董仲舒

Tung-lin 東林

Tung-lin lieh-chuan 東林列傳

Tung-lin shu-yüan chih 東林書院志

tzu-jan 自然

Wang An-shih 王安石

Wang Chi 王畿

Wang Ken 王艮

wang-shih 忘世

Wang Shou-jen, Po-an, Yang-ming 王守仁，伯安，陽明

Wei Chung-hsien 魏忠賢

wei-fa 未發

wei-hsüeh 僞學

wen 文

wo hsin-t'i 我心體

wu 悟

wu-chi 無極

Wu Chih-yüan, Tzu-wang, Ch'u-an 吳志遠, 子往, 蘧菴

Wu Yü-pi 吳與弼

Wu-ching po-shih 五經博士

wu-shih (not set on anything) 無適

wu-shih (without affairs) 無事

wu-wei 無爲

yang 陽

Yeh Mao-ts'ai, Ts'an-chih, Yüan-shih 葉茂才, 參之, 圍適

Yen Yüan 顏元

yu-chi 遊記

Zazen to seiza 坐禪と静坐

Wu-ching cheng-i 五經正義

wu-li 無理

wu-yü 無欲

Yang Shih, Chung-li 楊時, 中立

yin 陰

Yüeh Ching 樂經

Selected Bibliography of Works Cited

Baird, Robert. *Category Formation and the History of Religions*. The Hague: Mouton, 1971.

Bauer, Wolfgang. "Icherleben und Autobiographie im Älteren China." *Heidelbeger Jahrbücher* (1964) 8:12-40.

Bellah, Robert. *Beyond Belief: Essays on Religion in a Post-Traditional World*. New York: Harper & Row, 1976.

Bemporad, Jack. "Suffering." In Mircea Eliade, ed. *The Encyclopedia of Religion*. New York: Macmillan 1987.

Berling, Judith. "Paths of Convergence: Interactions of Inner Alchemy Taoism and Neo-Confucianism." *Journal of Chinese Philosophy* (1979) 6:123-47.

_____ . *The Syncretic Religion of Lin Chao-en*. New York: Columbia University Press, 1980.

Bowker, John. *Problems of Suffering in Religions of the World*. Cambridge: Cambridge University Press, 1970.

Busch, Heinrich. "The Tung-lin Academy and Its Political and Philosophical Significance." *Monumenta Serica* (1949-1955) 14:1-163.

Chan, Wing-tsit. *A Source Book in Chinese Philosophy*. Princeton, N. J. : Princeton University Press, 1969.

_____. "Chu Hsi's Completion of Neo-Confucianism." In Françoise Aubin, ed. *Études Song–Sung Studies, In Memoriam Étienne Balazs* (1973), ser. 2, no. 1, pp. 59-90.

_____, trans. *Instructions for Practical Living and Other Neo-Confucian Writings of Wang Yang-ming.* New York: Columbia University Press, 1963.

_____, trans. *Reflections on Things at Hand, The Neo-Confucian Anthology Compiled by Chu Hsi and Lü Tsu-ch'ien.* New York, Columbia University Press, 1967.

_____. "The Ch'eng-Chu School of the Early Ming." In William Theodore de Bary, ed. *Self and Society in Ming Thought.* New York: Columbia University Press, 1970.

Chang, K. C. *Art, Myth and Ritual: The Path to Political Authority in Ancient China.* Cambridge, Mass.: Harvard University Press, 1983.

Ch'en, Ting, ed. *Tung-lin lieh-ch'uan [Biographies of the Tung-lin].* 1711 edition.

Ch'eng, Hao and Ch'eng I. *Erh-Ch'eng i-shu [Surviving Works of the Two Ch'eng Brothers].* In Ch'eng Hao and Ch'eng I. *Erh-Ch'eng ch'üan-shu [The Complete Works of the Two Ch'eng Brothers].* Taipei, Ssu-pu pei-yao edition, 1969.

Ching, Julia. *Confucianism and Christianity: A Comparative Study.* Tokyo: Kodansha International, 1977.

Ching, Julia and Hans Kung. *Christianity and Chinese Religions.* New York: Doubleday, 1989.

Denny, Frederick M. and Rodney L. Taylor, eds. *The Holy Book in Comparative Perspective.* Columbia, S.C.: University of South Carolina Presss, 1985.

De Bary, William Theodore. "Individualism and Humanitarianism in Late Ming Thought." In William Theodore de Bary, ed. *Self and Society in Ming Thought.* New York: Columbia University Press, 1970.

_____. "Neo-Confucian Cultivation and the Seventeenth-Century 'Enlightenment.'" In William Theodore de Bary, ed. *The Unfolding of Neo-Confucianism.* New York: Columbia University Press, 1975.

_____. *Neo-Confucian Orthodoxy and the Learning of the Mind-and-Heart.* New York: Columbia University Press, 1981.

———, ed. *Self and Society in Ming Thought*. New York: Columbia University Press, 1970.

———. "Some Common Tendencies in Neo-Confucianism." In David Nivison and Arthur Wright, eds. *Confucianism in Action*. Stanford, Calif.: Stanford University Press, 1959.

———, ed. *The Unfolding of Neo-Confucianism*. New York: Columbia University Press, 1975.

De Bary, William Theodore and Irene Bloom, eds. *Principle and Practicality: Essays in Neo-Confucianism and Practical Learning*. New York: Columbia University Press, 1979.

De Bary, William Theodore, Wing-tsit Chan, and Burton Watson. *Sources of Chinese Tradition*. New York: Columbia University Press, 1960.

Eberhard, Wolfram. *Guilt and Sin in Traditional China*. Berkeley: University of California Press, 1971.

Eliade, Mircea, ed. *The Encyclopedia of Religion*. New York: Macmillan, 1987.

Fingarette, Herbert. *Confucius: The Secular as Sacred*. New York: Harper and Row, 1972.

Forke, Alfred. *Geschichte der neueren chinesischen Philosophie*. Hamburg: Friederichen DeGruyter and Co., 1938.

Fung, Yu-lan. *A History of Chinese Philosophy, Vol. I, The Period of the Philosophers*, trans. Derk Bodde. Princeton, N. J.: Princeton University Press, 1952.

Goodrich, L. Carrington and Chaoying Fang, eds. *Dictionary of Ming Biography, 1368-1644*. New York: Columbia University Press, 1976.

Hall, David L. and Roger Ames. *Thinking Through Confucius*. Albany, N. Y. SUNY Press, 1987.

Hastings, James. *Encyclopaedia of Religion and Ethics*. New York: Charles Scribner's Sons, 1921.

Hawley, J. S., ed. *Saints and Virtues*. Berkeley: University of California Press, 1987.

Hsü, Hsien, ed. *Tung-lin shu-yüan-chih* [*Records of the Tung-lin Academy*]. 1881 edition.

Hsü, Sung-peng, *A Buddhist Leader in Ming China: The Life and Thought of Han-shan Te-ch'ing (1546-1623)*. University Park, Penn.: Pennsylvania State University Press, 1979.

Hu Chih. *K'un-hsüeh chi* [*Recollections of the Toils of Learning*]. Appendix to Kuo Tzu-chang, ed. *Heng-lu ching-she hsü-kao*. 1902 edition.

Hua, Yün-ch'eng, ed. *Kao Chung-hsien kung nien-p'u* [*Chronological Biography of Kao Chung-hsien*]. Appendix to Ch'en Lung-chen, ed. *Kao-tzu i-shu* [*Literary Remains of Master Kao*]. 1876 reprint edition.

Huang, Siu-chi. *Lu Hsiang-shan: A Twelfth Century Chinese Idealist Philosopher*. New Haven, Conn.: American Oriental Society, 1944.

Huang, Tsung-hsi. *Ming-ju hsüeh-an* [*The Records of the Ming Scholars*]. Taipei, Ssu-pu pei-yao edition, 1965.

————. *Sung-Yüan hsüeh-an* [*The Records of the Sung and Yüan Scholars*]. Taipei, 1975.

Hucker, Charles. "The Tung-lin Movement of the Late Ming Period." In John Fairbank, ed. *Chinese Thought and Institutions*. Chicago: University of Chicago Press, 1964.

James, William. *Varieties of Religious Experience, A Study in Human Nature*. New York: Modern Library, 1929.

Jung, Chao-tsu. *Ming-tai ssu-hsiang shih* [*History of Ming Thought*]. Taipei, 1969.

Kao P'an-lung. *Ching-tso shuo* [*A Discussion of Quiet-Sitting*]. In Ch'en Lung-cheng, ed. *Kao-tzu i-shu* [*Literary Remains of Master Kao*]. 1876 reprint edition.

————. *Ching-tso shuo-huo* [*A Later Discussion of Quiet-Sitting*]. In Ch'en Lung-cheng, ed. *Kao-tzu i-shu* [*Literary Remains of Master Kao*]. 1876 reprint edition.

————. *Fu-ch'i kuei* [*Rules for "Returning in Seven"*]. In Ch'en Lung-cheng, ed. *Kao-tzu i-shu* [*Literary Remains of Master Kao*]. 1876 reprint edition.

_____. *I-tuan pien* [*Criticism of Heterodoxy*]. In Ch'en Lung-cheng, ed. *Kao-tzu i-shu* [*Literary Remains of Master Kao*]. 1876 reprint edition.

_____. *Kao-tzu ch'üan-shu* [*Complete Works of Master Kao*] (ed. Hua Hsi-min). 1742 edition.

_____. *Kao-tzu i-shu* [*Literary Remains of Master Kao*] (ed. Ch'en Lung-cheng). 1876 reprint edition.

_____. *Kao-tzu wei-k'o-kao* [*Unpublished Manuscripts of Master Kao*]. Rare Book Collection of the Peking National Library, reel no. 797, Library of Congress, Washington D. C..

_____. *K'o-lou chi* [*Recollections of the Suitable Loft*]. In Ch'en Lung-cheng, ed. *Kao-tzu i-shu* [*Literary Remains of Master Kao*]. 1876 reprint edition.

_____. *K'un-hsüeh chi* [*Recollections of the Toils of Learning*]. In Ch'en Lung-cheng, ed. *Kao-tzu i-shu* [*Literary Remains of Master Kao*]. 1876 reprint edition.

_____. *San-shih chi* [*Recollections of Three Seasons*]. In Ch'en Lung-cheng, ed. *Kao-tzu i-shu* [*Literary Remains of Master Kao*]. 1876 reprint edition.

_____. *Shan-chü k'o-ch'eng* [*An Agenda for Dwelling in the Mountains*]. In Ch'en Lung-cheng, ed. *Kao-tzu i-shu* [*Literary Remains of Master Kao*]. 1876 reprint edition.

_____. *Shui-chü chi* [*Recollections of the Water Dwelling*]. In Ch'en Lung-cheng, ed. *Kao-tzu i-shu* [*Literary Remains of Master Kao*]. 1876 reprint edition.

Katz, Steven T. *Mysticism and Religious Traditions*. Oxford: Oxford University Press, 1983.

Keightley, David N. "The Religious Commitment: Shang Theology and the Genesis of Chinese Political Culture." *History of Religions* (1978) 17: 211-55.

Keng, Ting-hsiang. *Keng T'ien-tai hsien-sheng wen-chi* [*Collection of Literary Works of Keng Ting-hsiang*]. Taipei, 1970.

Kengo, Araki. *Bukkyo to Jukyo* [*Buddhism and Confucianism*]. Kyoto, 1963.

Kieckhefer, Richard and George Bond, eds. *Sainthood: Its Manifestations in World Religions*. Berkeley: University of California Press, 1988.

Kupperman, Joel. "Confucius and the Nature of Religious Ethics." *Philosophy East and West* (1971) 21:189-94.

Lau, D. C., trans. *Confucius: The Analects (Lun-yü)*. Middlesex: Penguin Books Ltd., 1979.

————, trans. *Mencius*. Middlesex: Penguin Books Ltd., 1970.

Legge, James. *The Chinese Classics, Vol. I, Confucian Analects, the Great Learning and the Doctrine of the Mean*. Oxford: Clarendon Press, 1893.

————. *The Chinese Classics, Vol. III, The Shoo King or the Book of Historical Documents*. Oxford: Clarendon Press, 1893.

————. *The Chinese Classics, Vol. IV, The She King or the Book of Poetry*. Oxford: Clarendon Press, 1893.

————. *The Religions of China*. London: Hodder and Stoughton, 1880.

Levering, Miriam. "Scripture and Its Reception: A Buddhist Case." In Miriam Levering, ed. *Rethinking Scripture: Essays from a Comparative Perspective*. Albany, N. Y.: SUNY Press, 1989.

Little, David. "Human Suffering in a Comparative Perspective." In Rodney L. Taylor and Jean Watson, eds. *They Shall Not Hurt: Human Suffering and Human Caring*. Boulder: Colorado Associated University Press, 1989.

Little, David and Sumner B. Twiss, Jr. "Basic Terms in the Study of Religious Ethics." In Gene Outka and John P. Reeder, Jr., eds. *Religion and Morality: A Collection of Essays*. Garden City, N.J.: Anchor Books, 1973.

Liu, Ts'un-yan. "Lin Chao-en (1517-1598), The Master of the Three Teachings." *T'oung Pao* (1967) 53:253-78.

————. "Taoist Self-Cultivation in Ming Thought." In William Theodore de Bary, ed. *Self and Society in Ming Thought*. New York: Columbia University Press, 1975.

Lu, Hsiang-shan. *Hsiang-shan ch'üan-chi* [*The Complete Works of Lu Hsiang-shan*]. Taipei: Ssu-pu pei-yao ed. 1970.

Maslow, Abraham. *Religions, Values, and Peak Experiences*. New York: Penguin Books, 1976.

Matsunaga, Alicia. *The Buddhist Philosophy of Assimilation: The Historical Development of the Honji-Suijaku Theory.* Tokyo: Sophia University, 1969.

Metzger, Thomas A. *Escape from Predicament: Neo-Confucianism and China's Evolving Political Culture.* New York: Columbia University Press, 1977.

Ming-shih [*History of the Ming Dynasty*]. Taipei: Ssu-pu pei-yao edition, 1965.

Munro, Donald. *The Concept of Man in Early China.* Stanford, Calif.: Stanford University Press, 1969.

Neville, Robert C. *Soldier, Sage, Saint.* New York: Fordham University Press, 1978.

Okada, Takehiko. *Zazen to seiza* [*Buddhist and Confucian Meditation*]. Tokyo, 1972.

Olney, James. *Metaphors of Self: The Meaning of Autobiography.* Princeton, N. J.: Princeton University Press, 1972.

Pascal, Roy. *Design and Truth in Autobiography.* Cambridge, Mass.: Harvard University Press, 1960.

Shih, Vincent Y. C. "Metaphysical Tendencies in Mencius." *Philosophy East and West* (1963) 12: 319-41.

Shryock, John. *The Origin and Development of the State Cult of Confucius.* New York: Paragon Reprint Corporation, 1966.

Smith, Wilfred Cantwell. *The Meaning and End of Religion.* New York: Harper and Row, 1978.

Staal, Frits. *Exploring Mysticism: A Methodological Essay.* Berkeley: University of California Press, 1975.

Streng, Frederick. *Understanding Religious Life,* 3rd ed. Belmont, Calif.: Wadsworth, 1985.

Sung-shih [*History of the Sung Dynasty*]. Taipei: Ssu-pu pei-yao edition, 1965.

T'ang, Chun-i. "The Development of the Moral Mind from Wang Yang-ming to Wang Chi." In William Theodore de Bary, ed. *Self and Society in Ming Thought.* New York: Columbia University Press, 1970.

Taylor, Rodney L. "Acquiring a Point of View: Confucian Dimensions of Self-Reflection." *Monumenta Serica* (1979-1980) 34:145-70.

_____. "Compassion, Caring and the Religious Response to Suffering." In Rodney L. Taylor and Jean Watson, eds. *They Shall Not Hurt: Human Suffering and Human Caring.* Boulder: Colorado Associated University Press, 1989.

_____. "Journey Into Self: The Autobiographical Reflections of Hu Chih." *History of Religions* (1982) 21: 321-38

_____. "Neo-Confucianism, Sagehood and the Religious Dimension." *Journal of Chinese Philosophy* (1975) 2: 389-415

_____. *The Confucian Way of Contemplation: Okada Takehiko and the Tradition of Quiet-Sitting.* Columbia, S.C.: University of South Carolina Press, 1988.

_____. *The Cultivation of Sagehood as a Religious Goal in Neo-Confucianism: A Study of Selected Writings of Kao P'an-lung (1562-1626).* Missoula, Mont.: Scholar's Press/American Academy of Religion, 1978.

_____. *The Way of Heaven: An Introduction to the Confucian Religious Life.* Leiden: E. J. Brill, 1986.

Taylor, Rodney L. and Frederick Denny, eds. *The Holy Book in Comparative Perspective.* Columbia, S.C.: University of South Carolina Press, 1985.

Taylor, Rodney L. and Jean Watson, eds. *They Shall Not Hurt: Human Suffering and Human Caring.* Boulder: Colorado Associated University Press, 1989.

Tu, Wei-ming. *Humanity and Self-Cultivation: Essays in Confucian Thought.* Berkeley: Asian Humanities Press, 1979.

_____. *Neo-Confucian Thought in Action: Wang Yang-ming's Youth (1472-1509).* Berkeley: University of California Press, 1976.

_____. "Pain and Suffering in Confucian Self-Cultivation." *Philosophy East and West* (1984) 34: 379-88.

_____. "The Confucian Perception of Adulthood." *Daedalus* (1976) 105:113-27.

_____. "The Confucian Sage: Exemplar of Personal Knowledge." In J. S. Hawley, ed. *Saints and Virtues.* Berkeley: University of California Press, 1987.

_____. "Toward a Third Epoch of Confucian Humanism: A Background Understanding." In Irene Eber, ed. *Confucianism: The Dynamics of Tradition.* New York: Macmillan, 1986.

_____. "Yen Yüan: From Inner Experience to Lived Concreteness." In William Theodore de Bary, ed. *The Unfolding of Neo-Confucianism.* New York: Columbia University Press, 1975.

van der Leeuw, G. *Religion in Essence and Manifestation.* New York: Harper and Row, 1963.

Wach, Joachim. *Sociology of Religion.* Chicago: University of Chicago Press, 1971.

_____. *The Comparative Study of Religion.* New York: Columbia University Press, 1961.

Waley, Arthur, trans. *The Analects of Confucius.* New York: Vintage Books, 1938.

Weber, Max. *The Religion of China: Confucianism and Taoism.* New York: Free Press, 1951.

Wilson, John F. "Modernity and Religion." In Mircea Eliade, ed. *The Encyclopedia of Religion.* New York: Macmillan, 1987.

Wu, Pei-yi. "The Spiritual Autobiography of Te-ch'ing." In William Theodore de Bary, ed. *The Unfolding of Neo-Confucianism.* New York: Columbia University Press, 1975.

Yang, C. K. *Religion in Chinese Society.* Berkeley: University of California Press, 1961.

Yeh, Mao-ts'ai. *Hsing-chuang [Annals of Conduct].* In Hsü Hsien, ed. *Tung-lin shu-yüan-chih [Records of the Tung-lin Academy].* 1881 edition.

Index